INTER-ECONOMY COMPARISONS
A CASE STUDY

Publications of the
Institute of Business and Economic Research
University of California

INTER-ECONOMY COMPARISONS A CASE STUDY

A COMPARATIVE STUDY OF INDUSTRIAL DEVELOPMENT, CURRENCY DEVALUATION, AND INFLATION

by Leonard A. Doyle

UNIVERSITY OF CALIFORNIA PRESS 1965
BERKELEY AND LOS ANGELES

University of California Press
Berkeley and Los Angeles

Cambridge University Press
London, England

A research study under coöperative arrangements among the following:

In the Republic of Indonesia: P. N. Pabrik Semen "Gresik," Surabaja, East Java; Bank Pembangunan Indonesia; Department of Basic Industry and Mining; State Accounting Office, Department of Finance

In the United States of America: Institute of Business and Economic Research, University of California, Berkeley, under a grant from the Rockefeller Foundation; The Permanente Cement Corporation, Kaiser Center, Oakland, California

Institute of Business and Economic Research
University of California, Berkeley

The opinions expressed in this study are those of the author. The functions of the Institute of Business and Economic Research are confined to facilitating the prosecution of independent scholarly research by members of the faculty.

Acknowledgments

This study was made possible by the encouragement of many individuals associated with the agencies listed, as well as by others in Indonesia and in the United States. President-Director Soemanang of Bank Pembangunan Indonesia, Dr. Darmawan Mangunkusumo, Chairman of the Board of Directors, President-Director Sarimin Reksodihardjo of P. N. Pabrik Semen "Gresik," and Mr. Paul Rogers, Vice-President and Controller of the Permanente Cement Corporation, all approved the project and authorized full access to the records and personnel of the two cement enterprises which are the subject of this investigation. The study itself is a part of a larger study of industrial development in Indonesia. The major study represents a coöperative venture among several agencies of the Government of Indonesia. For the larger study I am particularly indebted to Mr. Chaerul Saleh, Minister of Basic Industry and Mining; Dr. Zakaria Raib, of the Bureau of Industrialization of the Department of Basic Industry and Mining; Professor Sumardjo, Head of the State Accounting Office in the Department of Finance; Ir. Saksono, President-Director of the State Agricultural Enterprises; and Mr. Sardjoe Ismunandar, President-Director of the Nationalized Manufacturing Enterprises. Dr. Mohammad Sadli, Acting Director of the Institute for Social and Economic Research at the Faculty of Economics of the University of Indonesia at Djakarta, was most generous and helpful in encouraging and supporting my research on industrial development problems in Indonesia.

My debt to the executives of P. N. Pabrik Semen "Gresik"

could be acknowledged properly only by a full roster of names, for I have imposed on technical and administrative personnel and on the accounting and sekretariat group at all levels. President-Director Sarimin not only authorized the staff to give me all assistance possible, but provided help and counsel as the study progressed. I should like particularly to acknowledge the help and counsel of Ir. Padjo Soerjodiningrat, Production Manager of Gresik during the period of the field work and now President-Director; Sdr. Mohammad Arifin, Administrative Manager; Sdr. Soeriokoesoemo, Legal Advisor; and Sdr. Tony Dano, Chief Cost Accountant. Special thanks and appreciation are due Mrs. Marjatoen Winarto for the arduous task of typing the tables and preparing the stencils for the original draft of the study. Members of the sekretariat at Gresik were unfailingly generous and coöperative in making arrangements with officials and in assisting with correspondence and other details. Sdr. Arifin gave me the benefit of his counsel and experience at every stage of the investigation, read preliminary drafts of the manuscript, and made many helpful suggestions for improving the presentation. A special word of thanks and appreciation is due Gresik for the extraordinary hospitality of the staff of its Guest House.

Mr. C. MacArthur Carman, Technical Advisor of P. N. Pabrik Semen "Gresik," helped me at every stage with his enormous technical knowledge of Gresik in particular and of the cement industry in general, and provided the fine hospitality of his home during my stay at Gresik. Mr. Louis Wheeler, Project Manager of the Morrison-Knudsen International Corporation, contractor for the original Gresik plant and its expansion program, was most helpful, as were members of his engineering and administrative staff, in providing information and in showing me the plant during construction and the initial operations when I visited the plant in 1956 and in 1957.

In the United States I imposed greatly on a long and pleasant professional and personal association with Mr. Paul Rogers, Vice-President and Controller of Permanente Cement Corporation, and on the manager and controller of the Cushenberry plant of Permanente at Lucerne, California. When I returned to the United States to revise the draft prepared in Indonesia, Mr.

Ronald Hohnsbeen, who succeeded Mr. Rogers as Vice-President and Controller of the Permanente Cement Corporation when Mr. Rogers retired, was most generous in providing additional information about Cushenberry and in taking time from a busy schedule to read the first draft of the study. The work of photographing and multilithing the tables for the study was done by Permanente Cement Corporation.

My colleague in the Graduate School of Business Administration, Professor William Vatter, read the first draft and made many valuable suggestions for revising and improving the manuscript.

Particular thanks are due the Rockefeller Foundation; Professor Richard Holton, Director of the Institute of Business and Economic Research of the University of California at Berkeley; Professor E. T. Grether, former Dean of the Graduate School of Business Administration at Berkeley; and President Clark Kerr for making possible the somewhat unusual Faculty Fellowship which permitted me to return to Indonesia for the coöperative research program of which this study is a part.

It is a pleasure to acknowledge the work of Mrs. Jan Seibert, who planned the form of the tables and typed them, and of Bob McIlroy, who checked the computations and footings of the tables and the text references to the tables. My wife has encouraged and assisted me at every part of the larger study of industry in Indonesia, and of the study of Gresik and Cushenberry. What may be good and useful in this study is due to the help and encouragement I have received from so many persons. The errors of fact, computation, and interpretation are mine.

Leonard A. Doyle

Walnut Creek, California

Contents

PART III. ACHIEVEMENTS AND PROBLEMS OF
THE GRESIK PLANT

APPENDIXES

* Included with Indonesian edition only. See reference in text, p. 12.

I

Introduction

In the future the number of independent developing countries that were former colonies of Western nations will increase. If the recent past is an indication of the future, many of the new countries will select some form of socialism for industrial development rather than private enterprise. This will be done because there is not enough private national capital and management for the large industrial projects with political and economic appeal, and because private foreign investment and management will be regarded as perpetuating the colonialism recently cast off. The newly developing countries may be expected to prefer foreign loans and grants from governments or international agencies to private foreign investment. If these predictions are accurate, the Western private enterprise countries may feel that they are being asked to encourage and subsidize an economic and political system too close to that of their opponents in the cold war. But to refuse to provide assistance for socialist projects may be to risk the loss to the communist bloc of many otherwise neutralist countries.

Economic aid to developing countries as a matter of political strategy is of recent origin, and it is fair to say that it is still an experiment that has not been vindicated by satisfactory progress in most recipient countries. To a large extent economic aid is more a political factor in the cold war than a program to be evaluated in terms of the presumed objective of development in the recipient countries. We do not yet know how to provide really effective assistance to developing economies. The Marshall Plan in Europe was very successful in rebuilding industrial economies, but it was intended to rebuild physical capital and reinvigorate an existing system of enterprise. It did not have to develop a system of industrial or commercial enterprise out of a primitive agricultural or nomadic grazing economy, nor did it have to solve the problem of developing a political structure suitable for a system of industry and commerce. The plants and machinery and utilities that were built or repaired in Europe were, for the most part, integral units of the oldest industrial nations of the world. The European authorities knew what they needed, and how to use it to advantage once it was in operation.

The fact that an effective mechanism for economic development of nonindustrial countries has not been found is one of the major challenges of our time. In the effort to find one or more workable programs we need both general theories of development and factual data about specific projects. Factual data concerning specific development projects must be related to general theory for the purpose of testing its adequacy and usefulness, and to see where additional theoretical work is necessary. Studies of specific projects, however, should not be regarded as social or industrial laboratory experiments to test specific theories. The investigator has no control over the experiment; rather it is his task to discover and evaluate the facts. These are not always easy to acquire in a complex industrial situation, and in a newly developing country the difficulties are likely to be more numerous than in an industrial society.

The present study represents the first of what is hoped will be a series of coöperative international industry studies. It is, first of all, an attempt to compare the capital cost of two modern plants, one in a newly developing country, Indonesia, and the other in an industrial economy, the United States. Second, it is an attempt to compare the operating costs and output of the two plants for the period July, 1957 through June, 1960. Third, it is an attempt to measure and evaluate the contributions of the Indonesian plant to the economy of Indonesia.

The study is concerned with the Gresik cement plant of the Department of Basic Industry and Mining of the Republic of Indonesia, and the Cushenberry plant of the Permanente Cement Corporation in the United States. The Gresik plant is located at Gresik near Surabaja in East Java. The Cushenberry plant is near Lucerne in the Mojave Desert of Southern California. Both plants were completed and began operation in 1957, and are of United States design and manufacture. The United States plant started production in April and the Indonesian plant started production in July. The two plants use the same process of making cement, the wet process, and each was originally constructed to operate with two rotary kilns. The United States plant had a larger original capacity than did the Indonesian plant. Although there would be definite advantages in comparing the investment required and the production costs of two plants of the same capacity, the fact that the United States plant was of larger capacity does permit some useful analysis of the extent of the economies of scale and the relevance of this for the most suitable capacity to be sought for the first plant in a particular industry in a newly developing country.

Indonesia inherited a substantial number of state enterprises from the Netherlands with the transfer of sovereignty at the end of 1949. In addition to such public utilities as post and telegraph, railroads, electricity and gas, and a national airline, the government operates tin mines, coal mines, solar evaporation salt beds, and a number of agricultural estates. From the beginning of its independence it was expected that the Government of Indonesia would play a major role in financing industrial development, but the form of ownership of new industries was not definitely fixed. It was hoped and expected that national enterprises would play an important role in industry, and a special bank, Bank Industri Negara (State Industrial Bank), was established to provide investment capital to national enterprises. The national enterprises could be either private, government, or mixed enterprises, and might also be a combination of central and provincial government participation. Bank Industri Negara, in general, provided long-term capital, but on occasion also provided working capital.

The new Government of Indonesia assumed the general position of the former Netherlands Indies government with respect to foreign investment of nationals other than those of the Netherlands, and established new regulations concerning Dutch private enterprises, which also assumed the status of foreign enterprises with the transfer of sovereignty. Indonesia thus inherited a legal and government system based on private enterprise but with a large amount of state industrial and mining enterprises. When sovereignty was transferred most private businesses were Dutch or Chinese, or other foreign, chiefly United States or Western European. Indonesian citizenship was made available to both Dutch and Chinese residents. Relatively few Dutch availed themselves of the opportunity to become citizens, but many of the Chinese engaged in business in the cities and larger towns became citizens as soon as possible.

The new government sought to redress the balance between foreign and national enterprises by legislation and regulations designed to restrict or curtail the position of foreign enterprises and to encourage the development of new national enterprises and the expansion of old enterprises. Private enterprise and parliamentary democracy were the economic and political bases for development following independence, and within this framework the Gresik cement plant was planned and built. The plant was completed and began operation in the middle of 1957. In this year, however, major changes in the Indonesian political, economic, and social structure were set in motion. In 1957 "guided democracy" was introduced by President Sukarno, and at the end of November Dutch private property in Indonesia was taken over and Dutch nationals were required to leave Indonesia. The take-over of Dutch enterprises was followed by their nationalization and the development of the concept of "guided economy" as the economic counterpart of "guided democracy" in political affairs. Some form of socialism is the vehicle for industrial development in Indonesia in the future. A rebellion in West Sumatra and Northern Sulawesi in 1958 was suppressed quickly, but sporadic guerilla activity continued in a number of provinces and security expenditures continued to represent an important part of the government budget at the time of the field work for this study late in 1960.

The entire period of operation of the Gresik plant with which this study is concerned, from July, 1957, through June, 1960, was one of great political, economic, and social change in Indonesia. The Gresik operating experience therefore has not been that of a plant conceived, built, and operated in a peaceful socialist society, but rather that of a plant conceived and built under one political and economic system and operated from the start under conditions of significant political and economic change, of which not the least was that of continuous and rapid inflation. In an important sense the Gresik plant is a microcosm of the problems of industrial development in Indonesia in its recent critical years. The fact that the plant was successful from the start led to a 50 per cent expansion program that was well under way at the time of the study. This expansion program, as we shall see, provided valuable evidence of the extent of increases in the cost of construction over the time interval involved, and insight into the financial problems to be expected in future major industrial development projects in connection with a new Eight-Year Development Plan adopted in the second half of 1960.

The Gresik cement plant is typical of the financing arrangements preferred by the newly independent countries. Virtually all the dollar exchange was provided by the United States Export-Import Bank under a 25-year loan at 5¾ per cent interest. All expenditures requiring local currency were provided by the Government of Indonesia. The government also provided the foreign exchange required for certain of the initial exploration and planning, for the salary and expenses of the technical advisor, and for much of the imported material used in work done directly by local contractors for the government. Assistance funds for the training program and the related operating-training contract were provided by the International Coöperation Administration in Indonesia.

The chief purpose in comparing the investment in a modern plant in a developing country with the investment required in an advanced industrial country was to obtain factual data on the nature and importance of social overhead capital. Social overhead capital is usually treated as a separate investment problem for developing countries rather than as a part of the investment required for a particular enterprise. This is done on the assumption that such investment is necessary for several industrial enterprises rather than just one. Thus an industrial park project might include utilities, streets and roads, housing, transportation for goods and workers, schools, municipal government buildings, and the like. Large single enterprises in new locations without prior industrial development present a good example of what may be called *minimum requirements for social overhead capital,* if the facilities are primarily for the individual plant and not for an industrial community involving plants other than the one in question. The data made available by both enterprises permitted a rather complete and detailed analysis of the nature of the particular social overhead capital required at Gresik but not at Cushenberry, and its cost both in foreign exchange and in local currency.

One of the strongest arguments for the type of arrangement at the Gresik plant is that from the start of production all top managerial and technical positions were held by Indonesians, although none had previous experience in cement production. Training for twenty-three top technical and administrative personnel began in the United States, about a year before the plant was scheduled for completion, and usually was a combination of academic work and on-the-job observation at United States plants. For approximately the first year of operation the Indonesian managers and technical staff worked with American operating personnel provided by the Morrison-Knudsen International Corporation under an operating contract with the Indonesian government. The Indonesian personnel assumed an increasing share of responsibility and before the end of the contract period were discharging all the responsibilities of their positions, and most of the foreign personnel were able to leave ahead of their originally scheduled departure.

The Gresik plant illustrates a fact that is often overlooked in discussions of industrial development—the long time period often associated with planning and financing the first large plants in a newly independent country. The Gresik plant, in fact, was not a project originally conceived and executed by the new Indonesian government, but had been under consideration for a long time. The first geological survey of the Gresik limestone deposit was made by Dr. Ir. L. J. C. van Es of the Bureau of Mines of the Netherlands Indies government in 1935. Plans for a plant were made before the Japanese occupation, and the Japanese also seem to have planned to exploit the Gresik deposit. After the transfer of sovereignty at the end of 1949 the Government of the Republic of Indonesia had Dr. F. Lunfer make another survey. In 1953-54 the White Engineering Company of the United States made a survey. Based on the White report, negotiations were entered into between the Indonesian government and the MacDonald Engineering Corporation for the construction of a plant under Export-Import Bank financing. These negotiations were not successful, and the Morrison-Knudsen International Corporation eventually obtained the construction contract. The final plans for the plant were in part the work of White and of MacDonald, but were chiefly the product of the American technical advisor, Mr. A. J. Anderson, and the H. K. Ferguson Company, an affiliate of the Morrison-Knudsen Company. In addition to assisting in planning the plant layout and equipment, the technical advisor acted as the representative of the Government of Indonesia in checking the construction work in relation to the plans, and in approving such changes as appeared desirable during actual construction. The use of an independent technical advisor was in conformity with Export-Import Bank requirements, and has proved to be a valuable feature of the Gresik development. Mr. Anderson, who started work in 1955, was succeeded by Mr. C. MacArthur Carman in 1957. After the operating success of the plant was assured, Mr. Carman concentrated his time and efforts on plans and negotiations for a 50 per cent expansion program. At the time of the field work for this study the expansion program was in the hands of a team of engineers and staff members appointed from the regular Gresik staff. The Morrison-Knudsen International Corporation again handled the procurement and construction program, and financing was by the Export-Import Bank for the foreign exchange and the State Development Bank for the rupiah requirements. The third kiln was in operation by the end of 1961. The original plant was completed in May, 1957, approximately three months ahead of schedule, and regular operations started in July of that year after satisfactory completion of the trial runs.

The cement plant at Gresik is owned and operated by a limited corporation, P. N. Pabrik Semen "Gresik." The share capital of this corporation in turn was owned by the Bank for State Industries, Bank Industri Negara. Bank Industri Negara secured part of its original rupiah capital from the Department of Finance and part through the public sale of bonds. In the case of Gresik, the Department of Finance handled the foreign exchange arrangements with the Export-Import Bank and the actual transactions passed through the central bank, Bank Indonesia. The rupiah equivalent of the foreign exchange appeared first as participation of the Department of Finance in the capital of Bank Industri Negara, and then went to P. N. Pabrik Semen "Gresik" as a loan. Thus the capital for the plant was set up in the form of a loan from Bank Industri Negara to the cement corporation rather than in the form of stock participation.

The direct contribution of the Department of Finance in terms of foreign exchange included three major categories of expenditures:

1. Cost of initial engineering surveys and plans for the plant, plus salary and related expenses of a resident foreign technical advisor.
2. Payments to foreign contractor for constructing the plant and taking it through trial runs.
3. Costs of training Indonesian technical and administrative personnel.

The foreign exchange for the first category of expenditures was paid by the Government of Indonesia from its own current foreign exchange funds; the costs of the second category were derived from a loan of approximately $14,000,000 from the United States Export-Import Bank; and the funds for the third category represented a grant from the International Coöperation Administration of the United States Government. In approximate figures, the foreign exchange for the three categories was as follows:

1. Initial surveys, planning, and technical advisors ......$ 150,000
2. Payment to Morrison-Knudsen International for machinery, equipment, ocean freight, insurance, salaries, and related expenses of construction, costs of administrative and supervisory personnel, and fees 13,587,392
3. Payments of International Coöperation Administration for sending Indonesian personnel during initial training period of operation of about a year ... 200,000

Total $13,937,392

Of the three categories, the first two, in the amount of $13,737,392, represent the foreign exchange cost to the Government of Indonesia, that is, what it has paid already or is obligated to pay in the future. The Export-Import Bank loan was made for a period of 25 years at an interest rate of 5¾ per cent. Interest is payable semiannually on the unpaid balance of the loan. In all, the Government of Indonesia borrowed a total of approximately $15,800,000 for the Gresik plant, of which about $2,200,000 was for spare parts. For the purpose of measuring the investment in the plant, the expenditure for spare parts is excluded, since these become a part of current operating expenses when they are charged out of the inventory.

Although the author and the executives of the two plants originally expected the study to be made entirely in terms of the cost data developed by the accounting procedures of the two plants, it became apparent that this procedure would be satisfactory only for the purpose of comparing the original investments in the two plants. To develop comparable costs of production, similar costs would have to be treated in the same way for both plants. To evaluate the contribution of the Gresik plant to the economy of Indonesia, the problem of inflation would have to be met by developing a specific solution for measuring and evaluating the effects of price changes.

Although the original cost data for the investment in each plant were satisfactory for comparative purposes, it was found that the cost systems at the two plants did not treat the most important cost items in the same way. The Gresik cost system was originated by the American group that operated the plant during the training period, and omitted capital costs entirely, as well as the large group of cash costs associated with the social overhead capital and general administration. After discussions with the administrative personnel at Gresik it was decided that the study should be expanded to include an *ex post* accounting procedure designed both to recognize inflation and to analyze its consequences. A corollary of this was that the accounting conventions adopted should be of general use to the Government of Indonesia for the purpose of developing pricing policies for existing government manufacturing industries, and for making investment decisions for future industrial development.

The decision to develop a theory of cost determination suitable for the needs of the Indonesian cement plant in particular and for a socialist planning operation in general did not mean that the original intention of making a comparative study was abandoned, but rather that the use of actual book costs did not seem as useful as the alternative. The alternative, in effect, retained current cash costs and developed new costs of capital. The new costs of capital were for capital consumption in the form of depreciation, and for capital use in the form of interest. In the decision to approach capital cost in its relation to the problem of inflation, there was a significant advantage in being able to apply the same depreciation and interest rates to each plant. The accounting procedure of the two plants involved substantial differences in depreciation rates, and also substantial differences in the cost accounting treatment of indirect costs, such as repairs and maintenance, utilities, and administration. By using the same cost accounting procedure for each plant, and applying the same depreciation rates and interest rates, it was possible to develop production costs which, as far as possible, reflect the real economic and technical differences between the two plants operating in two different economies.

The experience of the Gresik cement plant to date is not so much an illustration of how socialist industrial development takes place under a fixed and definite procedure as it is an illustration of how socialism is evolving in Indonesia. President Sukarno uses the term "Socialism à la Indonesia" to indicate that the Indonesian form will not be patterned after that of any other country, but will evolve in conformity with the particular needs of Indonesia and the particular character and personality of the Indonesian people. The encouragement given by the Indonesian officials to this study indicates a lack of dogmatism and a willingness to consider new or different approaches to the problems of accounting, finance, and management.

The writer wants to make it clear that the study *was not done at the request of the Indonesian government.* It was proposed by the author, and both the Indonesian officials and Permanente Cement Corporation agreed to coöperate by making data and personnel available. Although the report makes many specific proposals for accounting and actually employs the proposals in developing the data, the proposals are the sole responsibility of the author and do not represent official policy of either the Indonesian or the Permanente plant. The proposals for general policy in future pricing and those concerning financial and management policy in state enterprises in Indonesia are the views of the author and do not represent actual practice at the time of the study.

The primary object of the study was to find out as much as possible about the problems—including, of course, finding out what the problems really are in an economy and society quite different from those of the investigator. The complete freedom given by the Indonesian officials to investigate and to recommend solutions and procedures is evidence of the sincerity of Indonesia's foreign policy of "neutralism" or nonalignment with other power blocs. In its development Indonesia has expressed the desire to search for what is best for it without regard to the source of the ideas or the material. In dealing with the complicated problems of the Gresik plant the writer believes that the professional tools of analysis of the accountant and economist are as suitable for the needs of a socialist economy as for those of a private enterprise economy. Accounting and economics should not be nationalist or ideological but rather tools for international use.

In using the analytical tools of economics and accounting it is necessary to know, or at least to assume, something about the objectives of the economic unit to be analyzed. When a new social, political, and economic system is evolving, the goals and hence the needs of a particular unit may not be a matter of agreement to all concerned. In arriving at a workable policy for the development of its industrial sector, Indonesia truly must evolve organizations and procedures suited to the personality and character of its people. The proposals set forth in this study were developed after long discussions with executives at the Gresik plant and members of its board of directors. The proposals, however, are not the result of either a formal vote or of any sort of consensus, but solely the responsibility of the author and represent his present understanding of the needs of Gresik in particular and of industrial development in Indonesia in general. The proposals set forth in this study are intended to promote discussion and criticism, both in Indonesia and in the United States.

Because this is an attempt to compare economic enterprises in two different economies and cultures, it required the preparation of extensive statistical and accounting data from the records of each enterprise. Publication of the detailed basic tables appears necessary for those actually involved with the administration of the cement plant in Indonesia and for the officials concerned with general policy recommendations. The tables referred to in the Contents and the text as Appendix A and Appendix B have been multilithed and will be inserted in a pocket at the back of the copies available in Indonesia. A limited number of copies of the tables comprising Appendix A and Appendix B are available at the Institute of Business and Economic Research, University of California, Berkeley, for readers in other countries. All references to Appendix tables have been retained in the text. Supplementary tables for chapters 2, 3, 6, and 7, designated by chapter number and table number, appear as Appendix 1.

It is hoped that the detailed cost data in the appendixes will be of use to teachers and students of accounting and administration in Indonesia as well as to those concerned specifically with the cement industry. The flow-sheet method of computing unit and total costs for continuous process plants has the merit of showing exactly how the costs are accumulated by production departments and then assigned to the output or product as it flows through from raw material to finished product.

It was stated earlier that this study deals with three rather distinct but related issues. Part I, Capital Investment Comparisons, consists of a single chapter (Chap. 2) and is concerned with measuring and evaluating the significance of the initial capital investment in the fixed assets of the two plants. To make the data on investment both comparable and meaningful, it was necessary to develop the data by functional departments. The reason for this lies in the diverse nature of the economies of the two countries. As Chapter 2 attempts to point out, the plant in Indonesia, although of smaller capacity, required an investment approximately twice that of the United States plant. This was, to a limited extent, the result of an unrealistic official rate of exchange between the currencies of Indonesia and the United States, but primarily the greater cost reflected the need to build many things in Indonesia that were already available to the plant in the United States. Many readers may be surprised at the proportion of the cost differences represented by social overhead capital.

Part II, Comparison of Operating Costs and Output, is concerned with the comparative operating costs of the two plants in the period July, 1957, through June, 1960. Part II consists of chapters 3–6. Chapter 3 is concerned with the problems of developing useful costs of capital consumption (depreciation) and capital use (interest). This would be a difficult task if the economies of the two countries were stable, or even if they were both unstable but moved in the same direction at the same rate. During the period covered by the study, the United States economy experienced a general upward movement in prices, but the economy of Indonesia experienced the most severe inflation of its short history as an independent nation. The theories and related procedures employed by the writer may be unsatisfactory to some readers. To have used the valuation and depreciation methods actually employed by the two enterprises in their own accounting would have been unsatisfactory. By developing what the writer hopes is a reasonably consistent theory and actually employing it in the accounts, the interested reader has a solution to evaluate.

Chapter 4 is an explanation of the cost accounting procedures employed to develop the basic data in Appendix A and Appendix B. Appendix A includes the details of the investment cost, the revisions of investment cost, and the depreciation rates in tables A-1 and A-2. The detailed costs for 1958, 1959, and the first six months of 1960 are shown in tables A-3 to A-14 for the Gresik plant. Appendix B includes the details of the investment cost, the revisions of investment cost, and the related depreciation in tables B-1 and B-2. The detailed costs for 1957, 1958, 1959, and the first six months of 1960 are shown for Cushenberry in tables B-3 through B-10.

Chapter 5 presents a theory and related procedures for inter-economy cost comparisons under inconvertible currency. It points out the difficulties to be expected in using the procedure, and some of the advantages and limitations of such comparisons.

Chapter 6 explores the differences in the unit costs of production for the two plants and attempts to evaluate the differences in relation to the economies and political and social systems of the two countries. Emphasis is laid on the fact that the Gresik plant in Indonesia is even more labor-intensive than it is capital-intensive in comparison with the United States plant. The purpose of this analysis is to get at the question of the extent to which low pay for workers and managers in a developing economy does or does not result in lower unit cost for labor in the unit cost of the product. It is hoped that readers in both countries will find the results worth working through the somewhat involved analysis and the statistical tables.

Part III, Achievements and Problems of the Gresik Plant, consists of chapters 7 and 8. Chapter 7 is concerned only with the Gresik plant, and attempts to measure its achievements in terms of profit or loss, its contribution to the foreign exchange problem of Indonesia, the flow of funds from the enterprise to the parent bank and to the Department of Finance, and the general social contributions in the context of the goals of economic development.

Chapter 8 deals with some of the problems which appear to

be emerging in the new Eight-Year Development Plan of Indonesia. The Gresik experience is the primary basis for the views and suggestions put forth, but the writer also drew on the findings of an extensive survey of current industrial problems in East Java and in Central Java. The material in that chapter is concerned chiefly with problems of organization and of financial relationships.

PART I

Capital Investment Comparisons

II

Investment in the Two Cement Plants

The nature of the plant and equipment that a newly developing country should install is one of the most important considerations in its industrial development program. The problem cannot be approached entirely from the point of view of cost if, as is likely, the efficiency and productive life of the plant and equipment depend upon the combined competence of managers and workers. Industrial development for a new country is as much a process of acquiring human skills and experience as it is of acquiring physical capital. If a country decides, on principle, to use only the managerial and technical talents of its own people, it may want to employ modern technology, but not necessarily the size or design of plant best suited to an advanced technical society. A plant large enough to provide the economies of scale necessary to be competitive in the domestic market appears desirable; but, beyond this, other considerations become important. Even competitive costs may not be possible, and many enterprises may require either direct or indirect subsidy.

For a socialist economy the important risks associated with large and complex production units may not be those of the market but those of operating the plant efficiently in the short run, and in extending the long-run life of the plant as far as possible. A large and complicated plant may be cheaper in an industrial economy than in a developing one because of the differences in the relative costs of capital and labor in the two economies. In a developing economy the money investment in a given plant may be much higher than for a plant of similar capacity in an industrial economy because of the need to construct important items of social capital already present in an industrial society. If a developing country starts with a higher investment, and cannot secure the same output per year or as many years of service life, obviously the capital cost per unit of actual output will be even higher, in relation to similar costs in a plant in an industrial economy, than if calculated from the original capital investment. The higher costs of capital may, of course, be offset by lower labor costs, but this is unlikely when the plant itself is not labor-intensive.

Cement is one of man's oldest manufactured building materials. Cement does not occur in nature, but is the result of chemical and physical changes in a combination of rather common materials, limestone, clay, silica, iron, and gypsum. The important feature of cement is that when mixed with water it "sets up" and becomes hard. The setting-up process need not be done with cement alone, but is better if the cement bonds to other hard material such as rock and sand. It is likely that the discovery of cement was the result of finding a deposit of limestone which contained enough of the other materials so that, after being burned or fired in a primitive kiln, it would set up into concrete when mixed with aggregate and water. Cement can be made in so-called upright kilns by the dry process, but this process is not satisfactory for making cement of uniform quality. Uniformity results from using a specific proportion of raw materials and processing them in a particular way.

The modern large-scale method of making cement is the wet process, in which the basic raw materials are added to water and ground in a ball mill to the necessary fineness. The ground material, called slurry, is stored in large tanks where the quality can be controlled very accurately by blending and mixing. The ground material in suspension in water is easily transported by pipes and pumps, and in the final blending operation the mixture can be thickened by drawing off excess water. The blended slurry is then introduced into a large rotary kiln where the water is converted to steam and drawn off through a stack, and where the necessary chemical change is produced to make the material set up when water is added. High temperatures are required for the chemical and physical change, and both temperature and timing must be carefully controlled. Of the machinery and equipment used in the wet process, the kiln ordinarily represents the largest single capital cost. The cash variable cost of fuel for the kiln, and of power to turn the kiln and operate the cooling fans and material-handling equipment, is the highest of the various separate production operations.

The burning and cooling operation is the most critical and important in making cement, not only because of the capital cost and the variable power and fuel cost, but because of possibilities for variations in yield. If the plant has modern dust-collecting equipment in the kiln process, the finely ground particles will not escape through the stack but will be captured and collected in such a way as to form units large enough to be carried out with the heavier burned material. A plant without proper dust-collecting equipment will deface the countryside for miles with the cement dust lost through the stack. For new plants the incremental cost of dust-collecting equipment usually is less than the discounted value of the cement production lost through the stack in the absence of the equipment. Even if this equipment did not pay for itself in increased output it may be regarded as a necessary social cost of production. In addition to the yield of burned material in relation to the dry material in the slurry, the kiln process is critical in terms of the yield of material per unit of time. The time factor again is divided into operation time and shut-down time. Is the equipment used to capacity when running? Is it run as long as possible? As we shall see, these were critical questions in the design and operation of the two plants.

Once the material is burned in the kiln it is in a form called clinker, and has the essential physical and chemical property of cement, that of setting up after being mixed with water. Because of this, all production operations after burning must work with dry material, and water as a vehicle for transportation cannot be used. The final stage in manufacturing cement is to grind the clinker to the desired degree and uniformity of fineness and to add one or more ingredients which will facilitate the setting and bonding performance of the cement. The most important additive is gypsum, which in standard Portland type cement is about 3½ per cent of the finished weight. The finish grinding, like the original raw grinding, is done in a ball mill. Here again the time required and the yield are critical. Good modern equipment permits accurate mixing of clinker and additives; a "closed circuit" of screens and material handling is used so that only material of the desired fineness can get out of the mill circuit and on to the storage silos. Material too coarse for the specifications is rejected by the screen and returned to the mill for grinding.

The cement producer has an opportunity to rectify minor deficiencies in the quality of a run of cement by blending cement of higher quality in the storage silos. This is done by a system of air pumps and air mixing and agitation in the silo.

Cement production by the wet process is capital-intensive, and much of the material-handling equipment of the plants of industrialized countries reflects the advantages of eliminating high-cost labor, high cost in the sense of pay per hour, and high cost in the sense that errors in weighing, measuring, and blending may be very expensive in terms of quality and customer reaction. An economical cement plant depends on a combination of the quality and location of the basic limestone with respect to the market, and of the ability of the market to absorb the output without great fluctuations in quantity over the year. Irregular use must be compensated for either by investment in storage facilities (the preferred method) or by investment in enough capacity to meet peak demand. Given the foregoing factors, the obvious problem of the cement producer is to get his basic capacity for as low a capital investment as possible, and then use this basic capacity to the maximum. For each of these factors there are several variables that may influence performance.

It seems best to use only approximate figures for the cement production capacity of both Gresik and Cushenberry. The capacity of equipment depends in part on the type of cement being produced and in part on the assumptions employed in the use of the equipment available. When the Gresik plant was under consideration and when it was completed and placed in operation the capacity was generally stated as 250,000 metric tons per year. The round figure used by the management at Cushenberry for production limited to standard Portland-type cement is 2,500,000 U. S. barrels per year, or, at 5.86 barrels per metric ton, about 426,600 metric tons. For convenience, a capacity of 425,000 metric tons will be used. The capacity of 250,000 tons in relation to 425,000 indicates that Cushenberry has a capacity approximately 1.7 times that of Gresik. When the field work was done in Indonesia, however, discussion with the production officials at Gresik and with the American technical advisor indicated that the figure of 250,000 tons was based on assumptions about maintenance and operating difficulties that would not be employed in rating the same plant for production in the United States. The evidence suggested that the capacity figure involved approximately 10 per cent more down time for the kilns than would be regarded as good practice in the United States. For measuring the cost of production capacity of the equipment actually installed, it would seem reasonable to use at least 275,000 tons as the Gresik capacity. The Cushenberry capacity of 425,000 tons would then be 154 per cent of that of Gresik. Accordingly, 150 per cent will be used in this study as a convenient indication of the capacity of Cushenberry in relation to Gresik.

The economies of scale in cement production ordinarily are substantial. In the United States it is usually the available market that limits the size of the individual cement plant rather than the diseconomies of size. Most of the large cement plants in the United States reached their present size by adding new units of equipment from time to time as the market grew. Essentially, the economy of scale problem relates to the individual kiln, and this in turn depends in part on the quality of the limestone and the type of fuel available. Given a satisfactory quality of limestone and clay, a two-kiln plant is usually considered the desirable *minimum* size. This permits efficient quarry operation and the use of an efficient size of grinding mills and the related material-handling equipment. A cement plant can be enlarged by adding kilns and grinding equipment if there is sufficient land available. Ordinarily, substantial economies result from adding units at a single location because of the ability to enlarge productive capacity without a proportionate increase in such overhead items as supervision, laboratory analysis, personnel and industrial relations, accounting, medical facilities, and so on.

The rotary kilns used in modern cement production vary in diameter, length, and rate of feed of the raw material, slurry. Slurry is a mixture of ground limestone, clay, silica, and iron; in the modern wet process, slurry is in suspension in water, and this liquid form permits economical movement by pipes and pumping units, and blending of the basic materials in accordance with the requirements indicated by laboratory analysis. The burning process in the kiln changes the chemical form of the basic material, and also removes both the water in which the material is suspended and any water in the material itself. The quality of the limestone influences the thickness of the slurry as it enters the kiln. A large percentage of moisture, particularly in the stone itself, requires more time in the kiln, and hence greater cost. Thus the quality of the material being burned influences the length of the kiln and the speed with which the material moves through the kiln.

If two cement plants have the same quality of raw material and identical markets, the one with the best quarry will probably have the lowest production costs. The quality of a quarry depends on its location with respect to the processing plant, the conformation of the deposit, and whether the material is broken or solid. A deposit of limestone that is broken in small sizes through natural action ordinarily requires less blasting and crushing than a deposit of hard strata or a mixture of small, loose particles and very large pieces. Locating the processing plant close to a mountain is usually very satisfactory because the rock can be moved by conveyor belt with little expenditure for power, since the force of gravity does much of the work in moving the rock. Given a sufficient volume, moving rock by conveyor belt is much cheaper than moving it by truck or monorail. Usually it is better to locate the processing plant at the base of a mountain of limestone and work down through the deposit of limestone than to start with a deposit where the material must be raised to the surface. The chemical quality of limestone varies, and the best deposit is one that requires little in the way of additives such as clay, silica, or iron. Variation in quality of rock in the quarry may be an advantage in that it permits ready blending of high-grade rock with low-grade rock to secure the quality required for the type of cement being produced. A relatively poor deposit requires additives; this is especially disadvantageous if the additives must be transported from a distance.

In view of the combination of physical, chemical, and mechanical factors which influence the production of cement, one would expect to find significant differences between two modern plants in the same country. For two plants in two different countries, one in a desert location and the other in the tropics, the differences may be substantial. Table 2–1 (Appendix 1) summarizes the investment in each of the plants considered in this study. The investment is expressed in U. S. dollars for each plant. For the Gresik plant in Indonesia the costs represent the actual dollar expenditures paid to the Morrison-Knudsen International Corporation plus the rupiah costs incurred by that company and by P. N. Pabrik Semen "Gresik" on its own account, converted at the official rate of exchange during the construction period of 11.475 rupiahs to one U. S. dollar.

The data of table 2–1 are arranged by function or department to show the type of facilities required in Indonesia but not at the United States plant. In some cases an investment was required at both Cushenberry and Gresik for the same class of facility, but the investment was much higher at Gresik. Where there was a significant difference in the type of equipment and the difference represented social capital available at Cushenberry but not at Gresik, the difference in dollar investment is shown in the last column of the table.

Table 2–1 shows that the total investment in Gresik was more than twice that at Cushenberry, but that the difference was mainly attributable to items of capital required at Gresik but not at Cushenberry. For the moment, therefore, we may say that the investment in comparable facilities at Gresik was $16,636,000

in relation to $14,540,000 at Cushenberry. Since the capacity of
the Cushenberry plant was at least 50 per cent greater than that
of the Gresik plant, should we conclude that the higher investment
per ton of capacity was the result of higher general construction
costs in Indonesia? The data of table 2–1 do not support this
interpretation. For comparable facilities, costs were higher in
Indonesia for the factory administration building and equipment,
the machine shop and warehouse, the quarry and related material equipment, and the storage silos, packhouse, and loading
facilities. These are all facilities influenced either by the location
in the tropics or by the state of development of the economy
(as distinguished from the stock of social capital). The difference
in cost of the administration building apparently was the result,
in part, of differences in methods of capitalizing costs, and of the
need for a larger number of administrative and technical personnel in Indonesia. With respect to cost, at Cushenberry the initial
complement of laboratory and office supplies was charged to expense, whereas the same items apparently were capitalized at
Gresik. This was a minor factor, however, compared with the
difference in the size of the staff.[1] The warehouse and the machine
shop had to be much larger in Indonesia than in the United
States: the warehouse, because of the need for maintaining a much
larger inventory of spare parts and operating supplies; the machine
shop, because it had to have much more equipment in order
to make the many things that in the United States can be obtained
from a manufacturer or an outside machine shop.

The difference in the cost of the quarry and related raw
material facilities reflects in large part the difference in the natural
qualities of the two deposits and their location with respect to
the processing plant. The Cushenberry plant is in a high desert
region in Southern California, and the limestone deposit is in a
mountain above and close to the processing plant. The rock is
generally soft and loose, requiring relatively little blasting, and
is conveyed to the storage areas by belt conveyors and moved
from each storage pile by gravity feeder tunnels at the bottom
of the storage area. The Gresik limestone deposit is about the
same distance from the plant as that at Cushenberry, but it is

---

[1] For details of these differences, see Chap. 6, and table 6–5 (Appendix 1).

in a low outcropping rather than a mountain. Because of the tropical location, covered storage for quarried rock is required, for the heavy tropical rains add moisture and make handling difficult, whereas nothing of this sort is necessary in the dry desert air at Cushenberry. Gresik employs trucks instead of conveyors to transport the limestone and the clay. The clay field at Gresik is at a distance from the limestone quarry and there is not as much clay material in the limestone as at Cushenberry; hence both capital costs and variable production costs tend to be relatively higher at Gresik.

The higher investment in storage and loading facilities at Gresik is the result chiefly of the differences in construction costs payable in dollars. When the Gresik plant was built there was no satisfactory supply of cement for the storage silos and other reinforced concrete structural requirements. All cement for the Gresik plant was imported from the United States; hence ocean freight and insurance had to be added to the cost incurred by Cushenberry.

The following facilities may be regarded as critical in the economies of scale for the two plants: raw grinding, kilns, and finish grinding. Since all processing equipment for the Gresik plant was purchased in the United States, the landed cost at the plant site in Indonesia would exceed that of the delivered cost at Cushenberry by approximately the amount of ocean freight and insurance—approximately 20 per cent of manufacturer's price on the heavy machinery and equipment. Cheaper construction labor in Indonesia might offset entirely or in part the additional costs of ocean freight and insurance. The comparable facilities for which costs expressed in dollars were higher in Indonesia than in the United States were, for the most part, not strictly determined by the production capacity of the processing equipment. If the critical processing equipment had a larger capacity, it probably would not have been necessary to spend proportionately more on the quarry, the office and laboratory, and the machine shop and warehouse. These items might be expected to contribute to the economies of scale.

Since the Cushenberry plant initially had a production capacity of finished cement of approximately 150 per cent that of the

Gresik plant in Indonesia, we would expect the processing facilities at Cushenberry to cost more than those at Gresik, even allowing for the 20 per cent added for ocean freight and insurance. This is borne out by table 2–1: the costs of raw grinding, kilns and related equipment, and finish grinding were $6,728,363 in relation to $5,620,058 for Gresik, or approximately 120 per cent. Although Cushenberry gained a definite advantage over Gresik by spending 20 per cent more dollars to secure 50 per cent more capacity, we are not justified in concluding that Gresik could have reduced its dollar investment per ton of capacity by using equipment of the capacity and type used at Cushenberry. Except for the kilns, there seems to be no important advantage in the size of the processing units. Although the Cushenberry plant invested 125 per cent of the amount at Gresik for grinding equipment, most of this advantage was apparently in the safety factor attributable to plant location. The Gresik plant employed five ball mills, two for raw grinding and two for finish grinding, and one "switch mill" that can be used for either raw or finish grinding. The switch mill is in part excess capacity as a safety factor in the event of breakdown in one of the mills—a risk not as great at Cushenberry where excess grinding capacity is not as necessary.

There is little question that the critical equipment for the economy of scale in cement processing is the kiln and related cooling equipment. Here for only 115 per cent of the Gresik cost the Cushenberry plant obtains 160 per cent in rated capacity. The Cushenberry kilns have a diameter of 12 feet, a length of 450 feet, and a rated output of 26.6 metric tons per hour. The Gresik kilns each have a diameter of 11 feet, a length of 375 feet, and a rated output of 16.5 metric tons per hour. Why were larger kilns not used at Gresik? Discussions with the technical staff at Gresik indicated that the larger kilns used at Cushenberry would not have been satisfactory for Indonesia. In part, this was because of cost and technical construction problems, for the larger-diameter kilns would have had to be cut in shorter sections for shipment as a result of limitations of cargo-handling equipment on the boats and at Gresik, and would have created substantial additional maintenance and operating problems. In part, the difference in capacity of the kilns is not one of kiln size but of the nature of the limestone at each location. The Gresik limestone has a higher water content; hence a given tonnage entering the kiln will emerge as a smaller tonnage of burned clinker, and take longer in the kiln.

GENERAL DETERMINANTS OF SIZE
OF THE GRESIK PLANT

The objective in designing the original Gresik plant was to obtain an efficient small plant which could be expanded. Instead of the market being the limiting factor on initial size, Indonesia had the problem of a limited supply of managerial and technical manpower. For practical purposes, the supply was zero and had to be developed during the construction period. It was thought that the managerial and technical problems of operating a small, flexibly balanced plant would be fewer than those of a larger plant. The two-kiln plant was selected as the most flexible and satisfactory, for the risks of failure of any one piece of major equipment are fewer with a two-kiln plant than with a single-kiln plant. The Gresik plant was large enough for the expected immediate market, and was believed to meet the objective of being staffed entirely by Indonesian personnel after a relatively short period of on-the-job instruction and training by foreign technical personnel. The plant was designed to provide room for the additional units required for at least one other kiln (a 50 per cent expansion in the original capacity). It was recognized that the total cost of the enlarged capacity might well be higher if the additional units were built in two stages rather than one, but the reduced staffing problem and related risks were believed to outweigh the advantages of lower over-all construction costs. Undoubtedly an important consideration in selecting the two-kiln design was the fact that, at the time of planning, Indonesia's economy was primarily one of private enterprise, and the influence of the Dutch in the industrial and marketing sectors of the economy was very important. It was not certain that the domestic market would grow rapidly, or that the government plant would be decisive in shaping import policies.

SOURCES AND NATURE OF THE INVESTMENT COST DATA

The cost data of table 2–1 are expressed in U. S. dollars. The fact that the total cost of the Gresik plant in dollars was more than double that of the Cushenberry plant suggests that the investment may have been too high. An excessive investment, in economic terms, certainly would be one in which the foreign exchange costs associated with the capital cost of a plant and the current operating expenses in foreign exchange produce a unit cost of product in foreign exchange alone that exceeds the landed cost of the product when imported. In evaluating investment in a developing economy it is necessary to distinguish between investment requiring foreign exchange and that involving local currency. For the latter it is desirable to determine the total expended on local labor and material and the total expended on imported material purchased from local suppliers. Table 2–2 shows the expenditures of table 2–1 for Gresik in both dollars of foreign exchange and rupiahs for local labor and material. Following the distinction between social capital expenditures and regular cement-producing facilities, expenditures for these two groups in foreign exchange and local currency are given in the accompany-

	Expenditures in foreign exchange	Expenditures in rupiahs converted to dollars at rate of 11.475 to 1
Facilities representing social capital:		
General administration	$ 1,413,606	$ 8,686,674
Ocean dock and oil storage	697,793	892,468
Diesel power plant	1,902,518	301,569
Water line and treatment plant	503,716	761,287
	$ 4,517,633	$10,643,998
Total expenditures	15,000,000	16,562,928
Difference: expenditures for cement-producing facilities	$10,482,367	$ 5,918,930

ing tabulation. It shows that the items of social capital included a larger percentage of local currency expenditures than did the facilities for making and storing cement. The cement-producing facilities, which were in general similar to those required at Cushenberry, involved a foreign exchange investment of $10,482,367. This compares with a total dollar cost at Cushenberry of $14,539,715. Since the Cushenberry plant had a production capacity of 150 per cent of the Gresik plant, the total dollar investment per ton of capacity at Cushenberry was approximately the same as the investment in foreign exchange alone per ton of capacity at Gresik.

Economic Consequences of Expenditures in Local Currency

In selecting industrial projects in a developing economy it may be desirable to favor those for which the ratio of local currency to foreign exchange is relatively low. In spite of the rather general belief that newly independent nations require enormous sums of foreign exchange for capital investment, the fact is that the chief limitation on industrial capital formation is often local currency rather than foreign exchange. This is particularly true of countries, such as Indonesia, that elect state enterprises rather than private foreign investment. State enterprises require the developing country to provide the local currency. Since, by definition, the economy is at a low stage of development, total savings are likely to be small, and so the savings come by way of the forced savings of inflation when the government, in effect, creates the money required for the investment in projects such as Gresik cement. It must be emphasized that for Indonesia, and probably for most other developing economies, the creation of additional money to finance industrial construction projects has the maximum inflation effect. This is because the economy has little or no surplus of the strategic factors of production to be brought into play as a result of the demand created by the spending capabilities of construction workers and local contractors. Indonesia has a good deal of unemployment, but it has little or no idle land or land producing below the maximum per hectare with existing techniques.[2] Similarly, it does not have idle shops or factories waiting to use local materials to produce necessities for the construction workers. The construction workers with their pay enter the market to compete for a limited supply of food, clothing, and other necessities. The immediate "multiplier effect," in terms of real income, is close to one for expenditures on construction. The plant is built and its cost represents real income, but there will be little or no increase in the production of consumer goods during the construction period. As an alternative to inflation, of course, the government can use foreign exchange to pay for importing more consumer goods, especially rice and clothing. If this is done, the local currency costs really represent foreign exchange; the case for private foreign investment is strengthened because the foreign investor would, in effect, import not only equipment but also food, clothing and other consumer goods for the construction worker.

Although the investment in capital goods represented by expenditures for labor and locally produced material may create an inflationary problem in Indonesia without an offsetting multiplier effect on consumption goods, the economic benefits are not solely those of getting the plant built but extend to training a substantial part of the operating force required to run and maintain the plant. In many ways it would be advantageous if the labor force required to build a plant in a developing country were equal in size and skills to that required to operate the plant. Usually, however, the construction labor force greatly exceeds the operating labor force; hence there is an unemployment problem when a plant is completed if the development program does not have another construction project scheduled to take up the slack in work opportunities. Although only part of the construction labor force could be kept on to run the Gresik plant, a substantial majority of the operating labor and especially the maintenance labor force was recruited from the construction labor force. Thus the construction of capital equipment in a

---

[2] Indonesia has large areas of land believed suitable for cultivation of food crops, but this land requires substantial capital investment before it will be very productive. Such land is chiefly on Sumatra, Kalimantan (Borneo), and Sulawesi (Celebes). To be suitable for rice culture, the land may require extra clearing of jungle growth, drainage, irrigation facilities, or all of these.

developing country provides a necessary training school for the operating and maintenance labor required for the operation of the plant.

PROBLEMS IN THE RATE OF EXCHANGE

In converting rupiah costs to dollars the official rate of exchange of 11.475 rupiahs to one U. S. dollar was used for all rupiah expenditures. This rate appeared the most satisfactory of those available, but is subject to the defect that some of the rupiah expenditures were incurred after the 11.475 rate was changed. A *de facto* devaluation of the rupiah started in May, 1957, and continued to August 24, 1959, when the rupiah was officially devalued to a rate of 45 to one U. S. dollar. The *de facto* devaluation was accomplished by the inauguration of a system of foreign exchange auctioning. Under the auction system the price paid by the purchaser of foreign exchange was expressed as a percentage of the official rate for the currency in question. When the system was inaugurated the rate on the U. S. dollar immediately went to about 200 per cent, and then advanced slowly but steadily to 332 per cent in 1958, at which level it was frozen by government action. At 332 per cent of 11.475, the final rate was 38.097 rupiahs to one U. S. dollar, and the official devaluation of August 24, 1959, established the rate of 45 to one U. S. dollar. Clearly the use of the investment at the end of 1959 presents problems of interpretation. The Gresik plant prepares a balance sheet only at the end of the calendar year; hence the additions for the year could be converted only at the monthly average rate for the year. The following are the book figures for depreciable assets at the end of 1957, 1958, and 1959:

Year	Investment	Increase over prior year
1957......Rp.	348,683,585	
1958.......	356,927,030	Rp. 8,243,445
1959.......	365,963,905	9,036,875

If we take the "frozen" rate of 332 per cent as an approximation of the monthly average for the years 1958 and 1959, the investment of approximately Rp. 17,000,000 in 1958 and 1959 would be decreased from $151,000 (at the 11.475 rate) to $45,500, or $105,500. This did not appear sufficiently large to warrant the use of separate exchange rates for 1958 and 1959. The change, if made, would be almost entirely in the category of general administration. Although the exchange auction system was inaugurated in May, 1957, it appeared from the available records and from discussions with the accounting personnel at Gresik and representatives of Morrison-Knudsen International that the rupiah investment in the last six months of 1957 was not very large, and that certainly there was little increase in either the prices paid for local material or for wages and salaries of construction workers. Since the plant officially began production in July, 1957, after completing a final trial run of at least 30 days, it seemed satisfactory to treat all 1957 rupiah expenditures as, in effect, made before the *de facto* devaluation.

As will be brought out in detail in Chapter 3, any error in failing to convert rupiah investments in 1958 and 1959 to dollars was substantially corrected in developing depreciation and interest costs by the use of construction cost revaluation indexes.

Perhaps the most important question raised by the devaluation of the rupiah concerns the possibility that the 11.475 rate in effect during the major construction expenditures was somewhat inaccurate. If the rate overvalued the rupiah, as subsequent devaluation would suggest, then use of the 11.475 rate to convert rupiah expenditures to dollars will give a dollar investment that is too high. The rupiah was not a convertible currency during the period under consideration, and unofficial market quotations for Djakarta were published in the official reports of the central bank, Bank Indonesia. The high and low unofficial market rates in Djakarta for the 1955–1957 period were as follows:

Year	High	Low
	Rupiahs per U. S. dollar	
1955	46.50	33.25
1956	36.12	29.50
1957	47.50	31.00

SOURCE: Bank Indonesia, as published in *Statistical Pocketbook of Indonesia,* 1959, by the Central Bureau of Statistics, Djakarta. Table 10, p. 193.

It might be argued that the rupiah was not worth more than one-third of its official value in terms of the dollar during the period of construction of the Gresik plant. On this basis the dollar value of the local currency expenditure of Rp. 190,059,591 could be reduced from $16,642,697 to approximately $5,000,000. Although the rupiah was overvalued during the period of construction of the Gresik plant, the relevance of this to a comparative study is qualitative rather than quantitative. The qualitative aspect relates to the implications of the overvaluation for the relative merits of government versus private foreign capital for a plant such as Gresik in a developing country such as Indonesia. Clearly an overvalued currency is a barrier to seeking investment by private foreign capital, for the foreign investor must buy the local currency with foreign exchange if he is to supply all the capital. A foreign investor is not likely to invest in a country with overvalued currency, particularly if he cannot secure a definite commitment concerning repatriation of capital at a rate of exchange reasonably close to that in effect when the original investment was made. In Indonesia, for example, it would take four times as many rupiahs to repatriate a dollar of capital after devaluation to 45 to one U. S. dollar as at the rate of 11.4. Serious overvaluation is thus a double barrier to private foreign investment: first, because the foreign investor might believe, as in the case of Gresik, that he pays three dollars for rupiahs that should cost one dollar; and second, because the overvaluation suggests the strong possibility of official devaluation after the plant is built, with the consequent difficulties of earning enough rupiahs to repatriate the number of units of foreign exchange actually invested in the plant.

Whatever one's views of the theoretical procedure necessary to compare investment in a country with an overvalued currency, the practical solution must be to accept the official rate for statistical purposes. To adjust for overvaluation or undervaluation would involve the investigator in the problem of deciding what free market rate should be used. The precise amount of overvaluation is not important for a study of this sort. As we shall see in the following chapters when we consider costs of production and measures of performance, the important theoretical and practical issues connected with currency valuation are not so much those associated with official overvaluation or undervaluation during the construction period or in connection with the loan agreement for the foreign exchange involved in the plant, but with the changes in both the internal value of the currency and the official foreign exchange value *subsequent to the start of actual production.*

Costs Not Included in Investment in the Two Cement Plants

In attempting to compare the costs of building two plants in two different countries the investigator encounters the usual difficulties of "omitted costs," in addition to those of converting the money costs to a common currency unit. The practice of omitting some costs from the capital account and charging such costs to current operations obviously is not possible for a new enterprise acquiring its first production unit, for usually it has no revenue against which such charges can be made. An established firm, however, can secure interest-free funds in the amount of the income tax rate applied to any capital costs it is permitted to charge to operations. Since the Gresik plant was the first plant acquired by the new corporation, P. N. Pabrik Semen "Gresik," and Cushenberry was a plant constructed by a corporation already operating in the cement industry, the possibility exists that some capital costs were omitted from the Cushenberry data. On the other hand, it is likely that some expenditures in connection with the Gresik plant in Indonesia were absorbed by other government agencies, particularly the Department of Finance and the Bank Industri Negara.

The investigator found that neither enterprise included interest on capital during the construction period as a capital cost. In a legal sense this might be viewed differently for Gresik than for Cushenberry because Gresik was built entirely with borrowed capital, whereas Cushenberry was financed out of earnings. The operating corporation, P. N. Pabrik Semen "Gresik," was established as a wholly owned subsidiary of the State Industrial Bank, Bank Industri Negara. The operating company was capitalized at only Rp. 2,000,000, and the actual investment in the corporation in both fixed and working capital was in the legal form of a loan. In spite of the legal device of the loan, Bank Industri Negara, to the best of the investigator's knowledge, did not accrue interest during the construction period. Since the Permanente Cement Corporation financed the Cushenberry plant out of earnings, it did not record any charge for interest on capital during construction. The effect of the two practices in the two countries therefore provides comparable costs with respect to interest during construction by eliminating this charge.

As for other possible exclusions, the investigator is satisfied that some did occur for each plant, but that their total amount was too small to warrant the extensive investigation required to obtain the costs. The costs omitted seem to be mainly of two sorts: the land for the quarry, and the initial surveys and plans required before the construction contracts were let. The omission of quarry land cost, on the whole, proved an advantage for a comparative study. If quarry land costs were included it would require some sort of valuation process, either alternative use, as indicated by a market price, or discounting the future yield of the quarry deposit. Either process of valuation would cause difficulties in comparing both investment cost and the subsequent cost of production.

Under Indonesian law, following the Roman law system of the Dutch, the government retains title to subsurface mineral rights. For this reason it was necessary to acquire only the land for the plant site and for housing. Payments to individuals and to the communities involved probably were included in a general account and did not appear as a specific item on the books. The land around the Gresik plant is of poor quality for agriculture, and is used chiefly for grazing and minor forest operations such as firewood and the produce of some of the trees. The traditional payments for damages for disturbing the social equilibrium were nominal, as are the continuing contributions to the surrounding communities since the plant started operations.

The quarry site for the Cushenberry plant was and still is owned by the Kaiser Steel Corporation, an affiliate of Permanente Cement Corporation. An important factor in the decision to build the cement plant at the site was the possibility of selling a part of the limestone to the Kaiser Steel Corporation. As we shall see in the examination of production costs, Kaiser Steel is billed for limestone on the basis of actual current cash cost plus depreciation on the facilities; hence it derives payment for the land from the low price at which it secures metallurgical grade limestone. The cement plant, at the same time, presumably obtains its own limestone for the production of cement at a lower cash cost plus depreciation—assuming that there are economies of scale in quarrying and handling the limestone. Although Cushenberry did not have to invest in land for the quarry, it may have invested in larger quarrying and material-handling equipment. If so, as table 2–1 shows, the investment was still much less than that required at Gresik. At Cushenberry the smaller investment not only provided 150 per cent of the capacity at Gresik, but a substantial additional increment. In general, Cushenberry will ship about one-third of the quarried limestone to Kaiser Steel.

Although no payment is included in the investment data of Cushenberry for the quarry site, the site for the plant was purchased by Permanente for approximately $92,000. This cost is not included in the investment data of table 2–1. Omission of the site cost seems consistent with the treatment of site cost at Gresik. The costs of surveys and plans not a part of the actual construction contracts could not be determined for either plant. The history suggests that such costs were larger for Gresik because of the longer time during which the project was under consideration and the number of separate surveys and plans. In terms of the value for a comparative study, such costs are better omitted, for they are usually not relevant to the final decision to build the plant.

In the monetary amounts involved, the most important item omitted from the costs of Gresik is the import duties on material and equipment. At the time the field investigation work was done in Indonesia, a final decision had not been reached by the Government of Indonesia concerning the treatment of import duties on capital equipment in the work performed by Morrison-Knudsen International. The writer is strongly of the opinion that a government enterprise should not be assessed import duties, and therefore did not include the proposed duties in the rupiah costs. The issues are very complex and very important, but the details are not likely to interest all readers. The problems associated with financing a plant such as Gresik in Indonesia, and the implications of assessing import duties, are discussed in the final section of this chapter.

SOCIAL CAPITAL AT GRESIK

The literature on economic development abounds with discussions of social overhead capital and its place in economic development. The general nature of social overhead capital is easy to describe, but a definition which enables one to analyze a particular project and decide whether it should be included in the category of social overhead capital is impossible. A part of the stock of capital of every community is used to provide services to the community in the work of producing and consuming goods and services. These items are not employed directly in production, yet they either are absolutely necessary or at least facilitate the work of the community. The concept of social overhead capital seems to have originated with writers concerned with the distinction between private and public enterprise. Social overhead capital is usually equated with things provided by the government: educational facilities, roads, communication services, police protection, harbors, and so on. For a newly developing country such capital items are necessary, but their productivity is associated with the complex of industry and commerce in the community rather than with a single enterprise.

In reality, however, the items of social overhead capital that are listed above relate to the organization of economic activity in the community. The fact that there are many different enterprises making use of particular facilities is what makes them "social" and "overhead." When the same facilities are constructed and used by a single large enterprise comprising the entire economic activity of a community, the services described must be performed, and they become a part of the capital investment in the economic unit. Thus an oil field, pipe line, refinery, and terminal operation may be the only economic unit in a particular region, and so will provide all roads, utilities, housing, health, educational, and recreational facilities, as well as transport in and out of the area. Any facilities originally provided by the oil operation and made available to other economic units in effect become social capital for such units.

Social capital can be viewed in at least two ways. The first is to consider it as investment made by one or more units not a part of a particular producing unit but providing services to that unit. If one were to use this concept, the social capital in an industrial project such as the Gresik cement plant would consist of facilities constructed by private or governmental units other than P. N. Pabrik Semen "Gresik" but used entirely or in part by Gresik. The second view of social capital is that it represents the investment required in a developing economy and not in an industrial economy. This definition can be used in comparing two industrial projects, but must be employed with discretion, for not all differences in the facilities required can properly be attributed to differences in the stages of economic development.

If a manufacturing plant in a developing country cannot draw on the same stock of social overhead capital that is available to a similar plant in an industrialized country, the enterprise must either acquire the necessary facilities on its own account or there must be a prior or concurrent construction of the necessary capital by other government or private agencies. Since some of the social overhead capital may require a substantial amount of imported material, and even imported construction equipment, one would expect all or much of the initial capital to be included in the construction program of a new plant. This facilitates both foreign and domestic credit arrangements. Such was the situation at Gresik.

Few industrial plants are completely static in the sense that they do not change production methods or production capacity with the passage of time. Improvements in production techniques and market growth may cause one enterprise to grow, and declining demand and stagnation in the industry may cause another enterprise to decline with time. In attempting to relate capital investment to output or to compare investment in one enterprise with that in another, the investigator is faced with the necessity

of defining the point in time at which he will measure investment. Seldom can this be the date at which production actually
begins, for in a large installation many things are not completed
by that time. With proper design, it is possible to start producing cement before most of the buildings that house the equipment are completed. The nature of the investment at Gresik
makes the selection of the proper date for measuring investment
both difficult and important. A certain amount of capital investment in most enterprises may be viewed as a part of "the
standard of living of the enterprise." This is particularly true
of capital additions once operations begin. Certainly in the
United States a profitable enterprise may have a standard of
maintenance and improvements that reflects its earnings. The
same may be true of a socialist enterprise. The pressures in a
socialist economy to use earnings for housing, education, and
recreation of the workers may be greater than those for "con-
spicuous consumption" in a private enterprise economy. The date
selected for measuring capital investment in the two plants was
December 31, 1959. This date was selected so as to include the
investment at Gresik in housing and related facilities, and the additional investment at Cushenberry subsequent to the start of
operations.

The use of the end of 1959 for plants starting production in
1957 may appear questionable to many readers. The fact that
Gresik invested Rp. 8,000,000 in 1958 and Rp. 9,000,000 in 1959
was the basis for concluding that the end of 1957 could not be
regarded as a satisfactory date. The use of the year-end figure for
1959 is not altogether satisfactory, for in 1960 the enterprise was
still building housing and related facilities. In 1960, however, the
contract for a 50 per cent expansion was signed and it is likely
that a part of the 1960 expenditures was for housing in anticipation of the needs of the expansion. At any rate, the data at the
end of 1959 were the latest available, for problems in general accounting were such that only an annual balance sheet was prepared and that several months after the end of the calendar year.

The first item in tables 2–1 and 2–2 for which Gresik expended
funds but Cushenberry did not is that of general administration.

In classifying investment expenditures between general administration and factory administration, an effort was made to include in the latter category those items constructed at both Gresik and Cushenberry and clearly associated with the administrative and technical requirements of a cement plant. This was facilitated by the fact that the construction costs for the administration and laboratory building at Gresik were incurred by Morrison-Knudsen International, and the available details were comparable with those available from Kaiser Engineers for the Cushenberry plant. The category of general administration at Gresik was used for the following: housing for staff and the monthly employees (over 250 units had been completed by November, 1960) ; an elementary school; construction costs for police and other security offices; a fleet of buses and trucks to transport workers to and from work; cars for executives; a guesthouse for visitors; a bungalow at the nearby mountain resort of Tretes; and such recreation facilities as an assembly hall, tennis and badminton courts, and a community swimming pool. With few exceptions the facilities constructed at Gresik would be owned or rented by the employees at Cushenberry. Police protection and schools and streets would be provided by public authority in the United States, and the employee and the corporation would share in their costs by paying taxes to a variety of government units. As we shall see in Chapter 6, money wages and salaries at Gresik for all categories of employees are very low. To compare money wages and money labor costs per unit of output at the two plants would be unsatisfactory and unrealistic if the money payments were intended to cover fewer basic necessities in one economy than in the other. The use of the category of general administration makes it possible to obtain a more useful measure of the cost of labor and management at Gresik in relation to that at Cushenberry. This can be accomplished by adding to money wages and salaries the depreciation and interest on the investment so represented.

The investigator concluded that three of the four groups of utilities might usefully be designated as social capital: the ocean dock and oil storage facilities, the diesel power plant and transmission lines and facilities, and the water line and water treatment plant. Whether these represent items of social overhead capital depends upon the definition employed. For practical purposes all the facilities are used exclusively by the Gresik plant. Thus it is not valid to say that they are utilities which, for the sake of convenience in financing, were charged to P. N. Pabrik Semen "Gresik" but are used for the benefit of other economic units as well.[3]

Of the three major utility installations, not all are equally "social overhead capital" even in the sense of not being required at Cushenberry. The ocean dock was required primarily to handle the oil required for the kilns and the diesel generators, but can also be used for other incoming material and for shipping cement by freighter. Basically, however, the dock and related storage facilities may be viewed as a choice between fixed and variable cost. At Cushenberry the company is able to buy both natural gas and electric power from a private utility. The requirements for natural gas are so large that the utility constructed a pipeline some 34 miles in length to serve the plant. The cost of this is in part met by Cushenberry in a higher gas rate for a period of years, but the gas supply represents a form of capital available in California but not in Indonesia. In Indonesia, however, bunker fuel oil and diesel fuel are available at prices among the lowest in the world. Thus for Gresik to invest in facilities necessary to use oil was to exchange a fixed investment for a low variable cost for oil. Certainly the variable cost of oil at Gresik is lower than the variable cost of gas and electricity combined at Cushenberry.

The diesel power plant is an example of capital investment required at Gresik and not at Cushenberry, and not one of preferring to generate power rather than buy it. Gresik had no choice but to generate its own power. Having the generating plant, however, makes a certain quantity of electricity virtually a free good.

The Cushenberry plant was able, even in a desert, to obtain an adequate supply of water by drilling a deep well. This cost

---

[3] It is not strictly accurate to say that the utilities are not available to any economic unit other than the cement plant, for the neighboring small communities obtain some benefit from the water and electricity, but this is for consumption rather than production and represents so small a fraction of the total supply as to be ignored.

was relatively nominal and far less than the cost at Gresik of bringing water from the Brantas River, a distance of over 20 kilometers, and then treating it for both plant and household use.

The last two items of table 2–1, the bag factory and the locomotive and railroad spur tracks, are somewhat unusual examples of differences in levels of economic development. Since the end of World War II the percentage of cement sold in bags in most areas in the United States has declined steadily until it is a very small percentage of total volume. Most shipments from cement plants in the United States are in bulk form, and again most of this is by special cement gondola carriers. In Indonesia all cement is sold in bags. Since all paper for the bags or the bags themselves must be imported, the Gresik plant had to choose between importing bags or making them. The economies of making bags are so great that investment in a bag factory is much to be preferred to the higher cost of importing ready-made bags. Here the saving in foreign exchange is important. Sacks are used in Indonesia primarily because of the humid climate, and also because of the nature of the transportation and storage facilities. The highway system is not adapted to the use of large cement gondolas, which would cause excessive damage to the roadbed; the railroad system is built for small freight wagons; and a bulk carrier would carry a relatively small quantity of cement. The chief disadvantage of bulk cement, however, is that most of the equipment for transporting and handling it would have to be imported, and the scarce foreign exchange should not be used for what is essentially labor-saving equipment in an economy with a great surplus of unskilled labor. In Indonesia the cement bag is a valuable good and not a nuisance to be burned as in the United States. One important use of cement sacks is in the manufacture of ceiling boards. The boards are made by hand in molds and consist of cement over a paper core of several layers of (usually) cement sack paper and a small quantity of fiber (such as cocoanut fiber or hemp). The enormous demand for ceiling board for both public and private construction has resulted in a market price for empty cement sacks that exceeds the cost of manufacturing the sacks.[4]

---

[4] The Government of Indonesia employs a simple but effective way of rationing

Table 2–1 shows that each plant invested in railroad facilities. The decision to treat the excess of the Gresik investment as social capital was made because the Gresik investment reflects the differences in the transportation system of the two economies. Both Cushenberry and Gresik were built in relatively isolated locations. Cushenberry was not served by a railroad, but the volume of limestone it would ship to Kaiser Steel was so large that the nearest railroad built a branch line to the plant site. The investment in plant switching and loading facilities at Cushenberry was treated as a cost to be associated with limestone shipped to Kaiser Steel and not with the production of cement. In Indonesia the railroad is a state enterprise. A line runs near Gresik, but the plant had to construct extensive switching facilities and a rather long connecting line to the nearest point on the railroad. As in the case of fuel for the kilns, Gresik had to make the investment in rail connections that was made by another enterprise at Cushenberry.

In summary, the investment shown on tables 2–1 and 2–2 as required for Indonesia but not in the United States should not all be designated as social overhead capital. The largest category, that of general administration, is perhaps best defined as a combination of social overhead capital and a reflection of important differences in the methods of paying and treating personnel in the two societies. The higher investment in utilities is a combination of differences in available energy materials and in the stage of industrial development. From the economic point of view, the higher investment in utilities at Gresik suggests that what is termed social overhead capital need not appear as a separate investment figure in a state budget or economic plan, but may, to a large extent, be incorporated in the investment totals of specific projects. The differences in the investment in the railroad facilities and the need for a separate bag factory are the result of differences in climate, of the stage of economic development, and of ownership relationships with respect to the railroad system of each country. The much higher investment in Gresik affords

the supply of paper for ceiling board by not permitting the import or sale of such paper. This limits the supply to used cement bags and forces manufacturers to administer a used-sack market, thereby creating some employment and making the foreign exchange on paper for cement sacks do double duty.

impressive evidence that the cost of so-called basic industrial capacity in a developing economy is likely to exceed by far the cost of similar capacity in industrial countries.

Cost of the Expansion Program at Gresik

The 50 per cent expansion program in progress at the time of the field work late in 1960, and completed by the end of 1961, increased its rated capacity to approximately the same level as that obtained with the original two-kiln plant at Cushenberry. The estimated cost in foreign exchange of the expansion program was in excess of $7,000,000, but a portion of this was for spare parts. The rupiah cost was budgeted at 400,000,000. By using a dollar cost of $6,500,000 for the new equipment exclusive of spare parts, and by converting the rupiah budget to dollars at the official rate of 45 to 1, the expansion totaled about $15,400,000, of which nearly $9,000,000 was in local currency. For practical purposes, therefore, the dollar equivalent investment per ton of production capacity was about the same as for the original plant, that is, about $54 in foreign exchange or $114 in total. This compares with the original Cushenberry investment of approximately $34 per ton.

We must conclude that, in terms of investment per ton of production capacity, the Gresik plant started production with a capital cost disadvantage of approximately 3.3 times that of the Cushenberry plant. Although this is a great differential when expressed as a multiplier, an investment of $114 per metric ton of capacity for so basic a construction material as cement may provide a fast recovery of the investment in terms of the saving in foreign exchange. The higher capital cost does not in itself mean that the combined cost of capital and current cash costs will be higher in Indonesia than in the United States plant, although certainly the Gresik plant starts with a handicap. Even a higher total cost for Gresik than for Cushenberry does not mean that the plant in Indonesia was not a sound commitment of available economic resources.

TREATMENT OF IMPORT DUTIES ON CAPITAL GOODS

The problem of import duties on the capital equipment imported for the Gresik cement plant points up an important fact concerning government policy. It is conventional to speak of "the government" and of "government policy." But these terms imply a definite mechanism for determining and carrying out top or overall policy. A corollary of this is that the process of government administration does not permit any individual department or agency to follow a policy or adopt procedures at variance with the central or top policy. In fact, however, the separate departments and agencies of any government engage in power struggles with each other at many levels. Within the same department there may be struggles for funds and for power that are inconsistent with the larger goals of the department itself, even if one ignores the more important goal of general state policy. The process of industrial development is, in the long run, an attempt to add to the economically productive resources of a nation. But in the short run, especially in a newly developing nation, the tangible capital formation involved in industrial development may not appear more important to the development of the nation than other types of government expenditures, and one should expect a struggle between groups and individuals for the very limited amount of currently available resources.

Because the nature of the struggle for resources is not always clear, it is useful to understand the administrative apparatus. A theory of monetary policy and resource allocation is not sufficient in practice; it must be related to the actual operation of the departments and agencies which implement the theory. Theories of fiscal policy abound for underdeveloped countries, but very often the results expected from the policies involved in the theories are not achieved. The administrative apparatus often develops an extraordinary capacity for frustrating the theoretical programs.

When the Gresik cement plant was built, at least six government departments or agencies were concerned in the financial arrangements. Gresik was to be a state corporation and its stock held by Bank Industri Negara. For convenience the present names of the departments (ministries) and agencies will be used; hence the State Development Bank will be used as the English equivalent of Bank Pembangunan, successor to Bank Industri Negara under the Eight-Year Development Plan of Indonesian socialism. The Indonesian name, P. N. Pabrik Semen "Gresik," will designate the state corporation owning and operating the Gresik cement plant.

The Department of Finance acted as the official agency of the Indonesian government in handling the foreign exchange represented by the loan from the United States Export-Import Bank; it assessed and collected import duties on the equipment and other items imported; through the Foreign Exchange Allocation Board (Lembaga Alat-Alat Pembajoran Luar Negeri, known in Indonesia by its initials, LAAPLN, pronounced *laplan*) it allocated foreign exchange to P. N. Pabrik Semen "Gresik"; and through its tax division it collected income taxes from the operation of the plant. The central bank of the Government of Indonesia, Bank Indonesia, dealt with all transactions in foreign exchange, and from time to time provided working capital loans to the cement plant. Permits for specific imports were issued by a subsidiary agency of the Foreign Exchange Allocation Board known as the Foreign Trade Bureau, or more familiarly by the initials for its Indonesian name, BDP (Biro Devisen Perdagangan).

The fact that the Department of Finance proposed import duties on P. N. Pabrik Semen "Gresik" is evidence of the point made in the first chapter that a country taking the road of socialism may often be influenced by its past experience with private enterprise. The Gresik plant antedated the decision to proceed entirely with state enterprises in the large-scale industrial sector (except possibly in the oil industry, where foreign contractors apparently may be employed in the future development of oil resources). Certainly the decision to include import duties represents the application of the principle that when private and government enterprise both are instruments of state development policy, there should be no discrimination in taxation. Not many countries, however, treat state corporations in exactly the same way as private corporations. Such state corporations are often exempt from at least some taxes, and often from almost all taxes.

At the time of the field work for this study (late 1960) the Department of Finance was proceeding with its proposal to impose import duties on Gresik; so it may be inferred that this policy may not have been considered in the light of its implications for the new Eight-Year Development Plan under which state enterprises will be the means of industrial development for basic industry. The issues in taxing state enterprise for capital imports seem important to the writer. The arguments appear valid not only for Gresik but for any major industrial project in Indonesia.

Import duties in Indonesia are payable in rupiahs on the basis of a rate schedule applied to the landed cost of the imports at the official rate of exchange. In the first ten years of independence, import rates were rather high, particularly on consumer goods. This is not the place for an extended examination of the advantages or disadvantages of import duties on consumer goods, but it is appropriate to consider the effect of import duties on capital goods, particularly when the items are clearly "capital" in the sense that they cannot be diverted to consumer use by sale after import. For example, a Chevrolet sedan may be imported for either business or personal use. If it is imported by a business enterprise and subsequently sold to a private individual for personal use, the intention of the government in granting the import license may be thwarted. A cement kiln or a grinding mill, however, will not be diverted to personal use.

From the financial point of view, it may be argued that imposing import duties on capital goods will be likely to reduce the volume of capital formation *by private enterprise*. In Indonesia, however, this is not necessarily true. The operation of inflation and of economic controls may result in a situation in which private individuals or corporations have accumulated substantial rupiah balances. These balances may well be much larger than required for the local construction costs of new plant and equipment and for the purchase of imported capital goods at the official rate of exchange. This means, of course, that the system of economic controls (including taxation of individual and corporate incomes) may not yet be operating in a satisfactory manner. The fact that the amount of foreign exchange regarded as currently available for capital imports is less than the demand at the official rate of exchange means that the government can, in effect, raise the domestic rupiah cost of imported capital by the use of import duties. When applied to private enterprises, this means that capturing inflation earnings from private enterprise, they may be less satisfactory when the state itself becomes the major instrument *existing funds* in currency or bank balances are transferred to the government, and if so the effect is to reduce inflationary forces in the private sector of the economy. Although rather high import duties on capital goods may represent an effective means of re- for the formation of physical productive capital.

What happens when the government imposes import duties on a state enterprise? Here it is useful to distinguish between two categories of state enterprises: those being formed for the first time and those already in existence. P. N. Pabrik Semen "Gresik" was in the first category when the initial two-kiln plant was built, and is in the second category when it adds another kiln after a period of operating the plant. For a new plant under construction, there was good reason for the Department of Finance to "defer" the import duties on the original construction. This was so because of the financial arrangements for the plant. The Department of Finance contributed the rupiah counterpart of the foreign ex- change borrowed from the Export-Import Bank. The use of a rupiah counterpart is necessary when two or more financial agen- cies are involved. This is important, for it means that this amount of money must be introduced into the monetary system through a series of accounting transactions. For the Department of Finance to have insisted on collecting import duties on the capital im- ported for Gresik would have required the Department itself to provide the funds, particularly since at the time of construction the State Development Bank had rather limited funds. But before considering the effect of the import duties, let us trace the rupiah counterpart of the foreign borrowing through the accounts of the various agencies concerned: the Department of Finance, Bank Indonesia, the State Development Bank, and P. N. Pabrik Semen "Gresik." For convenience we shall assume round figures based on a loan of $14,000,000 converted at the rate of 11.4 to 1, a counter- part of Rp. 159,600,000.

On books of Department of Finance, counterpart value of Export-Import loan

Dr. Dept. of Finance deposit with Bank Indonesia ...... Rp. 159,600,000

   Cr. Loan payable to Export-Import Bank .... Rp. 159,600,000

On books of Bank Indonesia, to record preceding deposit

Dr. Foreign exchange holdings, U.S. dollars .... Rp. 159,600,000

   Cr. Deposit liability to Department of Finance .... Rp. 159,600,000

On books of Department of Finance, to transfer rupiah funds to State Development Bank

Dr. Advances to State Development Bank .... Rp. 159,600,000

   Cr. Deposits with Bank Indonesia .... Rp. 159,600,000

On books of State Development Bank, to record receipt of advance from Department of Finance

Dr. Deposits with Bank Indonesia Rp. 159,600,000

   Cr. Advances from Department of Finance .... Rp. 159,600,000

On books of Bank Indonesia, to record clearing of check from Department of Finance to State Development Bank

Dr. Deposit liability to Department of Finance .... Rp. 159,600,000

   Cr. Deposit liability to State Development Bank .... Rp. 159,600,000

On books of State Development Bank, to record investment in P. N. Pabrik Semen "Gresik"

Dr. Capital investment in P. N.
    Pabrik Semen "Gresik" .... Rp. 159,600,000
  Cr. Deposits with Bank Indo-
    nesia .... Rp. 159,600,000
On books of P. N. Pabrik Semen
    "Gresik," to record advance
    from State Development
    Bank
Dr. Deposits with Bank Indo-
    nesia .... Rp. 159,600,000
  Cr. Loan payable to State De-
    velopment Bank .... Rp. 159,600,000
On books of Bank Indonesia, to
    record clearing of check
    from State Development
    Bank to P. N. Pabrik Se-
    men "Gresik"
Dr. Deposit liability to State De-
    velopment Bank .... Rp. 159,600,000
  Cr. Deposit liability to P. N.
    Pabrik Semen "Gresik" .... Rp. 159,600,000

The foregoing transactions are required to get the rupiah counterpart of the Export-Import Bank loan into the hands of the
Gresik cement enterprise. The next step is a series of payments to
Morrison-Knudsen International, the contractor for the Gresik
plant. The mechanics of these payments need not concern us,
and we can summarize them as follows:

On books of P. N. Pabrik Semen
    "Gresik," to record trans-
    fer of dollars in foreign ex-
    change
Dr. Investment in fixed assets ... Rp. 159,600,000
  Cr. Deposits with Bank Indo-
    nesia .... Rp. 159,600,000
On books of Bank Indonesia, to
    record disbursements of its
    foreign exchange acquired
    from Export-Import Bank

    to Morrison-Knudsen Inter-
    national
Dr. Deposit liability to P. N.
    Pabrik Semen "Gresik" . . . . . Rp. 159,600,000
    Cr. Foreign exchange holdings . . . . Rp. 159,600,000

With the completion of the foregoing transactions the accounts on the books of Bank Indonesia are all canceled. The Department of Finance has an asset in the form of a long-term receivable from the State Development Bank, and a liability to the Export-Import Bank in the amount of Rp. 159,600,000. The liability to the Export-Import Bank, however, is in dollars and not in rupiahs; hence a change in the official rate of exchange between the rupiah and the dollar will, in a practical sense, require a revaluation of the accounts in rupiahs affected by the unpaid balance of the dollar loan. The State Development Bank, after the foregoing transactions, has an asset in the form of its long-term receivable from P. N. Pabrik Semen "Gresik," and a liability to the Department of Finance. P. N. Pabrik Semen "Gresik" has assets in the form of equipment purchased with the loan and construction work done by Morrison-Knudsen International, and a long-term liability to the State Development Bank. The creation of Rp. 159,600,000 through the foregoing transactions was in itself not inflationary for the Indonesian economy because the money did not enter the domestic economy as payment for wages or salaries or goods or services.

The rupiah expenditures that did affect the domestic economy of Indonesia approximated Rp. 190,000,000. This amount was also advanced to P. N. Pabrik Semen "Gresik" by the State Development Bank. The State Development Bank does not publish sufficiently detailed statements to permit a definite statement about the source of the rupiah funds advanced to Gresik, but something can be said about the general policy of the State Development Bank to date. As Bank Industri Negara, it sold bonds to the public and received advances from the government. To the extent that it received capital from the sale of bonds, it did not add to the money supply but simply transferred funds from the private sector or other government sectors (if its bonds were bought by government agencies). To the extent that it received advances from the Department of Finance, the money supply was increased if the funds eventually came from increases in the advances of Bank Indonesia to the government. If the source of funds from the Department of Finance was taxes, then again the transaction represented a transfer of funds rather than an increase in the supply of money. Since it is not possible to determine the exact source of the rupiahs advanced to P. N. Pabrik Semen "Gresik" by the State Development Bank during the construction of the plant, we can only consider how each type of transaction would affect the accounts of the financing agencies. If the funds were secured by the State Development Bank from Bank Indonesia without the intermediary of the Department of Finance, the result would be an increase in the assets and liabilities of the two banks by Rp. 190,000,000. This in turn would appear on the accounts of P. N. Pabrik Semen "Gresik" as a part of the investment in plant and equipment (assets) and as a loan payable to the State Development Bank (liabilities and capital) . If the funds represented the proceeds of a sale of bonds, there would have been some combination of deposit transfer and currency transfer. Although we do not know how much of the rupiah financing of the Gresik plant was inflationary in character, the fact that advances of Bank Indonesia to the government, including government agencies, were substantially in excess of the rupiah expenditure for Gresik is sufficient reason for presenting the transactions entirely in inflationary terms. It is reasonable to consider the investment of rupiahs as representing money created by Bank Indonesia.

If P. N. Pabrik Semen "Gresik" must pay import duties, it must get the money either from the Department of Finance or from the State Development Bank. What would be the situation if the rupiahs came from the Department of Finance? It would obtain them either by reducing current expenditures, which is unlikely, or by borrowing from Bank Indonesia. If it borrows from Bank Indonesia it can, in theory, repay the advance received from Bank Indonesia; if so, there is no effect on the money supply and only a bookkeeping transaction which increases the assets and liabilities of P. N. Pabrik Semen "Gresik." But we would not expect the Department of Finance to reduce its obligation to Bank

Indonesia as soon as it received the proceeds of the duties. The import duties probably would be treated as current income on the government budget, and the effect would be inflationary. This is because the Department of Finance is under continuous pressure for funds, and the import duties, instead of appearing as income/outgo, become a device for government borrowing from the central bank.

It is not likely, however, that the Department of Finance would insist on collecting the import duties if it had to increase its own direct investment in P. N. Pabrik Semen "Gresik" by borrowing Bank Indonesia funds to advance to the State Development Bank. Instead, we might expect the Department of Finance to take the position that the State Development Bank should provide the funds for the import duties of its subsidiary corporations. This would mean that the State Development Bank would have to use its own funds. If it were operating with a fixed budget for capital investment, the effect would be to transfer funds intended by government policy for capital investment to the current receipts sector of the government budget. This is not inflationary, for a fixed sum is expended, and whether it goes for capital construction expenditures or current government expenditure is probably not relevant. What is relevant is that it seems to be a device for reducing capital formation while increasing the book cost of capital assets.

The State Development Bank may, however, use import duties as a reason for obtaining an advance from Bank Indonesia. If it has committed its available funds for development projects and then must pay a large assessment for import duties, it is possible that it might enlarge its capital by borrowing from Bank Indonesia. If it did, the result would be inflationary. The inflationary pressures here are somewhat different from those exerted by creating money to finance the local construction costs of capital development. Here the capital projects compete with other economic activities and the "forced saving" of price increases has the result of adding to the stock of productive capital. But to use capital formation as an excuse for borrowing from Bank Indonesia to pay import duties to the Department of Finance will have the effect of retarding economic development in forming real productive capital, whether the funds are borrowed from the central bank or represent the use of a fixed total amount assigned to the State Development Bank. The whole process of collecting the data for the Department of Finance to assess the duties is time-consuming and costly, and this alone is a good, if not sufficient, reason for not imposing import duties on capital goods for government corporations.

In the following chapters attention will be devoted to the problems of developing and using data on the cost of production of cement. To the extent that costs are relevant for establishing prices of government products, the assignment of a large percentage of the original rupiah cost in the form of import duties will add to the capital cost and so to the price paid by consumers.

In the following chapters the proposed import duties on the items supplied by Morrison-Knudsen International are not included in the capital cost for the purpose of computing depreciation and interest. Any import duties included in the price paid by P. N. Pabrik Semen "Gresik" when it bought on its own account from local suppliers are, of course, included in the capital cost. This is not because the writer believes that import duties of this sort are a proper and useful part of capital cost, but simply because there was no way of computing the amount of such import charges.

PART II

Comparison of Operating Costs and Output

III

The Costs of Capital—Depletion, Depreciation, and Interest

Of the many difficult problems of comparing investment cost and production costs for two plants in two countries having different degrees of economic development and different political systems, those of depletion, depreciation, and interest appear to be the most formidable. Here the investigator must select the theories and related procedures he regards as most useful under the prevailing conditions, and apply them as consistently as possible to the two enterprises. He may select the methods employed by one of the enterprises and adjust the accounts of the other to make them comparable, or he may select a method not used by either of the enterprises and adjust the accounts of each in accordance with the requirements of the theory selected. This study employs the second procedure. In developing the theory and related procedures, the objective was to serve the interests of the socialist system of Indonesia rather than the private enterprise system of the United States. It is hoped that the discussion will throw light on the problems of the United States as well as on those of Indonesia.

The procedure in this study was to base both depreciation and interest charges on the estimated reproduction cost of the tangible depreciable assets employed by the enterprise. It must be emphasized that this is a procedure or convention for arriving at charges for depreciation and interest, but it is not employed for arriving at a charge for depletion of the limestone or clay deposits. It must be emphasized also that the interest charge so developed is used to determine the cost of production of cement and to value the inventory in process and the inventory of finished cement. It does not include a charge for interest on working capital. The two enterprises have differing working capital problems. The Cushenberry plant is one of several plants operated by the Permanente Cement Corporation, and the writer did not have sufficient data to develop a useful estimate of the working capital employed by Cushenberry. Interest on working capital for Gresik is treated as a "period charge" for the purpose of measuring earnings and contributions to the economy. The problems related to this are discussed in Chapter 6.

DEPLETION PROBLEMS OF THE TWO PLANTS AND THEIR RELATION TO THE ECONOMIC SYSTEMS OF THE TWO COUNTRIES

After considering the problems, it is the conclusion of the writer that the purposes of the comparative study are best served by omitting any charge for depletion. This decision is in part one of expediency, and in part one of theory. The available records do not provide a useful cost figure for the limestone and clay deposits of either plant. As the writer understands the situation, the limestone for Cushenberry was acquired by Kaiser Steel Corporation and no value was assigned to it for the purpose of a sale to the Permanente Cement Corporation. Kaiser Steel Corporation in effect retains title to the deposit and it is exploited by Permanente Cement Corporation and the tonnage transferred to Kaiser Steel is invoiced at actual book cost of production. In any event, depletion charges under the tax laws now applicable in the United States are based on the value of the rock or clay when it enters the kiln process, and not on the cost of the deposit. In practice the value is really the cost prior to the kiln operation. Over the life of the deposit the depletion charges allowed for tax purposes will usually exceed by a substantial amount the original cost of the deposit. This means that the depletion "allowance" is really an adjustment of the corporate income tax rate.

In Indonesia another government agency handled many of the problems of making available to P. N. Pabrik Semen "Gresik" the limestone deposit at Gresik, and it does not appear that the costs of such acquisition were included in the capital investment of Gresik. Since, under Indonesian law, mineral and oil deposits remain the property of the state, payments were largely compensation to communities for damages in giving up traditional rights to the surface use of the land. As far as the writer could determine, the computation of taxable income for Gresik has not included a separate charge for depletion. Since one of the purposes of developing the accounting conventions used in this study was to provide a cost basis for determining or evaluating selling prices, it would seem that a depletion charge should be included. This, in fact, is accomplished through the depreciation and interest charges in that they involve the use of a book life of the plant and equipment substantially shorter than the expected useful economic life of the depreciable assets or the limestone and clay deposits. Neither socialist economic writings nor the general marginal analysis as applied to private enterprise provide a satisfactory theory of depletion for a natural resource exploited entirely for the domestic market. The value of a mineral deposit in a private enterprise society is essentially obtained by discounting over time the stream of earnings attributable to the quality and location of the natural resource. But for a socialist society to apply this concept amounts to selecting a particular price-output combination; hence the charge for depletion cannot be a factor in determining price. For this reason the writer believes that depletion can be handled satisfactorily by the use of a "social cost" involving the consumption of the depreciable assets at a rate faster than the expected physical deterioration of the assets.

DEPRECIATION ACCOUNTING UNDER INDONESIAN SOCIALISM AND UNDER UNITED STATES PRIVATE ENTERPRISE

Whether there is a difference between the objectives to be attained by depreciation accounting under socialism and under capitalism is an interesting question. Presumably the objectives should determine the method of computing depreciation and reflecting it in the accounts. It does not seem to the writer that socialism and capitalism, as economic systems, imply anything very definite about depreciation; hence we must examine the economic and political factors which influence depreciation accounting under each system.

Depreciation accounting is usually defined as the *systematic allocation of the cost of an asset to the periods of time during which the asset will be used by the enterprise.* Although a time period is usually employed, it is possible to employ the concept of use in assigning cost. Use may be defined in terms of units of output, but is more often related to the hours of use of the asset. In an economy characterized by relative stability of prices and a relatively unchanging technology, the problems of depreciation accounting are chiefly those of determining the economic life of the asset and then selecting the method of assigning the original cost minus scrap or trade-in value at the end of the useful economic life to the intervals of time over the period for which cost or financial data are required. Such a solution assumes that there are no institutional factors affecting the enterprise which would make any particular method of assigning cost more advantageous than another. The simplest method of assigning depreciation, given these assumptions, is the so-called straight-line, or equal annual charge, method. This method applies to the cost to be assigned an annual percentage obtained by dividing one by the number of years of estimated useful economic life and multiplying by 100. Thus the annual rate in percentage terms for an expected life of 10 years would be 10 per cent, and for 20 years the annual rate would be 5 per cent.

The economic life of an asset subject to deterioration with use and the passage of time is that period of time for which it will be more advantageous for the owner to continue to use the asset than to replace it with a similar or different asset. In the absence of technological change, the economic life ends when the cost of repairing and maintaining the asset exceeds the relevant annual cost of a similar new asset. Technological change alone or in combination with an expanding market may shorten the economic life of an asset. Perfect foresight concerning the future would permit one to know the economic life of an asset when it is acquired. If the known life were used in assigning depreciation, the so-called book-life of the asset would be the same as the time for which the asset actually is used before being scrapped or replaced. The difficulties of ascertaining historical data concerning the period for which depreciable assets are used perhaps explains the widespread use of conventional groupings of depreciable assets according to type, and of a conventional book-life for each group. The conventional groups and associated useful time periods usually have a basis in past experience, but for some assets the conventional useful life may be longer than the period for which certain firms and industries find it economical to use such assets. In general, enterprises do not object strongly to conventional time periods when they are shorter than the period of actual use.

Recent experiences in the United States and in Indonesia demonstrate that depreciation accounting is influenced by many economic and political factors which may make the systematic assigning of original cost over the estimated useful life by the equal annual charge method an unsatisfactory procedure for accounting for depreciation. Of the various factors, two appear of primary importance in Indonesia and in the United States: price inflation and income taxes. These two factors are important even if we assume that depreciation accounting will have no effect on the prices at which the enterprise sells its products. Here the primary issue is the division of monetary resources between the enterprise and the government agency collecting income taxes. A related issue, of primary importance in Indonesia but not so important in the United States, is the division of monetary resources between the owners of the enterprise and the enterprise itself. Obviously, depreciation accounting takes on added importance if accounting costs are a factor in determining the price and output policy of the enterprise.

Both Indonesia and the United States have high corporation income taxes; hence the effect of depreciation accounting on the distribution of monetary resources of an enterprise is of substantial importance in each country. To analyze the money income distribution effect of depreciation accounting, we shall start by assuming that the depreciation charges do not influence the prices charged by an enterprise, and that the straight-line method for the useful life is used. In each country the factor of general price inflation makes it possible for the income tax to be, in part, a tax on capital. This happens if depreciation charges are based on original money cost of the assets. General inflation will increase money income and, depending on the time lag between increases in prices and increases in costs, may increase the money costs of factors currently purchased. The difference between the two money measures is the margin for capital consumption charges (depreciation and depletion) and the return to capital in the form of profit. Profit in this sense includes the return on capital in the sense of imputed interest, the contributions of superior management (in excess of regular salaries), and any pure profit in the economic sense. If the depreciation charges must be based on original money cost, then the real cost of capital consumption is understated by a larger and larger percentage as the general price level advances, and profits are correspondingly inflated. If the inflated profits are taxed at the rate of 50 per cent, and the balance after taxes is distributed to the owners as dividends, it may be argued that both the government and the owners take a part of the real capital each year. This argument rests on the assumption that the enterprise is to maintain its real capital. As we shall see, however, the argument also applies if the enterprise does not plan to replace its depreciable assets and the distribution of the funds provided by operations is the major issue. Let us first examine the case in which the enterprise expects to replace its depreciable assets and continue indefinitely as a going concern.

The loss of real capital referred to in the preceding paragraph can be seen if we assume that the enterprise segregates in a special bank account the amount of the annual depreciation charges. If the prices of depreciable assets employed by the enterprise should increase by 100 per cent over the time such assets are used, the replacement fund would be only half the amount required to replace the assets at the end of their useful life. In order to avoid the possibility of distributing "real" capital through income taxes or dividends determined by "unreal" accounting income, depreciation charges should be based on the current replacement costs of the assets. This procedure will not provide sufficient funds to replace the assets even if the depreciation charges are funded, that is, deposited in a special bank account. This is so if price inflation is progressive over the life of the assets. Thus an asset costing $10,000 and having a useful life of 10 years would have an annual depreciation charge of $1,000. If the replacement cost advances $1,000 per year, it would cost $20,000 to replace the asset at the end of 10 years, but only $11,000 at the end of the first year. Depreciation for the first year would be only $1,100. The annual charges, based on current replacement cost, would be as follows:

Year	Estimated replacement cost at end of year	Annual depreci- ation charge	Cumulative total in re- placement fund
1	$11,000	$1,100	$ 1,100
2	12,000	1,200	2,300
3	13,000	1,300	3,600
4	14,000	1,400	5,000
5	15,000	1,500	6,500
6	16,000	1,600	8,100
7	17,000	1,700	9,800
8	18,000	1,800	11,600
9	19,000	1,900	13,500
10	20,000	2,000	15,500

As the tabulation suggests, basing periodic depreciation charges on estimated current replacement cost will not necessarily provide, over the life of an asset, total charges equal to the replacement cost at the end of the useful life. There is a solution for the enterprise, however, if it is able to invest the funds rather than accumulate them in a special bank account. The solution is to invest in assets which will appreciate in value because of the general inflation. If the enterprise can invest in common stocks or real estate, and its investment appreciates in money value at the same rate as the increase in prices of the depreciable assets it uses, then it can accumulate sufficient funds to replace the assets at the end of their useful life. The appreciation in value of the assets acquired *should not be regarded as income* (and hence not taxed) if the enterprise is to achieve the objective of maintaining its real capital.

In a private enterprise economy the issues involved in basing depreciation on current replacement cost are in part a matter of equity as between the government and the owners of the enterprises, and in part a matter of the use of the accounts of the enterprise by interested parties. If we continue with our assumption that depreciation charges do not affect prices, we may inquire if estimated replacement costs should be reflected in the accounts—assuming that depreciation on estimated replacement cost is allowed for the purpose of computing taxable income. The providing of funds for the replacement of assets is primarily a matter of financial practice by the management of an enterprise. Accounting can assist in forming the necessary policy, but does not guarantee wisdom. If replacement values are not reflected in the accounts, but depreciation is allowed on replacement [1] value for tax purposes, then the firm encounters a difficulty if it uses the same depreciation charges for its own accounts that it does in computing taxable income; the accumulated depreciation in time will exceed the original cost of the depreciated assets, and so result in a negative net money value for depreciable assets (original cost less accumulated depreciation). In the tabulation above, the negative value would appear at the end of the eighth year. If a firm is growing, however, the accumulated depreciation need not exceed original cost for all assets combined. To use depreciation based on replacement value in computing taxable income and then use depreciation based on original cost in arriving at profit for so-called published or book purposes presents a problem in evaluating performance of the enterprise by overstating the earnings and also understating the money value of the assets. If book profits are actually distributed to the owners, it would seem that

---

[1] In the Netherlands the necessity for basing depreciation charges on replacement cost has been urged by both the Netherlands Employers' Association and the Netherlands Institute of Accountants. The Netherlands government, however, has not permitted depreciation on replacment cost for tax purposes. On three occasions the French government recognized in part the economic justice of the concept of replacement cost by permitting additional depreciation when assets are replaced, the additional depreciation being approximately equivalent to that which would have been charged on the old asset according to official replacement cost indexes computed by the government.

the owners withdraw capital to the extent of the after-tax difference between depreciation based on current replacement cost and depreciation based on original cost.

The arguments for recognizing replacement cost of depreciable assets in the accounts and for basing depreciation charges on replacement cost in computing income for tax purposes and for the use of the enterprise have not yet been adopted by Western private enterprise governments or by professional accounting bodies. If, in the Western private enterprise countries there is no general acceptance of the procedure of recognizing replacement cost in the accounts and for tax purposes, are there sound reasons for attempting to use it in the socialist economy of Indonesia? In the writer's view, the advantages in socialist Indonesia are substantial. If a private enterprise economy faces the problem of having the income tax become in part a capital levy because of inflation, is not the same risk present under socialism? It is if state enterprises are subject to a high income tax, as they are in Indonesia. Thus, if it is possible to estimate with substantial accuracy the useful life of depreciable assets, and depreciation is computed during the useful life on the basis of current replacement cost, it should be possible to obtain an accurate measure of the profit to be divided between the Department of Finance and the agency "owning" a state producing enterprise. In terms of developing money costs for the purpose of determining the money selling price, replacement cost certainly is a better base than original cost, even if the source of capital funds is within the state and not from borrowing abroad.

The case for replacement cost under private enterprise is strongest when equity capital is the chief source of funds. A private enterprise that can finance all its depreciable assets by borrowing for a term equal to or longer than the useful life of the assets is able to shift the risk of price inflation to its creditors. But what about a socialist enterprise? Here the state is the owner of the enterprise, and whether the funds are advanced to a state enterprise through the use of stocks or of bonds makes little difference. If P. N. Pabrik Semen "Gresik" borrows its fixed capital from the State Development Bank and repays the loan in steadily depreciating rupiahs, the practical effect is to reduce the ability of the State Development Bank to invest in other state enterprises. In general, one would expect state agencies to use bonds rather than stocks. This is because bonds as contractual obligations seem to be more consistent with the welfare aspirations of Indonesian socialism than do common stocks. As a state enterprise, P. N. Pabrik Semen "Gresik" should employ accounting concepts which guard against reducing the *real capital* of the nation. Thus it requires replacement cost for pricing, and replacement cost for managing its finances, that is, satisfying the claims of the State Development Bank for repayment of the loan and the payment of interest in approximately equivalent purchasing power to that of the original financing. This in turn involves replacement cost as the basis for computing depreciation and interest for the purpose of pricing cement in the domestic market.

The case for replacement cost appears even stronger in a socialist economy when all or a substantial part of the capital of a state enterprise is borrowed abroad and *must be repaid in foreign exchange*. Here the primary factor influencing replacement cost is the official rate of exchange. For the Gresik plant the 1959 devaluation of the rupiah from 11.475 to one U. S. dollar, to 45 to one U. S. dollar, poses an important problem in pricing cement. The plant, after devaluation, has to generate approximately four times as many rupiahs to cover the payments of interest and principal to the Export-Import Bank. The foreign exchange debt reinforces the domestic capital argument for the use of replacement cost.

Time and Rate for Depreciation under Indonesian Socialism and under Private Enterprise in the United States

The preceding discussion assumed the following:

1. The useful economic life of depreciable assets can be estimated with substantial accuracy.

2. The annual depreciation charge is obtained by applying to the appropriate asset value base the percentage obtained by dividing one (year) by the number of years of the estimated useful life for the asset group and multiplying by 100.

The foregoing are the procedures of straight-line depreciation. The straight-line method is easy to apply and probably is the one most used in Indonesia. There are several other ways of computing the annual depreciation charge, however, and economic considerations have made some of these methods popular in both countries. The methods which are now favored by many enterprises and sanctioned by law in both countries are the so-called accelerated methods. Depreciation can be accelerated by using a shorter time than that for which one expects the asset to be used, by applying a higher percentage rate in the earlier years of the life of the asset, or a combination of the two. Indonesia for a time (the provision was eliminated in 1960) permitted a firm to depreciate its fixed assets in three years for tax purposes, and permitted the foreign oil companies not only to accelerate depreciation by using a period of seven years, but to start the depreciation period at the convenience of the enterprise. Once started, however, the depreciation had to be continued for the assets involved.

In the United States certain assets associated with national defense could be depreciated in 60 months. Starting in 1954 the income tax law permitted business firms to employ either the sum of the years' digits method or the double declining balance method. In each country the accelerated methods were intended to provide a stimulus to private investment. Neither country permits the use of replacement cost as the *base* for depreciation. In the writer's opinion, each country has relied on the no-interest loan feature of accelerated depreciation as a stimulus to investment. The no-interest loan is simply the difference between the income tax computed with the straight-line, normal-life method and that computed with the accelerated method. The firm can use the funds represented by the tax saving for debt retirement or additional investment or distribution to the owners—subject to the existence of legally available surplus. Presumably the availability of the funds in the first few years facilitates borrowing. The accelerated methods do not reduce taxes over the life of a firm, assuming that the tax rate is unchanged, but they do change their distribution over time. For a growth enterprise the accelerated methods have definite attractions.

If the accelerated methods shift the tax payments so as to make them smaller in the early years and larger in later years, do they have any advantages when the enterprise is a government unit? For the purpose of facilitating the use of funds for capital investment rather than for regular government expenditures, accelerated depreciation is an advantage to a socialist economy. The advantages are in the psychological and administrative areas in that more funds are retained in the capital formation sector. A new country has so many pressures for regular government expenditures that it is difficult to provide funds for capital formation, even when extensive use is made of deficit financing. A measure which gives additional funds to the authorities concerned with capital formation is an advantage, if the funds are available, only if the operating enterprises *earn the depreciation charges.* Accelerated depreciation is not a source of funds, but is a device for distributing funds provided by operations. Thus the higher depreciation charges in the first years of operation may be a stimulus to sound pricing of the product and to efficient operation.

If accelerated depreciation may be employed to advantage by the state enterprises in Indonesia, what life and rate should be used? In this study the 15 per cent declining balance method is employed, and is recommended to the authorities. A rate of 15 per cent, under the declining balance method, assumes a booklife of the assets of approximately 13 to 14 years. The so-called book-life in years should not be longer than the so-called economic life of the asset. The economic life is the period of time for which the asset may be used before it is desirable either to replace it or to scrap it. Replacement may occur either because the asset is obsolete or because it is worn out. Economic obsolescence is not likely to be as important in newly developing economies as in industrially advanced countries. On the other hand, there is good reason to believe that the physical life of equipment may be shorter in developing economies than in industrially advanced countries because of the shortage of skilled maintenance personnel, repair facilities, and adequate stocks of repair parts. All these shortages contribute to the eventual wearing out and breakdown of the machinery. The more complex the machinery, the more likely it is that the useful life will be shorter in a developing economy. Even if we allow for a shorter physical life for modern machinery and equipment in Indonesia, would this be less than the 13 to 14 years implied in the use of the 15 per cent declining balance method? The writer does not believe so.

What will be the consequences if the 13- to 14-year book-life is much shorter than the useful physical life? The advantage is in the retention in the capital sector of the economy of the funds provided by operations. This would be an advantage from the point of view of capital formation alone, but it may also be important in terms of financial administration if the foreign exchange for the plants is obtained through relatively short-term borrowing. The writer does not have at hand the data necessary for the development of either a simple or a weighted average repayment period for the existing foreign borrowing of Indonesia. The Export-Import Bank loans are for 25 years, but many of the government-to-government arrangements with European countries are reported to be for repayment periods of 10 years. The shorter term loans appear to have a somewhat lower rate of interest than the longer term loans. In the absence of specific information making the 13- to 14-year book-life too long in relation to the pay-off period for loans, the writer decided to use it as a life which affords the following advantages:

1. It seems to meet the test of being equal to or less than the probable physical life of the plants.

2. It seems to meet the test of being equal to or less than the average pay-off period in years of foreign loans for capital construction.

3. To the extent that the book-life is too short in relation to either the physical life or the pay-off period, it has the merit of directing funds to the capital formation sector of the economy instead of to the current expenditure sector.

USE OF AN INTEREST CHARGE AS A COST OF OPERATION FOR THE STATE ENTERPRISE

Interest may be regarded as a charge for the *use* of capital funds and depreciation as a measure of the *consumption* of capital. As was pointed out in the preceding chapter, the use of an interest charge in the cost accounts has the merit of bringing to the attention of all concerned the ability of the enterprise to generate sufficient revenue to cover all economic costs. As with depreciation, its value is largely as an analytical tool for management decision-making. The decisions are those of planning new investment and of establishing prices and expenditure budgets for existing enterprises.

The rate employed in this study is 7½ per cent per year. For the purpose of determining production costs the interest rate was applied to the same capital value for the fixed assets that was used for the 15 per cent depreciation. This means that it was applied to the declining balance of the fixed assets. The reason for this somewhat unusual procedure lies in the prevailing and probable future financial arrangements between Bank Pembangunan (State Development Bank) and the operating enterprises. The former Bank Industri Negara enterprises are required to distribute their products through a state trading enterprise, USINDO, which remits the proceeds of the sale, less a commission, to Bank Pembangunan. The bank in turn advances operating funds to the enterprises. Reduced to its fundamentals, this means that much of the cash generated by the state industrial enterprise is turned over to Bank Pembangunan. If this practice, or an approximation, is continued, it is desirable that the earnings attributable to the use of capital (interest) be treated as a deduction from taxable income by the operating corporations, and excluded from taxable income by Bank Pembangunan. This is not to say that in economic theory the return to capital does not constitute a form of income. It should be regarded simply as a budgetary or financial device for the purpose of making Bank Pembangunan a self-sufficient development agency concerned exclusively with financing income-producing enterprises. This implies, and the writer recommends, that Bank Pembangunan, under the Eight-Year Development Plan, should not be responsible for investments in public works. Such economic development projects should be incorporated in the expenditure budgets of the appropriate ministries. To include them in the responsibilities of Bank Pembangunan would be to invite the rapid depletion of its funds with no sure prospect for replenishing them from the current budget. As the writer understands it, Bank Pembangunan will derive its initial capital from the proceeds of the monetary devaluation of August 24, 1959. Subsequent additions will come from the earnings of the state enterprises. It appears sound to confine the activities of the bank to income-producing enterprises.

We may now inquire: Why an interest rate of 7½ per cent? There were two reasons for its use. The first is that at the time of the study it was the interest rate of Bank Pembangunan. For a capital-short economy the rate is not excessive if used as a target for selecting projects for investment or for measuring the minimum acceptable achievement of an operating enterprise. The second and important practical reason for this particular study was to reduce the burden of computations. Since 7½ per cent is half of 15 per cent and was applied to the same base value, it eliminated an extra computation requiring a calculator. When time was limited and a calculator not always available, the time saved in computing and checking was substantial. Here again the writer directs attention to the principle involved. If the principle seems useful for Indonesia, the specific rate can then be decided.

COMPUTATION OF REPLACEMENT COST FOR THE GRESIK AND CUSHENBERRY PLANTS AND OF THE CHARGES FOR DEPRECIATION AND INTEREST

The use of replacement or reproduction cost or any cost other than the amount of cost originally recorded in the accounts of the enterprise presents the problems of arriving at the new cost, and of developing a procedure for treating it in the accounts.

The computation of replacement cost presents fewer difficulties when only one currency unit is involved than when foreign exchange must be considered. Because this is so, we shall examine first the use of the method in relation to the investment in the Cushenberry plant in California. The data available at the time of the field work in Indonesia relate to the percentage change in costs over a total period of approximately four years. No information is available concerning the change from one year to the next, but for the major pieces of equipment purchased in the United States by Morrison-Knudsen International for the expansion program at Gresik there was a price increase of approximately 20 per cent. To simplify the computation a rate of 5 per cent per year was used. This in effect involves compounding; hence at the end of four years the asset value will be increased by more than 20 per cent. Thus an asset that was acquired in 1956 for $1,000.00 is assumed to cost $1,050.00 at the end of 1957; $1,102.50 at the end of 1958; $1,157.63 at the end of 1959; and $1,215.51 at the end of 1960. The estimated replacement cost at the end of each year was used as the value for the purpose of computing the depreciation and interest charges. The details of the computation are shown in Appendix table B-2. The method of computing the depreciation charge and the interest charge will be considered in the following section.

The Gresik plant presents more difficult problems for estimating replacement cost. This is because part of the cost originally incurred was in foreign currency. Would it be inconsistent to use a 5 per cent annual increase in costs in the United States for the Cushenberry plant and not apply a similar percentage increase to the foreign exchange costs at Gresik? In strict logic, yes, if the primary object is comparison of operating costs between the two plants. But if the objective is to develop a valuation and cost procedures for the Government of Indonesia, then the issue is different. It does not appear sensible to tie replacement cost for imported capital equipment to the price level of a single country such as the United States unless there is no other country in which the equipment is available. Since the objectives are primarily the pricing of Indonesian cement and the internal management of rupiah funds, it seemed to the writer to be most useful to limit the computations of replacement cost to changes in the domestic cost level and to changes in the official rate of exchange. This method will *understate* the Gresik costs in relation to those at Cushenberry for the years used for the cost comparison, the year 1959 and the first six months of 1960.

Table 3–1 (Appendix 1) shows how Gresik assets are revalued at the end of each year. A weighted average percentage of cost increase is developed: the original cost in dollars converted to rupiahs at 11.475 to 1 is multiplied by the factor representing the rate of exchange between the rupiah and the dollar at the end of the year. During the period of the *de facto* devaluation of the exchange auction system, the year-end auction rate was used. When there was a *de jure* devaluation, the factor was the official year-end rate divided by the original official rate of 11.475. The local costs in rupiahs were considered to have increased at an average compound rate of 10 per cent per year. The two new rupiah values are then added and the total is expressed as a percentage of the original total. The weighted average percentage figures are shown in the first column of table 3–1. New computations are made each year in which there is a change either in the rate of exchange or in the local cost level.

For reasons set forth in detail in Chapter 4, the writer believed it desirable to determine depreciation and interest cost for each separate production department. This meant that the original cost of all assets in each department (of which there are 17 at Gresik) had to be ascertained both for the part acquired with dollars and the part representing local rupiah expenditures. Since the ratio of dollar cost to rupiah cost is different for each department, the percentage adjustment for each department will not be the same as for all assets combined. Some readers will question the value of the additional work required to develop departmental costs, but the possible benefits seemed to outweigh the disadvantages of the additional work.

Table 3–1 shows the method of developing a weighted index number for the purpose of revaluing the assets for each department at Gresik at the end of each year. We must now proceed from this technique to the computation of the actual base to be used each year, and to the application of the 15 per cent rate for depreciation and the 7½ per cent rate for interest. This is done in table 3–2 for the same department used for table 3–1. When the machine shop and warehouse were completed by the Morrison-Knudsen International Corporation, the total rupiah cost was Rp. 6,336,473, of which Rp. 3,935,675 represented the conversion of $342,978.22 at the rate of 11.475. The revaluation at December 31, 1957 (see table 3–1), involved an auction exchange rate of 270 per cent on the rupiah-from-dollar cost and a rate of 110 per cent on the local rupiah cost, or a weighted average rate of 209.38 per cent. The revised value of Rp. 13,267,201 was the original rupiah value for the purpose of computing depreciation and interest. The depreciation of Rp. 995,040 is 15 per cent of the value for one-half year, since the plant produced only from July through December in 1957. The interest charge of Rp. 497,520 is, of course, half the depreciation charge, or 7½ per cent.

The balance, or net book value, of the investment in the machine shop and warehouse at December 31, 1957, was Rp. 12,-272,161, that is, the difference between the new value of Rp. 13,-267,201 and the depreciation for six months of Rp. 995,040. This net value became the base for the 1958 charge, and would have been used at the end of 1958 if there had been no change in the *de facto* rate of exchange or in the construction cost index in Indonesia. Since the auction rate moved to 330 per cent of the official rate by the end of 1958 and the construction cost index moved to 110 per cent of the 1957 index, it was necessary to revalue again—using the weighted average index of 119.79 per cent. This, applied to the net book value on table 3–2, gave the revised net value of Rp. 14,700,822 for the assets and Rp. 1,191,958 for the depreciation reserve account. The depreciation for 1958 was 15 per cent of the revised net value (declining balance), or Rp. 2,205,-123, and the interest 7½ per cent, or Rp. 1,102,562. The same procedure is repeated at the end of each year.

Because of limitations of time, understanding, and equipment when the field work was done, the percentage figures of column 1 of table 3–1 were recorded to the second decimal instead of to the third decimal place. Thus the revaluation obtained by the use of the percentage figures will differ slightly from the revaluations actually used to compute the percentage relationships. The revaluation figures and the depreciation charges were computed by using the two-place percentage figures. Appendix table A-2 summarizes the results of the revaluations and the associated depreciation charges for each department at Gresik for the years 1957–1960. Table 3–3 shows how the computations of table 3–1 and table 3–2 were combined to produce the annual asset revaluations and associated depreciation figures. The computations of table 3–2 provide the *net revaluation* each year, and the proper depreciation charge. The computations of table 3–3 are required to provide the gross revaluations of both the asset account and the allowance for depreciation.

Note that the balance of Rp. 12,495,699 at December 31, 1958, in the first column of table 3–2 is the same as line 12 in the 1958 column of table 3–3. This is the declining balance which would be the basis for the 15 per cent depreciation charge in the following year if there were no revaluation because of domestic inflation or change in the official rate of exchange, and no addition to that category of assets. The allowance for depreciation for 1958 of Rp. 3,397,081 on line 11 of table 3–3 is the same as the balance at the end of 1958 in the column headed "Allowance for depreciation" in table 3–2. Both table 3–2 and table 3–3 show the adjustment of the allowance for depreciation when the assets are revalued, and the annual charge based on the revalued amount. The amount shown on line 13 of table 3–3 is the net amount that will be added to the credit side of the balance sheet. The total added, of course, will be the sum for the seventeen departments. Attention is directed to the fact that the *net revaluation is the amount that reasonably can be recovered in the future price of cement.* The adjustment of the balance sheets is shown in tables 7–7 and 7–8B for liabilities and capital, and in tables 7–6 and 7–8A for assets. Computations similar to those of tables 3–1 and 3–2 were made for each of the seventeen departments at Gresik for each year. The resulting adjustments are summarized in Appendix table A-2.

RECOGNIZING THE ANNUAL REVALUATION IN THE ACCOUNTS

In private enterprise countries there is substantial support in the business community and in the accounting profession for the view that the annual depreciation charge should be based on replacement cost. Until now, however, no government has sanctioned depreciation on replacement cost for tax purposes. Perhaps because of the refusal of governments to recognize the economic arguments for depreciation based on replacement cost, the business community and the accounting profession have not reflected in published financial statements the results of increased reproduction costs of fixed assets. Inflation in the United States has created many problems with respect to the meaning and usefulness of published financial statements. In 1960 the American Institute of Certified Public Accountants launched a two-year study of accounting postulates and principles, and it is likely that a major factor in developing the research program was the impact of inflation on the usefulness of statements which do not recognize inflation.[2]

If assets are revalued each year to reflect changes in the value of the monetary unit, or in the replacement cost of the assets, what entries should be made on the books of the enterprise, and how should the revised values be treated on the balance sheet of the enterprise? This study employs separate accounts for the increase in both the fixed assets and the allowance for depreciation. The offsetting net credit is treated as an adjustment of the liability of P. N. Pabrik Semen "Gresik" to the State Development Bank. This is in accordance with the view that the objective of the accounting procedure is to preserve the real investment capital of the State Development Bank by having it secure funds with substantially the buying power of those originally invested. In a private enterprise economy the credit would be to a net worth account with a title something like "Surplus from revaluation of assets."

In 1957 there would be no adjustment of the "Allowance for depreciation." In terms of table 3–3, the amount of Rp. 6,930,728 would be added to the fixed assets and to the account with the State Development Bank. The total of all departments was Rp. 294,407,328 for the end of 1957. At the end of 1958 the revaluation developed in tables 3–1 and 3–2 would be recorded as follows:

Debit: Revaluation of assets . . . . Rp. 2,625,579
      Credit: Addition to allowance
          for depreciation resulting
          from revaluation of assets . . . . Rp.   196,918
          Revaluation of assets,
          State Development Bank . . . . Rp. 2,428,661

---

[2] Of the six research studies published by the American Institute of Certified Public Accountants, two deal specifically with inflation problems. See Robert T. Sprouse and Maurice Moonitz, *A Tentative Set of Broad Accounting Principles for Business Enterprises*, Study No. 3, 1962; and Accounting Research Division, *Reporting the Financial Effects of Price-Level Changes*, Research Study No. 6, 1963.

For all groups of assets combined for P. N. Pabrik Semen "Gresik," the fixed assets accounts at December 31, 1957, would be shown as follows on the balance sheet:

Fixed assets subject to depreciation, valued
    at original acquisition cost .... Rp. 347,864,380
    Add revaluation because of change in
    value of rupiah 294,407,328
Estimated current acquisition cost .... Rp. 642,271,708
    Less allowance for depreciation
    on basis of reproduction cost 48,170,411
Net book value at December 31, 1957 .... Rp. 594,101,297

Appendix table A-2 gives details of the separate departments for the years 1957–1960. The implications of the method are discussed further in the following chapters.

DEPRECIATION AND INTEREST CHARGES IN RELATION TO PRICE DETERMINATION UNDER PRIVATE ENTERPRISE AND UNDER STATE ENTERPRISE

Two important theoretical and practical problems relate to depreciation accounting and, by implication, to the development of a cost of capital in the form of an interest rate applied to total assets. The first is the relation of such charges to prices for the products produced and sold. The second is the relation of the charges to the distribution of the funds provided by the operation of the enterprise. The major importance of the latter is the distribution of the funds between the government in the form of taxes, particularly income taxes, and between the business unit itself and its state agency owner. The problem of the distribution of funds was discussed above. Let us now consider the pricing problem.

The conventional approach to pricing of products under private enterprise is that the object of the enterprise is to select the combination of selling price and output which will provide the maximum difference between total revenue from the sale of the product and current operating costs, excluding depreciation, depletion (if applicable), and capital charges. Depending upon the nature of the market, the firm may actually be free to establish a price for its product, or it may have to accept a price established by competition or a regulating agency and adjust its output to that price. In any event, the theoretical solution is to maximize the cash margin before depreciation and capital use charges. Neither depreciation, depletion, nor interest charges will affect the price established by competitive forces. If the price is established by a government agency, however, some measures of depreciation, depletion, and capital return may be employed to arrive at a fair price. Nevertheless, a fair price which includes charges for the consumption of capital (depreciation and depletion) and the use of capital (interest) may be meaningless if the effective demand in the market does not permit the sale of enough units of the product or service to generate the total revenue required.

But what about the specific case of cement pricing in Indonesia? The supply of cement in Indonesia comes from two sources; imports and domestic production from Gresik and from a smaller plant at Padang, West Sumatra. The domestic price of imported cement is influenced primarily by two factors: the landed cost in terms of foreign exchange, and the import duty. In the short run the domestic market price may fall below the landed cost plus duty, but this is unlikely and certainly will not persist very long. It is obvious that the rupiah cost of imported cement is a function of the official rate of exchange applicable to the commodity. Thus a devaluation of the rupiah with no change in price in terms of the foreign currency will result in a proportionate increase in the rupiah cost of imported cement. The proportionate change will continue if the import duty remains the same percentage of the landed cost in rupiahs.

Events since the opening of the Gresik plant in 1957 make it necessary to examine the possible relationships between the rupiah cost of imported cement and the price permitted to Gresik. For practical purposes these are comparable prices, for the distributor takes over the imported cement at the harbor and the state trading enterprise, USINDO, takes over Gresik cement at the plant after it is bagged and loaded. The two prices cannot be much different for very long without creating problems for either or both the importer or Gresik. If the rupiah cost of imported cement is higher than that for Gresik, we would expect cement to continue to be imported only if there is unfilled demand at the higher price after all Gresik and Padang cement is sold, and that a black market for domestic cement would be likely. If the price of Gresik cement at the factory is higher than that for imported cement, we would expect the *retail* price of imported cement to be as high as that for Gresik, either officially or through the black market.

The significance of the preceding paragraph is that the market forces will tend to equalize the retail prices of the two cements even though there may be a significant difference at the factory or harbor level. Having committed economic resources to a big cement plant in Indonesia, the owner of the plant, the government itself, *should not follow a pricing policy which creates a black market in its own product.* The minimum factory price for Gresik cement should always be the rupiah cost of imported cement, including duty. If the final retail price obtained by adding the conventional markups is too high in the sense that the market will not take the available supply, that is, domestic production plus imports, the government should then examine the factory price of Gresik in relation to its full economic cost. If the price is higher than necessary to cover such costs, it might be argued, on grounds of consumer welfare, that the factory price of Gresik should be reduced. But the practical result of this would be to stop imports, simply because the distributor-importer could not compete. Certainly this would be the sensible result for the Indonesian government and the Indonesian people, for it would make little sense to force the government plants to reduce output just to keep them in a pro-rata position with the imported product. The obvious difficulty with having one government agency in Indonesia import cement and another distribute the domestic production is that a state trading firm importing cement is likely to behave just like a private capitalistic firm and resist reductions in imports unless price control is used as suggested.

It would seem necessary to examine the domestic cost and factory price position at least once a year in order to determine the steps to be taken with respect to changing the import duty on cement, imposing quotas, or both. With this in mind the writer has attempted in this study to develop a sound full economic cost for the Gresik plant—and not so much a particular cost as a method of arriving at such a cost. The practical significance of the method and results is explained at length in Chapter 7.

Not only is full economic cost necessary for pricing Gresik cement and regulating imports of cement; the economic cost is necessary for planning further investment in the Indonesian cement industry. In order to plan effectively, the economic cost should include an approximation of the opportunity cost of capital, that is, the rate of return available in alternative domestic investment. This is a neglected area of both economic planning and the theory of economic development. Economic development theory generally neglects the problem because it is much simpler for the theorist to assume that this is known than to worry about computing the rate. But the government can ignore this consideration only at the risk of putting its scarce investment capital into relatively unproductive uses, or dissipating it in projects which have political appeal but are a drain on and not an addition to the nation's income.

In the future Indonesian planners will need measures of capital consumption cost (depreciation) and capital return (interest), which represent *minimum desirable targets*. The depreciation base and the depreciation method plus the related interest computation employed in this study are intended to suggest a solution to this critical problem.

What has been attempted is a theory and procedure which can be analyzed and discussed. The object was not to establish an impregnable position so much as an understandable position and method. If the writer succeeds in this primary objective, the method and procedure can be discussed intelligently, revealing the weaknesses, which are conceded in advance, and advancing a more useful theory and related procedure.

IV

Cost Accounting for Cement Production

The manufacture of cement at both the Gresik and Cushenberry plants is by the wet process, and the technical differences in the production processes of the two plants are minor. The Gresik plant uses equipment obtained chiefly from Kennedy Van Saun, and Cushenberry uses F. L. Schmidt equipment. In making standard Portland cement, limestone or other calcareous material is combined with clay, silica, and iron. The first production process is that of raw grinding. The raw materials are mixed in approximately the required proportions and ground in a ball mill. During grinding, water is added, and after grinding the mixture is transferred to slurry blending tanks. In the blending tanks the mixture is sampled and analyzed and any necessary adjustments are made in the mix. The slurry contains the minimum amount of water required to maintain the ground material in suspension so that it may be moved by pumps. From the slurry blending and thickening tanks the material enters the kilns.

The cement kilns at each of the plants are the modern horizontal rotary type. The kilns at Cushenberry are gas-fired with oil as a stand-by fuel. The kilns at Gresik are oil-fired. Of the three separate steps in the manufacturing process, the kiln operation is the most expensive. The kiln operation is costly both in its direct variable cost and in the cost of capital equipment. The variable costs of most importance for the kiln operation are fuel to convert the slurry to clinker, and electric power to turn the kilns and operate the cooling and material-transporting machinery. The end product of the kiln process is, chemically, cement, but in the form of clinker which needs further processing, aging, and blending.

The final process is finish grinding. Cement must have both chemical and physical properties which determine rate of hardening, length of time required for "setting up," and strength. The chemical properties of the finished cement depend on the properties of the clinker from the kiln and on the material added to the clinker during finish grinding. The physical properties of the finished cement are chiefly those of its chemical composition and its "fineness" and uniformity of fineness and mixture. At each plant the facilities are very satisfactory for blending the additives, primarily gypsum, with the clinker. The finish grinding mills are good, and each plant has equipment which produces a uniform fineness of ground material. For the latter each employs a closed-circuit mechanism which automatically sorts out particles too coarse for the desired product and returns them to the grinding mill.

The finished cement is transferred by air pump to concrete storage silos. The silos contain equipment for aerating the cement, keeping it in motion to improve blending and to prevent caking or lumping. Samples are drawn from the finished silos so that any differences in quality can be minimized by blending the cement as it is drawn from the silos by air pump and transferred to the smaller storage hoppers for bulk loading (as at Cushenberry) or bagging (as at Gresik).

From the start of production through the period of this study the Gresik plant produced only standard Portland cement. The Cushenberry plant has produced a large number of different types of cement, but the major part of its output has been standard Portland cement.

METHODS AND PROBLEMS OF DETERMINING THE COST OF PRODUCTION

The investigator who attempts to compare the costs of producing cement at two different plants is seldom able to do a completely satisfactory job. It is seldom possible to obtain completely satisfactory production costs at any single cement plant. In comparing the costs of producing cement at two different plants, even when accounting is in the same monetary unit, the primary objective must be to minimize differences in the way in which costs are classified, and then to minimize differences in the way in which costs are assigned to the product.

In order to develop the most useful comparative costs for Gresik and Cushenberry the writer found it necessary to employ a cost accounting procedure somewhat different from that used by either enterprise. By so doing, maximum uniformity of treatment was secured. The cost accounting systems at the two plants are of the type called "actual cost" systems. An actual cost system is intended to develop costs without reference to a predetermined standard or budget cost. A so-called standard cost system usually has the primary objective of relating, at strategic points, all or the most important costs incurred to the standard costs computed for that operation. This may mean that the computations required to take all the costs through the various processes and intermediate inventory points are made only for the planned or budgeted costs. The actual costs of separate operations are related only to the standard costs for the operation, and the variation from standard is determined. The sum of the separate variations is usually disposed of on the periodic income statement, where no effort is made to designate it as cement produced, cement in intermediate or final inventory, and cement sold. Standard-costing is a tool of the principle of management by exception. This means that management determines in advance of actual production what the costs and yields should be. In evaluating actual production the management concerns itself primarily with operations which did not function as expected or planned. The emphasis on reporting costs is to show where departures from expectations occurred and the amount of money involved.

An actual cost system does not purport to show the relation between what happened and what was expected to happen. The reader of the statements must judge for himself the significance of the data provided. Actual costs, for effective use by management, require *ex post* analysis by the operating management or a staff

person acting on behalf of operating management. Both Cushenberry and Gresik employ this approach to costing cement
production. The writer discussed with operating and accounting
personnel at both the Gresik and Cushenberry plants the advantages of using a standard cost system for internal management.
The executives agree as to the general desirability of standards
and hope to use them when additional operating experience provides a basis for establishing the standards.

This study employs the actual costs of the two plants, but uses
the depreciation and interest costs developed by the methods discussed in the preceding chapter. If we distinguish between current
cash costs and non-cash costs, the cash costs used in the study are
those obtained from the two plants, whereas the non-cash costs of
depreciation and imputed interest are not the same as those of
the plant accounts. The study includes as manufacturing costs a
large group of costs not so classified at Gresik, namely, the costs
of general administration. The method of valuing inventories in
process is slightly different from that used at Gresik, but is substantially the same as that employed at Cushenberry.

What Is Process Cost Accounting?

The simplest way of arriving at the cost of production for cement
is to take all the costs incurred for the time period involved and
divide them by the number of tons or barrels of cement produced.
This would be relatively satisfactory if the product passed through
only one process. But in making cement there are several processes
and, more important, there are intermediate storage points for
the material. Cement making is a continuous process, but it would
be unwise to arrange the sequence of production so that an equipment failure at any point would mean stopping the whole plant.
Good cement plant design is intended to minimize the difficulties
of equipment failure at any one point and this is accomplished by
the use of intermediate storage facilities. Thus the quarry operation can feed limestone direct to the raw grinding mills, but it
can also put it in a storage pile for better blending. By this arrangement the quarry can operate during daylight hours only,
and it can stop production entirely for a period of time without

shutting off the supply of crushed rock for the raw grinding mills.

In the raw grinding process it is possible, from a technical point of view, to use either one big mill or several smaller ones. One large mill may cost less and produce lower grinding costs, but it subjects the following operations to shutdown when it cannot operate. Both of the plants in this study employ two raw grinding mills. It is theoretically possible to use mixing equipment of such great accuracy, flexibility, and precision that a highly uniform blend of raw material can be obtained. In theory, this might eliminate the need for slurry blending equipment. But the slurry blending tanks are also storage tanks, and so can feed the kiln for a certain length of time even if the raw grinding mills are out of operation. In addition, slurry tanks reduce the investment in feeder equipment by allowing some corrections in blend subsequent to raw grinding.

One big kiln might be more economical than two if it operated continuously. But here again the danger of breakdown is magnified, as are the problems of repair and maintenance. Clinker can be fed direct to the grinding mill feed bins at the beginning of finish grinding, and so in theory there is no need for a clinker storage area. But to do this requires installation of additional capital equipment to cool the clinker when it emerges from the kiln, eliminates the all-important blending operation, and again increases the possibility of loss of production if the kiln is stopped.

Because of the use of intermediate storage points, the sum of the output of the separate processes is unlikely to equal the amount of finished cement produced within a certain time. This is very important in relation to the length of the time period. Intermediate inventory changes may have important effects on unit costs in a short-time period, but over a long period the effects tend to average out and become unimportant. For this reason the costs of production for a year are likely to be more accurate than are those for a single month—unless the enterprise is prepared to spend both capital and labor to measure very accurately both quantity and quality of material in the intermediate storage areas. The difficulty of measuring intermediate inventories is an important factor in favor of a standard cost system which can concentrate on the individual production processes and neglect inventory changes. Hence the fundamental reason for a standard cost system is not better or more accurate cost data but lower unit costs of production. The lower costs are achieved by defining efficiency and then correcting the operation as soon as possible after it begins to go out of control. Many enterprises employing standard cost systems develop daily cost variances, and some determine them several times a day.

In process cost accounting, costs are recorded both by type of expenditure and for the department or process responsible for the cost. Thus labor may be classified as operating and maintenance, and the time cards may show in what department the worker was employed. Similarly, spare parts and operating supplies may be classified into several categories at the time of purchase, and when they are issued from the stockroom or warehouse the document may show the department in which they will be used. Fixed assets can be classified according to the department in which they are used, and the depreciation and interest assigned as a cost of the particular department.

Placing Departmental Costs on a Comparable Basis for the Two Plants

It is to be expected that the similarities of the two cement plants would produce similar groups of costs for elements which may be termed "inanimate," and that differences in the economies and cultures of the two countries would result in substantial differences in the costs relating to the employment of people. There is little difference in the accounting procedures of the two enterprises with respect to material, fuel, supplies, repair parts, power, and the like. But for the cost of management and labor the differences are many and important.

To ascertain comparable costs by departments or processes, it was necessary to analyze the systems of cost classification employed at each plant. In two different cultures, costs related to human effort vary not only in amount but in specific details. This was a fundamental part of the study of the two plants. To understand and interpret the differences, it was necessary first to ascertain the total amounts. The plan was to group the costs of each plant in a small number of categories corresponding as closely as possible to the following economic categories: management; labor required to operate the plant; labor, repair parts, and facilities to maintain the plant; purchased materials entering into the product or its containers; major supplies for the operation of the producing departments; the cost of utilities or energy; the consumption cost of capital (depreciation) ; the cost of capital (interest) ; and the cost of external resources.

Although the preceding categories of cost would appear satisfactory for a study of economic and social problems, it became clear early in the investigation that it would take too much time to group the costs in such categories—and that the most important difference between the two economic systems was in the categories which economists sometimes describe as resources *internal* to the firm and resources *external* to the firm. The plant in Indonesia must have resources considered as internal to the firm which for Cushenberry are external to the firm. The difficulty is that the resources turned out to affect virtually every major category of cost. This being so, it seemed most useful to retain as much as possible the broad cost categories of the Gresik plant and to rearrange the costs of the Cushenberry plant to fit the Gresik categories.

After the decision to use the Gresik cost categories, the next problem was to develop the costs of capital consumption (depreciation) and capital use (interest) for each plant. This was a formidable task for Gresik because the accounting records showed the original cost of fixed assets according to type, that is, permanent buildings, temporary structures, machinery, mobile equipment, office and laboratory equipment, and the like. In addition to this, the Gresik plant maintains two separate and distinct accounting departments, one for general accounting and one for cost accounting. The cost accounting department employs a system developed by the Americans during the initial operating contract period, whereas the general accounting department employs a Dutch system. The cost department does not develop full costs but only direct cash costs, excluding the large amount for general administration. This means that the monthly cost statements do not include any charges for capital or for general administration. The investigation disclosed that the costs excluded may represent

over 75 per cent of what may be regarded as the real economic
cost of production. The percentage of economic cost excluded depends upon the concepts of valuation, depreciation, and interest.
The substantial inflation experienced by Indonesia makes it very
important to include not just some costs for capital, but costs
which are related to the needs of a socialist state. This problem
was the subject of the preceding chapter and need not be covered
again.

The omission of general administration from the costs prepared
by the cost department presents another important problem in
attempting to adapt the practices of advanced industrial countries
to newly developing countries. In the first six months of operation
of the Gresik plant, the period in which the cost accounting
system was developed, the costs of general administration were
small and in about the same relation to regular production costs
as they are for a plant in the United States. But it is precisely in
this area that the Government of Indonesia expects a new industrial enterprise to contribute to economic and social development,
and it is here that the social and psychological forces of Indonesian society are brought to bear on management to increase expenditures. To exclude this area of expenditure from
production cost in Indonesia is likely to be a very serious omission.
To deal with this important problem the investigator analyzed
the costs included and decided that the most useful way of
treating these costs in the study would be to consider them as a
special category having no significant counterpart at the Cushenberry plant. The result of this decision is that two categories of
administration expense will be found in the Gresik statements:
general administration and plant administration. The category
of plant administration is roughly comparable to that of general
overhead in the Cushenberry accounts, but there are many differences.

Meaning and Treatment of Indirect Costs

One of the most troublesome aspects of cost analysis is the
vagueness and ambiguity of some of the terminology. Economists
have found the categories of *fixed* and *variable* cost to be of

great value in constructing theories of behavior for the individual firm. Accountants and business managers have found that the categories of *direct* and *indirect* cost are useful in dealing with the operating problems of the individual firm. The two sets of categories are not equivalent. What is a fixed cost to the economist may be either a direct or an indirect cost to the accountant and business executive. What is a variable cost to the economist may be either direct or indirect to the accountant. The two sets of concepts are of great value in analysis, and neither should be regarded as theoretically superior to the other.

The great advantage of dealing with cost determination in relation to functional departments is that it permits us to start with *exclusively direct costs*. By so doing it is possible to develop useful information concerning the extent to which such costs are either fixed or variable with respect to the volume of production. It is important to emphasize, however, that very few of the direct costs of a manufacturing enterprise are independent of managerial control. This is very important in dealing with the problems of socialism, for here the various government agencies, either singly or in combination, determine both the monetary cost of the unit of labor or material and the number of units to be used. As the study will reveal, many costs which are variable in relation to volume of production in the Cushenberry plant are fixed in total at Gresik. As a preliminary generalization, it may be said Cushenberry has more items of variable cost than does Gresik. But because of differences between the two economies the fewer variable costs at Gresik may represent a larger percentage of total cash cost over a wide range of output than is true of Cushenberry over the same range of output.

If we start with the proposition that departmentalization makes *all* costs direct costs at the outset, by what procedure do indirect costs emerge? In process cost accounting the fundamental distinction between direct and indirect costs lies in the nature of the departments themselves. Of the various functional departments, only a few are concerned with the physical production of cement. These are called the direct production departments. The indirect departments are those concerned with the maintenance and repair of capital equipment, and those concerned with producing mechanical energy or utilities. In full process accounting the costs of the various indirect departments are assigned to the direct producing departments, and then the costs of the producing departments are assigned to the product or products produced. The first is termed *cost distribution* and the second is called *cost assignment* or determination.

To assist the reader who is not trained in cost accounting, the development of process costs and their assignment to the product may be illustrated by employing the concept of tanks of water. Accounting included the following separate stages or actions:

1. Determining the *direct* costs of each department. In terms of our illustration, this is equivalent to putting water in each of the separate tanks. The amount of water placed in each tank or department depends chiefly on the function of the department. Thus some tanks receive water in direct proportion to the amount of cement produced, whereas the amount of water placed in another tank has little relation to the amount of cement produced.

2. Distributing the water in the tanks classified as indirect to those classified as direct. This is "cost distribution" and, in terms of our mechanical illustration, may be regarded as emptying the indirect tanks into the direct tanks.

3. Flowing the water through the direct tanks into the storage silos. Physically this is the process of converting limestone, clay, silica, iron, and gypsum into finished cement and placing it in the storage silos. Unlike the second process, this does not of necessity require emptying the tanks. Some of the tanks have water in them at the start of the period (i. e., they have an inventory of material in partly finished form) and at the end of the period; but the amount or level of water may change. If the time period is long, say a year, the volume of water flowing through may be so large in relation to volume remaining that the latter may be ignored in the accounts without significantly affecting the result.

The writer did not make significant changes in the method of moving the water from the indirect tanks to the direct tanks or from the direct tanks to the finished silo. That is, the *basic system of accounting was not changed*. The writer did the following:

1. Added one big tank at the top, that of general administra-

tion, and ran its contents through the system. The Gresik accounting system also has this tank, but its system is to transfer its contents direct to the last tank, *cost of cement sold.*

2. Changed the amount of water placed in every tank by adding the costs of depreciation and interest. This is where the writer departed from the actual book costs at both Gresik and Cushenberry. The departure consisted of two important things: (a) increasing the amount of depreciation by using a larger base, and (b) using interest when neither enterprise did so in its accounts. The two enterprises both charged depreciation on their books. Cushenberry did not include it in the cost of production in 1957, but did in subsequent years. Gresik did not in any year run depreciation through the cost accounts, but pumped it directly to the statement of profit and loss.

To employ the procedure indicated, it was first necessary to ascertain whether there were any duplications in the book costs, or beginning water level. This meant going through each account for each year and removing all costs which represented distributions or assignment from other departments. In simple terms, it was necessary to reverse the flow of costs and start with the original direct charges to the separate departments and add the appropriate amounts for depreciation and interest.

Having divided the total water (original direct charges, including depreciation and interest) among the separate departments, or tanks, the next task was to pump out the water, or costs, of the indirect departments into the direct production departments. To do this it was necessary to decide whether any indirect department would receive water, or costs, from any other indirect department. Almost all full-cost systems employ the principle that some or all of the indirect departments should receive charges from certain of the others. This is based on the idea that the department receiving the charge receives some service or benefit from the department from which the charge is made. For example, the houses included in the costs of general administration use water and electricity provided by the power and water departments. The power and water departments receive administrative services from both general administration and factory administration. The maintenance department does work for the administrative departments and the power plant and water department as well as for the cement-producing departments.

In this approach to cost distribution, both the order of distribution and the appropriate bases for making the charges must be selected. The accountant may employ a system of simultaneous equations, the arithmetic method of successive approximations, or a so-called order of clearing. The equation or approximation systems have the virtue of intellectual nicety, but seldom are employed because they take a great deal of time or computing equipment. The essentially arbitrary nature of the distribution seldom warrants the investment in equipment or time. The order-of-clearing system involves arranging the accounts, or tanks, in two or more levels and pumping only from those on a higher level to those on lower levels. Where a department at a lower level clearly benefits a department at a higher level, the practical solution is to start the clearing process by transferring a certain percentage of the direct cost of the lower-level department to the appropriate upper-level tank, or department.

The order-of-clearing procedure employed for Gresik may be summarized as follows:

1. Four levels are used: administration departments, maintenance, utilities, and producing or operating departments.

2. The clearing is started by assigning the following percentages of the original direct charges for the power and water departments to the other indirect departments.

	Power	Water
General administration	1.5	30.0
Factory administration	0.5	. . .
Maintenance	4.0	1.0
Water	3.0	

The percentages were those regularly used by the cost department at Gresik and were developed by discussions among department heads. The writer found no reason to alter the percentages.

3. Cost of general administration (including charges for power and water) was assigned to all other departments except factory

administration on the basis of the rupiah cost of operating and repair labor.

4. Cost of factory administration was assigned to all other departments except general administration on the basis of the rupiah cost of operating and repair labor.

5. Maintenance department costs were assigned to all departments except general administration and factory administration on the basis of direct charges for repair labor and repair parts and supplies.

6. Pier and oil storage department costs were assigned as follows: 25 per cent to the power department and 75 per cent to the kiln department.

7. Power costs were assigned approximately on the basis of connected horsepower as follows:

	Per cent
Clay department	2.0
Limestone quarrying and crushing	4.0
Raw grinding	35.0
Kiln	22.0
Finish grinding	30.0
Packing	4.0
Bag manufacture	3.0
Total	100.0

It is apparent that the method of distributing power cost does not permit the development of useful data on power usage by the operating departments. The expansion program will reduce this difficulty by installing meters for the most important consuming departments.

8. Water costs are distributed according to the following percentages developed by an engineering survey and conference:

Clay department	30.0
Raw grinding	66.0
Kiln	4.0
Total	100.0

DIFFERENCES BETWEEN THE GRESIK AND THE CUSHENBERRY SYSTEMS OF DISTRIBUTING COSTS

The indirect costs of the two plants reflect the differences in the stages of economic development in the two countries. For the important group designated as general administration at Gresik there is a counterpart at Cushenberry in the "real" sense but not in the accounting sense. In the real sense, many of the costs in the general administration group in Indonesia appear as direct money costs of salaries and wages in the United States. In a sense the Indonesian system is paternalistic and the system in the United States is individualistic. The extent to which it is proper to regard the Indonesian system as an inherent feature of either underdevelopment or of socialism is not clear to the writer. Certainly the system goes back to the colonial period of the Dutch; it is found in all the countries of Southeast Asia and in most so-called underdeveloped countries. Cushenberry does not have the same problems with respect to distributing the costs of maintenance and of utilities that are encountered at Gresik. At Cushenberry the utility services are purchased from another enterprise. The more arbitrary allocation by "percentages based on connected horsepower or engineering survey" at Gresik is avoided at Cushenberry by the use of an extensive system of meters. In effect this permits Cushenberry to treat as direct charges of the producing departments what are "distributed" charges at Gresik. Again this does not mean that the Cushenberry arrangement is better, only that it is different and leaves less room for arbitrary allocations. What may be of more importance, particularly for a short period such as we are concerned with in this study, the purchase of energy from sources outside the firm may lead to lower costs per unit of energy because the forces of inflation do not operate with equal effect in the two areas. Certainly the procedure employed in this study whereby assets are revalued each year to reflect changes in the price level will tend to produce results favorable to Cushenberry and adverse to Gresik for items internal to the firm at Gresik and external to the firm at Cushenberry.

The differences in the proportion and nature of direct charges and distributed charges reflect the differing role of taxes in the two economies. Indonesia relies chiefly on taxes on imports and exports. We can anticipate that the reliance on import duties in Indonesian finance will tend to make the costs of purchased materials and supplies relatively higher than in the Cushenberry plant. Indonesia has a highly centralized system of government and the governmental units comparable to cities, counties, and states in the United States have little or no taxing authority (or if they have, it is not used; so the results from the point of view of this study are the same). For practical purposes we can say that the Gresik plant *pays no local taxes in rupiahs.* But what is important is that Gresik itself is a municipality providing housing, transportation, schools, police and fire protection, utilities, and other services. These costs for the most part are in the general administration category. Cushenberry is assessed local taxes on a property valuation basis, and so these taxes as well as insurance can be and are made as direct charges to the departments on the basis of the value of the assets employed.[1]

Tentative Conclusions on the Major Elements of Cost for the Two Plants

Although this chapter is concerned with the methodology of cost accounting for the two plants and not with specific costs, it is appropriate to anticipate the cost comparison by suggesting that for every major category of costs there is reason to expect significant differences between the two plants. Except for imported items the two firms buy in different markets. Ocean freight and insurance and the use of import duties produce significant differences in the unit cost of imported items for each plant. In a very important sense we must compare two economies, two political systems, and two cultures.

The Cost Flow Sheet and Its Use in Determining the Cost of Cement Produced

Let us now consider the third and last step in the cost accounting procedure used for determining the cost of cement produced at

---

[1] The "value" used is the original cost. The distribution of such charges would be different if net book value were used—if there are different depreciation rates for different types of equipment.

Gresik and at Cushenberry. The first stage was to determine the direct charges by departments; the second was to assign or distribute the costs of the indirect departments to the departments which actually produce the cement. The first two stages concern problems associated with what each plant must provide for itself, and what each can buy from sources external to the plant. In the third stage we approach common ground, for the two plants use nearly the same method of producing cement, and very similar equipment. As we saw in Chapter 2, the two plants do not have the same designed capacity.

Several forms of flow sheets are used in the cement industry. The differences are slight and usually reflect differences in the use and size of the intermediate storage areas and in the assignment of certain items of overhead cost. In a study of this sort it seemed advisable to employ a work-sheet technique which showed clearly and exactly what was done with the data at each stage of production. A presentation in which the final cost movement from one process to the next has the appearance of a descending staircase is easier for the non-accountant to follow than a more compact flow sheet.

Flow sheets were prepared in Indonesia for the Gresik plant for 1958, 1959, and the first five months of 1960. The costs for the five months were used in preparing the profit and loss statement for this period of 1960. At the end of the field work, data were obtained for June, 1960, and costs were computed for the first six months of 1960. For Cushenberry, cost data were developed for 1957, 1958, 1959, and the first six months of 1960. In the time available it was not possible to convert the data for the six months of operation in 1957 to a form completely comparable with that available from January, 1958, to the time of the study. Table 7–1 does, however, develop the total unit costs for 1957 for Gresik.

The detailed cost computations for the Gresik plant comprise Appendix A of this report, and those for Cushenberry comprise Appendix B. The first two tables in each appendix provide details concerning the costs of the fixed assets, their distribution by departments, the annual revaluation of the assets to reflect changes in the cost of replacement, and the computation of the depreciation charges and interest charges. For each of the three periods (1958, 1959, and 1960) there are two tables or schedules for the Gresik plant. The first table shows the direct charges by major expense category for each department, and then the assignment or distribution of the costs of the indirect departments to the production and distribution departments. The second table for each year is the cost flow sheet which takes the costs of the cement-producing departments and from them develops the cost of the cement produced and the intermediate inventories. For 1959 and the first six months of 1960, costs at Gresik were also computed on a cash basis, that is, excluding depreciation and interest.

For the Cushenberry plant it was necessary to prepare three separate schedules or tables for each year. The first table provided a detailed explanation of the changes made in the Cushenberry costs as derived from the Corporation's statements. The changes are of two sorts, those involving reclassification and those concerned with substituting the 15 per cent declining balance method of depreciation applied to original cost adjusted for price changes, and to the addition of the $7\frac{1}{2}$ per cent interest charge. These schedules are not included in the Appendix because of their bulk, limited reader use, and the confidential nature of the detailed items of cost. The second table for Cushenberry developed the costs of quarrying and crushing limestone, and divided them between the cement plant and the steel plant. The third table is the cost flow sheet for the cement-producing departments. In this the costs assigned to cement rock enter the raw grinding process, and the treatment or derivation of cost is the same as for the Gresik plant.

It is probably fair to say that no cement plant has absolutely accurate data concerning the quantities processed, produced, or on hand. Some of the weight figures are not derived from actually weighing the material but from counting the loads carried and applying an average weight per load. Some weights are scale weights, but the scales are the so-called feeder scales and the recorded weights may be off from time to time because of dirt in the mechanism or other difficulties. Cement production control men at both plants are concerned with the production of a very high quality of product, one that *exceeds* minimum technical specifications for standard Portland type cement. Continuous sampling and checking and weighing at strategic points produce production quantity data which are adequate for most purposes. From the point of view of this study the least satisfactory quantity data are those for the quarry and clay departments and for raw grinding. Gresik does not maintain book inventories for limestone rock in the various stages, or for the amount of material in the slurry tanks. The Cushenberry data for production at the quarry and the crushing stations did not always agree with the quantity data used for raw grinding. After attempting several ways of handling the raw-material costs and quantities, a procedure was developed which seemed to satisfy the demands of logic in that the quantity passing out of one process is the same as that entering the next when there is no intermediate storage. Where there is an inventory the quantity in inventory is always reasonable in relation to reported movement in and out—a complicated way of saying that there are no "negative" or "impossible" inventory quantities.

The cost flow sheet used in this study employs three sets of data for each process: the total quantity in metric tons, the total cost in rupiahs or dollars, and the cost per metric ton. The first item on the flow sheets for the cement-producing departments for each plant is the quantity produced. For Gresik there is only one figure, expressed in metric tons. For Cushenberry there are two, the United States measure, and this measure converted to metric tons. United States cement plants, frequently to their own confusion, use tons through the quarrying and crushing operations, and United States barrels for the rest. Since the primary use of this report is likely to be with respect to the Gresik plant, it seemed sensible to employ the metric ton as the unit of production and to express unit costs as either rupiahs or dollars per metric ton.

On each flow sheet the metric ton figure on the first line is the number of tons emerging from that process during the time period involved. At each plant the quantity actually remaining in the processing machinery at the end of a given period is so small that it can be ignored. But it is not true that the weight of product emerging from a process is the same as that entering the process. In some operations there is a weight loss, either through chemical changes or dust loss through the stack, as in the kiln. The quantity leaving one process need not be the same as that entering the next process even when there is no intermediate inventory. This is so because it may be necessary to add another material. The chief problem in modern cement production concerns the production of the kiln in relation to the production of finish grinding. The kiln produces clinker, which ordinarily is stored for a time. Clinker is then drawn from storage and additives such as gypsum are mixed in as the material is introduced in the finish-grinding ball mills.

The objective of the cost flow sheet is to make certain that the tonnage figures are all accounted for. To attain this the flow sheet is divided into two sections, one for *processing costs* and one for *material costs*. The processing costs of each department are simply the original direct costs assigned to it plus the distributed costs from the other administrative, maintenance, and utility departments. On the Gresik flow sheets the processing costs are items 1 to 18. On the Cushenberry flow sheet for cement production they are items 1 to 16. In each case the last-numbered item is the total and the others are details of the total.

Let us now see what happens to the material. A mixture of limestone, clay, silica, and iron is placed in the raw grinding mills. Each of these is shown as a separate money amount, a separate tonnage (if ascertainable), and a cost per ton. The processing costs of the raw grinding department are added to the material costs of limestone, clay silica, and iron to obtain the cost transferred to the kiln. In the cost procedures at each plant, no processing loss is developed for the raw grinding department, and no inventory shown for slurry.

In the kilns the water is removed from the slurry and much material is thrown out of the stack because of chemical changes and because the dust-collecting equipment is not 100 per cent effective. Because of these two physical factors the weight of clinker emerging is much less than the weight of slurry entering. Since the processing costs of the kiln are related to the clinker produced rather than to the weight of slurry entering, the slurry units must be reduced for the processing loss and the unit cost increased. The burned clinker then enters a storage bin.

Since production costs vary from one period to another, it is necessary to adopt some convention for valuing the inventories at the points where they occur. In this study the weighted-average method or convention was used. This is general practice in the industry. Readers not familiar with inventory costing methods will note from the cost flow sheets that the weighted average is computed by adding both the money amount and the tonnage of production for the period to the money value of the inventory on hand at the beginning and the tonnage on hand. The total money amount is divided by the total quantity to obtain the weighted average cost per metric ton. This is then used to price the tons withdrawn from the inventory and sent to the next process. The same method was employed at Gresik to cost the inventory of finished cement and so to obtain the cost of cement sold or consumed by the plant.

DETERMINATION OF COSTS AFTER THE CEMENT IS PRODUCED

The scope of this study did not include data for Cushenberry after the cement is finished and placed in the storage silos. Because of the importance of the depreciation and interest methods proposed and employed in the study, the analysis was carried through for Gresik to include the preparation of the profit and loss statements and the balance sheets.

CASH COSTS AT GRESIK

Although the writer prefers the use of full economic costs for Gresik, there are advantages in having costs computed on other bases. Since depreciation and interest are arbitrary in the sense that they were developed by the author, cash costs only were developed for the year 1959 and the first six months of 1960.

The procedure was identical with that used for full costs, except that the intermediate inventory of clinker was valued at the average cost for the period. The computations for 1959 comprise Appendix tables A-7 and A-8 and for 1960 Appendix tables A-11 and A-12.

Having developed the methods of measuring investment and of determining production costs, we may now turn to the more interesting questions of the actual amount and behavior of costs and the reasons for and significance of the differences disclosed.

V

A Theory and Technique for Inter-Economy Cost Comparisons Under Inconvertible Currency

Most of the literature on foreign exchange in relation to the preparation and interpretation of accounting statements is concerned with the viewpoint of only one of the countries concerned, that of the country whose investors have operations in a foreign country.[1] The central problem in such cases is convertibility of the currency of the country in which the operations of the subsidiary are conducted—convertibility directly or indirectly into the currency of the country in which the investor (parent firm) is domiciled. If the currency is not effectively convertible in fact, accountants usually hold that using the official rate of exchange of the foreign country will not provide very useful data for the managerial-investor groups of the parent company. To see the general issue, let us take the 1961 official rate of exchange in Indonesia of the rupiah for the dollar of 45 to 1 and look at the case from the point of view of a hypothetical United States cement firm having a wholly owned subsidiary operating in Indonesia. At the time of writing, and for the period covered by this study, the Indonesian government did not permit the transfer of earned depreciation or of profits by foreign enterprises other than oil companies. Under such circumstances, would it be meaningful for the parent company in the United States to convert the rupiah

---

[1] S. R. Hepworth, *Reporting Foreign Operations*, Bureau of Business Research, School of Business Administration, University of Michigan, Ann Arbor, 1956, embodies this approach.

accounts of its Indonesian subsidiary into dollars at either the official rate of exchange or the free market rate in Singapore? Would the resulting dollar figures be significant? The essential test is to ask: Can the dollar figures be added to the dollar figures of the firm in the United States to obtain a meaningful balance sheet or income statement? The answer is in the negative, for there is insufficient evidence that the critical dollar figures are *realizable.*

Accounting for foreign exchange is dominated by considerations relevant to the balance sheet and the income statement. But does the test of realization apply to the cost statements? In the writer's view it is not the primary test. A firm in the United States can make a useful comparison of both the total cost and the separate components of total cost for a cement factory in the United States and one in Indonesia by converting the dollar costs of the factory in the United States to rupiahs at the official rate of exchange. The problems of inter-economy cost comparisons are essentially the same whether the objective is to gain insight into the problems of two plants owned by the same firm or two plants owned by nationals or the government in the countries concerned.

To compare the costs of production of similar plants in two different political units with differing economic environments, it is necessary to be certain that similar types of costs are treated in the same way, and that the same conventions or procedures are used for each plant for the items of cost which are largely matters of managerial policy, particularly inventory valuation and depreciation. Assuming comparability in terms of classification and methods of valuation, the next obstacle to be overcome is that of ascertaining a comparable monetary unit. The preceding chapters have indicated that the writer was given full access to data at each plant and complete freedom to reclassify the data and to use such inventory valuation and depreciation methods as he thought appropriate. Assuming that comparability can be achieved in terms of classification and valuation, what limitations arise in terms of the selection of the rate of exchange to convert the separate money costs to a common monetary unit?

Two issues emerge in inter-economy cost comparisons: absolute figures and relative figures. The test of actual or potential realization dominates financial accounting for foreign subsidiaries; hence it is necessary that the rate of exchange used be one at which the currency can actually be converted. In inter-economy cost comparison the primary problem with the rate of exchange would seem to be its effect on relative costs rather than on the absolute amount of cost. A rate of 45 rupiahs to the dollar will obviously provide a different rupiah or dollar figure from a rate of 11.475 to the dollar. If a rate of 45 to 1 provides a cost for depreciation per ton of cement produced of 200 rupiahs for Gresik and 75 rupiahs per ton for Cushenberry and a rate of 11.475 to 1 provides a cost of 51 rupiahs for Gresik and 19.12 rupiahs for Cushenberry, is one rate better than the other? Are real costs higher when the rate of exchange is 45 to 1 than if it is 11.475 to 1? The illustration and questions suggest that if our concern is with changes in relative costs we should not be as concerned with the particular rate of exchange as with the fact that it should be constant. Clearly, if our objective is to measure relative changes in cost resulting from inflation and from changes in efficiency, we might do so by using a constant rate of exchange.

But inflation is one of the dominant factors in our problem. A constant rate of exchange does not provide useful relative costs of capital, for the relative unit costs will be influenced only by changes in the relative rates of output. A second fundamental difficulty with a constant rate of exchange is encountered if the official rate is altered and imports are an important element of cost for the plant in whose currency unit the costs are expressed. Thus, if we use the official rate of 11.475 to 1 that prevailed during the construction period of Gresik and Cushenberry and express all costs in rupiahs, the rupiah costs for Gresik will jump sharply relative to those for Cushenberry for an item such as maintenance supplies when the official rate of exchange is changed to 45 to 1. We could, of course, deflate the Gresik costs for the effects of changes in the official rate of exchange. This would solve one problem only by creating another, that of ruling out a significant consequence of inflation in Indonesia, the necessity of continuous or periodic official devaluation of the currency. We may conclude that the use of a constant rate of exchange is not completely satisfactory if it is not also the official rate of exchange during the period covered by the investigation.

Although the issues in this study are primarily those of the Gresik plant and the Indonesian economy, they also concern the foreign investment program of the United States. Does it make sense, from the point of view of evaluating the problems and achievements of Gresik, to convert the Cushenberry costs to rupiahs at the official rate of exchange applicable during the accounting period? The Indonesian government can ration its supply of foreign exchange so as to buy cement abroad rather than to produce it in Indonesia. It is possible to say that one of the choices available to the government was between building the plant at Gresik, and building or buying one in the United States or contracting for the output of a plant abroad. Assume that Indonesia entered into a contract to buy cement from the Permanente Cement Corporation on a cost-plus basis, the basis being costs as determined under the accounting procedure employed in this study, i.e., current cash (under the accrual interpretation) costs plus depreciation using the 15 per cent declining balance applied to estimated current replacement cost, *plus* 7½ per cent interest applied to the same base used for computing depreciation charges. Assume, further, that the Government of Indonesia would buy from Permanente the same tonnage that it could produce at Gresik, and that Permanente would produce the quantity it did in fact produce at Cushenberry and sell in the United States market the excess over the Indonesian purchases. In terms of the Indonesian *internal* financial structure, it would convert the Cushenberry costs to rupiahs at the official rate of exchange. The only problem would be to determine how often Permanente would obtain payment from Indonesia. If we assume that Indonesia paid *each month* for current cash costs of actual shipments and at the end of each year for depreciation and interest (profit), we would, for practical purposes, establish a rate of exchange for converting dollar costs to rupiahs. If we base the annual depreciation and interest charges in rupiahs at Gresik on the estimated replacement cost at the *end of the year*, we have a procedure comparable to that of converting such charges at Cushenberry at the official rate of exchange of the rupiah for the dollar at the end of each year. Converting current cash costs at Cushenberry to rupiahs at the average rate for the year is approximately equivalent to monthly billing of such costs, assuming equal monthly production.

The procedure proposed for converting the dollar costs of Cushenberry to rupiahs is only in part an application of the concept of "opportunity cost" to Indonesia. It omits the cost of transportation and insurance. The purpose of the cost comparison attempted is not to determine whether Indonesia should have built the Gresik plant or contracted for the same tonnage with the Permanente Cement Corporation under the terms implied by the accounting procedures and the rate of exchange. If this were the objective, the transportation and insurance costs should be added to the manufacturing costs of Cushenberry. Our purpose is to gain insight into the nature of the technical problems of comparing production costs in two dissimilar economies. The opportunity cost comparison would require that we include the alternative of buying cement from any other supplier offering a landed cost in Indonesia (in terms of foreign exchange) below that of the implied arrangement with Permanente. We shall attempt this comparison and analysis in Chapter 7, but only in terms of the realized costs at Gresik in relation to the existing import prices of cement imported into Indonesia.

The present problem is to examine the proposed procedure to see what it will do and what it will not do. Perhaps the first thing to examine is the extent to which the rate of exchange will not affect relative rupiah costs at all. The method of computing depreciation and interest is to apply the appropriate rates to a declining balance that is adjusted each year to reflect changes in the estimated replacement cost. For the Gresik plant the investment in depreciable assets consisted of expenditures involving foreign exchange and those involving labor and material from local sources. At the official rate of exchange, during the construction period, of 11.475 to 1, the rupiah investment was approximately half in foreign exchange and half in local expenditures. The procedure employed to revalue the fixed assets is to revise the foreign exchange cost to reflect changes in the official rate of exchange, and for local expenditures to adjust for an estimated annual increase of 10 per cent. No adjustment is made for any change in the prices in foreign currency of the equipment or other items acquired abroad. On the other hand, an annual inflation factor of 5 per cent was used to revalue all the dollar investment in fixed assets at Cushenberry. If we were consistent in valuing assets involving dollar expenditures, the rate of exchange would not affect the relative costs for depreciation and interest on a given original dollar cost of plant. This is so because the factor representing a revaluation of the rupiah from 11.475 to 1 to 45 to 1 (a factor of approximately 4) would increase the rupiah base by approximately 400 per cent, but would also increase the rupiah equivalent of the dollar depreciation charge at Cushenberry by the same percentage. Differing rates of exchange will produce different *rupiah* amounts of depreciation per $1,000 of original investment, but the amount will be the same for each plant because the method of computing interest and depreciation is the same for each plant.

The fact that an inflation factor of 5 per cent per year was used for Cushenberry and no percentage inflation factor was used for the foreign exchange component of the Gresik plant means that the rupiah amount of depreciation and interest for $1,000 of original investment at Cushenberry will exceed the rupiah amount for the same original base of $1,000 at Gresik by 5 per cent in the first year, and at a compound rate of 5 per cent each year thereafter. This is independent of the rate of exchange used.

The portion of the Gresik investment expenditure representing local costs will, under the method employed, increase at the compound rate of 10 per cent. Under the declining balance method, the 10 per cent inflation factor will provide higher rupiah depreciation and interest charges than would be the case if construction costs were stable, but will not cause the rupiah total of depreciation and interest to increase. Even an inflation factor of 15 per cent will not provide a constant rupiah amount of depreciation under the declining balance method, for the 15 per cent rate for depreciation is applied to a base increased by 15 per cent, but the base itself is decreased each year by 15 per cent before the inflation factor of 15 per cent is applied.

The combined effect of the declining balance method and the revaluation techniques can be seen from a calculation of depreciation using an original investment of $1,000 for Cushenberry and $2,000 at Gresik, of which $1,000 was in foreign exchange converted at 11.475 to 1 and local rupiah costs of 11,475. The results will be shown first under the assumption of no change in the official rate of exchange for the rupiah in terms of the dollar, i.e., 11.475 to 1.

CUSHENBERRY

	U.S. dollars
Original cost	$1,000.00
Revaluation for construction cost increase of 5 per cent	50.00
Base for depreciation in first year	$1,050.00
Depreciation in first year at 15 per cent	157.50
New (declining) balance	$ 892.50
Revaluation for construction cost increase of 5 per cent	44.63
Base for depreciation in second year	$ 937.13
Depreciation in second year at 15 per cent	140.57
New (declining) balance	$ 796.56
Revaluation for construction cost increase of 5 per cent	39.83
Base for depreciation in third year	$ 836.39
Depreciation in third year at 15 per cent	125.46

GRESIK

	Cost in foreign exchange	Cost in rupiahs	Rupiah total
Original investment	$ 1,000	11,475	—
Convert dollars to rupiahs at 11.475 to 1	11,475	—	—
Original investment in rupiahs ...	11,475	11,475	22,950
Revaluation for construction cost increase of 10 per cent	—	1,148	1,148

	Cost in foreign exchange	Cost in rupiahs	Rupiah total
Base for depreciation in first year	11,475	12,623	24,098
Depreciation in first year at 15 per cent	1,721	1,893	3,614
New (declining) balance	9,754	10,730	20,484
Revaluation for cost increase of 10 per cent	—	1,073	1,073
Base for depreciation	9,754	11,803	21,557
Depreciation in second year at 15 per cent	1,463	1,770	3,233
New (declining) balance	8,291	10,033	18,324
Revaluation for cost increase of 10 per cent	—	1,003	1,003
Base for depreciation	8,291	11,036	19,327
Depreciation in third year at 15 per cent	1,244	1,655	2,899

If the official rate of exchange remains at 11.475 to 1 during the three-year period, the conversion of dollars to rupiahs provides the following comparative results:

Year	Cushenberry		Gresik	Gresik as a percentage of Cushenberry
First	$157.50	Rp. 1,807	Rp. 3,614	200.0
Second	140.57	1,613	3,233	200.4
Third	125.46	1,440	2,899	201.3

Although the actual percentages move against Gresik, the difference is negligible and for practical purposes remains at 200 per cent (or the original 2 to 1 ratio of investment). Now let us assume that the official rate of exchange falls from 11.475 to 1 to 45 to 1 in the third year. There would be no change in either the rupiah costs or the percentages in the first two years.

In the third year the depreciation for Gresik would be computed as follows:

	Cost in foreign exchange	Cost in rupiahs	Rupiah total
Balance (declining) at end of second year	Rp. 8,291	Rp. 10,033	Rp. 18,324
Revaluation:			
For change in rate of exchange from 11.475 to 1 to 45 to 1	24,223	—	24,223
Construction cost increase of 10 per cent	—	1,003	1,003
Base for depreciation	Rp. 32,514	Rp. 11,036	Rp. 43,550
Depreciation in third year at 15 per cent	4,877	1,655	6,533

In the third year Gresik would have a depreciation cost in rupiahs of 6,533. Cushenberry would have no change in its dollar cost, but it would be converted to rupiahs at 45 to 1, hence would be $125.46 × 45 or Rp. 5,646. The Gresik depreciation is now 115.7 per cent of that of Cushenberry, in rupiahs. The effect of the method is relatively favorable to Gresik, for its percentage changes from 201.3 to 115.7. Since interest is always one-half of depreciation for each plant, the relative costs will be exactly the same for interest as for depreciation. For the ratio to remain at 2 to 1, the construction cost index in Indonesia would have to move upward by a factor of 3.95 in the third year. The results in our example for the third year suggest a significant *relative gain* to the Indonesian plant because of a currency devaluation substantially in excess of the rate of increase in local construction costs. Indonesia did gain, but to do so it had to use its own labor and materials for approximately half of the original cost, and then have the index of such costs advance by a smaller percentage (in the example assumed, 10 per cent in one year) than the change in the official rate of exchange (in the example for the third year, 295 per cent). Is the result a real gain or an illusion? If we employ the "real opportunity cost" view, the gain is illusory, since it would probably require as much rubber, tin, petroleum, and other exports to buy cement after devaluation as it did before—from the point of view of the whole Indonesian economy. It may also be argued that building the plant in 1956–57 required fewer dollars of foreign exchange than after the third year, but this is not necessarily a real advantage. Whether there is a real advantage would seem to depend on the terms of trade of Indonesian exports relative to cement manufacturing equipment, and on the terms of foreign borrowing.

IMPLICATIONS OF THE METHOD FOR RELATIVE CURRENT EXPENDITURES

We shall now consider the costs representing expenditures in each production period. Does the procedure of converting the dollar costs of Cushenberry to rupiahs at an annual average of the monthly average official rate of exchange give an advantage to either plant? A stable official rate of exchange would seem to provide a better relative comparison than a fluctuating rate. If there is no change in the official rate, the Cushenberry dollar costs converted to rupiahs will provide a cost per metric ton in rupiahs which depends on the efficiency of the Cushenberry plant and the level of costs in the United States factor markets in which Cushenberry obtains management, labor, supplies, energy, and the like. Similarly, the rupiah costs of Gresik will be a function of the plant efficiency and of changes in the Indonesian market for management, labor, supplies, energy, and so on. In any year in which there is a change in the official rate of exchange which is greater, in percentage terms, than the rate of increase in the local factor markets in Indonesia, the conversion procedure will provide a relative advantage to Gresik. In other words, the procedure may be expected to provide "leads" and "lags" if the official rate is not changed frequently. Gresik costs will lead those shown for Cushenberry (on an absolute and relative basis) in a period in which inflation is not accompanied by a corresponding change in the official rate of exchange, and in a period in which the official rate is changed the Cushenberry costs will appear to "jump" relative to those for Gresik. The foregoing will be true only for salaries and wages in Indonesia and for purchases of material produced in Indonesia. It will not be true for costs represented by imports unless there is a significant time lag between payment and use.

SUMMARY AND WARNINGS

The procedure for converting dollar costs at Cushenberry to rupiahs is in itself an independent variable influencing the absolute rupiah costs for all elements of cost, and usually influencing the relative costs. We may expect also that the procedure will always operate to the relative advantage of Gresik and adverse to Cushenberry in any time interval in which there is a *de facto* (as with the exchange auction system of 1957 and 1958) devaluation of the rupiah in relation to the U. S. dollar, or a *de jure* devaluation (as in the August 24, 1959, change to 45 to 1 from the frozen auction rate of approximately 39 to 1). Just how important the relative change is, depends on several factors. For depreciation and interest, it depends on the proportion of original investment in local expenditures in Indonesia and on the relative movements of construction cost indexes in each country. For current outlays it depends on the proportion of Gresik costs represented by imports.

The procedure of using the official rate of exchange rather than a constant rate of exchange is not superior in all respects. Each procedure has limitations in a dynamic situation, but it seems to the writer that the use of the official rate of exchange in the manner proposed will provide more useful insights into the nature and behavior of costs in the two plants and in the two economies than would the use of a constant rate of exchange.

Would a free market rate be better than the official rate? It does not appear so to the writer. The reason is in the factors which influence the free market rate. Indonesia is an archipelago, and some of its most important export products, notably smallholder rubber and copra, are produced in Sumatra and Sulawesi, both close enough to Singapore to permit extensive smuggling. The free market rates for the Indonesian rupiah in Singapore and in Hong Kong usually are virtually the same because of arbitrage transactions. The supply of rupiahs in the free market comes chiefly from capital flight and from Indonesian traders who want to buy goods in Singapore or Hong Kong for smuggling into Indonesia. The demand comes mostly from traders who smuggle rubber and copra from Indonesia and who prefer to bring rupiahs back rather than commodities, and from foreigners who live in Indonesia or visit there and prefer to buy rupiahs at the free rate. The factors affecting the supply of and the demand for rupiahs in the free market often are influenced as much by political developments in Indonesia as by the relationship between the prices of consumer goods in Indonesia and the official rate of exchange. This being so, the writer is convinced that significant changes in the free or black market rate do not accurately reflect changes in the domestic purchasing power of the rupiah. The free market rate would seem to introduce more problems than it solves in terms of measuring relative inflation in the two economies.

As was shown above, a change in the official rate of the rupiah that is greater in percentage terms than the inflation in the domestic factor markets used by Gresik will result in a greater comparative rupiah cost increase for Cushenberry than for Gresik. With the free rate this result would be magnified when political developments caused the rupiah to fall, and the reverse when easing of political conditions caused the free rate to rise. There seems little logic in using a conversion procedure which would provide for Gresik a relative improvement during disturbed political periods and a relative decline when the political situation improved. The official rate as used in the procedure to be followed appears to provide more useful insight into the effects of inflation and has the merit of being a definite and known rate, whereas the effective free rate is hard to determine and an effective average rate for a year would be difficult to compute.

A final warning concerns the possibility that the cost inflation factor of a compound rate of 10 per cent per year for capital construction costs in Indonesia is too low. Between the end of 1956 (effectively the construction period) and the end of 1959, the money supply in Indonesia increased by about 140 per cent; that is, the supply at the end of 1959 was about 240 per cent of the supply at the end of 1956. This suggests a compound rate of over 50 per cent per annum for construction costs. The chief component of the local construction cost, however, is wages and salaries, and these were held down during the period 1957–1960 by a combination of unemployment, particularly in East Java, where the Gresik plant is located, and government policy. Certainly the compound annual rate of 10 per cent should be regarded as a minimum rate. In terms of gaining insight into the problems of a developing economy in which industrialization is regarded as the most important means of dealing with substantial (and increasing) unemployment, it appears logical to believe that wage rates will lag substantially behind prices, and that the margin will increase as the rate of increase in the money supply accelerates.

Having posted a number of warning signs concerning the difficulties to be encountered in using the methods proposed, particularly those for revaluing assets for depreciation and interest, and in the use of the official rate of exchange, we may now compare costs and output at Gresik and Cushenberry.

VI

Production and Production Costs at Gresik and Cushenberry

The cost comparisons of this chapter are based on the detailed work sheets contained in the tables of Appendix A and Appendix B. The data cover all or parts of the four years 1957–1960. The Cushenberry plant operated for the last nine months of 1957, and the Gresik plant for the last six months of 1957. Data for 1958 and 1959 are for the calendar years; data for 1960 is for the first six months.

Any attempt to compare costs must deal with the great difference in capital investment per ton of cement-producing capacity and the implications of this for differences in costs represented by current cash expenditures. Since the capital investment in Gresik was much higher than that in Cushenberry, the writer felt that the methods used should not be such as to widen this initial difference. In fact, as the discussion in the preceding chapter showed, the procedures employed favor Gresik to some extent, particularly for 1959 and 1960.

In the writer's opinion, the attempt to compare the costs of the two plants in terms of the monetary unit of one of the countries should be concentrated primarily on the year 1959 and the first six months of 1960. In both 1957 and 1958 the combination of fiscal and political problems in Indonesia affected the output at Gresik in adverse ways beyond the control of the Gresik management. The moving *de facto* rate of exchange in the last six months of 1957 and part of 1958 would complicate the comparison problems. In fact, only for the first six months of 1960 do we have an accounting period during which the official rate of exchange was unchanged.

TOTAL COSTS AND CASH COSTS

As was explained in Chapter 4, the flow-sheet method of developing full costs for a continuous process plant provides a final cost of finished product which is a combination of the costs of the current period and those carried forward from prior periods in inventories, and each of these in turn represents a combination of cash and non-cash costs. This method of developing costs is useful for many purposes, particularly as a basis for pricing and for determination of periodic profit or loss and the periodic statement of financial position (balance sheet). For purposes of cost comparison, however, it is desirable to have the unit cost of production of finished cement according to the major elements of cost: current cash costs and the non-cash costs of depreciation and interest. For the year 1959 and the first six months of 1960 the Gresik costs were computed in two ways: the full costs, including depreciation and interest (see Appendix table A-6 for 1959 and table A-12 for 1960), and current cash costs only (Appendix table A-8 for 1959 and table A-14 for 1960). In developing cash costs alone, the effect of inventories can be eliminated by pricing the in-process or intermediate inventory of clinker at the unit cost of the accounting period, and this was done in Appendix tables A-8 and A-14 for illustrative purposes. The total cash costs incurred in all producing departments were converted to a cost per metric ton by the following procedure:

1. The total amount of each element of cost was expressed as a percentage of the total cash cost.

2. The percentages of (1) were applied to the total unit cash cost of cement to obtain the unit cost per metric ton by elements of cost.

The computations of unit cost by elements are shown in tables 6–6 through 6–11 in Appendix 1.

By using the cash costs in the way described, the difference between full cost per metric ton and cash cost per metric ton represents, approximately, the non-cash costs of depreciation and interest for all departments combined. The procedure eliminates depreciation and interest from the administrative, service, and utility departments as well as from the so-called production departments. In tables 6–6 through 6–11 no attempt was made to value the inventory of clinker at the costs for the current period; hence there is no difference in total unit cost between the full cost basis and the unit cost used to derive the so-called cash cost per metric ton.[1] If there was no depreciation or interest in a particular element, such as operating labor, the unit cost is the same for the full-cost method and the cash-cost method. For utilities, however, the cash cost excludes not only depreciation and interest for the utilities themselves, but similar charges included in general administration and factory administration assigned to the utilities departments.

Table 6–1 shows the output of finished cement for the two plants for 1957, 1958, 1959, and the first six months of 1960. The cost per metric ton of finished cement is shown first in total and then by the following subdivisions: cash costs, depreciation, and interest. The data of table 6–1 suggest the following general conclusions:

1. The total tonnage of finished cement produced was larger at Cushenberry than at Gresik in each period, but the rate of increase over the total time was somewhat greater for Gresik—as indicated by the rising percentage figures.

2. The total costs per ton for Cushenberry were lower in the two periods for which they were converted to rupiahs than those at Gresik.

3. Total cost per metric ton in rupiahs at Gresik increased every period over that of the preceding period, whereas total

---

[1] Readers interested in cost accounting procedure will note that the cash costs per metric ton in Appendix tables A-8 and A-14 are slightly higher than those used in tables 6–6 and 6–7 in Appendix 1. The difference is the result of using a weighted average of beginning inventory and cement yearly costs to value the clinker inventory in the flow sheets of the appendix tables. Tables 6–6 and 6–7 in effect employ the LIFO (last-in, first-out) assumptions.

cost per ton in dollars at Cushenberry decreased in every period from the amount in the preceding period.

4. In every period, cash cost per ton at Gresik represented a smaller percentage of total rupiah cost than at Cushenberry. These percentages are not shown in table 6–1, but are as follows:

	1957	1958	1959	1960
Gresik	25	29	38	47
Cushenberry	49	57	62	65

The fact that Gresik was able to increase its output at a slightly faster rate than did Cushenberry does not support the view that a state enterprise in a newly independent country will be unable to deal effectively with the complications of a modern industrial plant. Rather, it supports the general thesis of socialism for a developing economy that the periodic recessions of a private enterprise economy need not have their counterpart in the heavy industry sector of a socialist state even if the country exports raw materials to the industrial countries and experiences wide fluctuations in the earning of foreign exchange as a result of market fluctuations in the industrialized private enterprise countries. The recession starting in the latter part of 1959 and continuing throughout 1960 affected the market for Cushenberry, and the problems of getting established in a new market area seem to have influenced the rate of output in 1957 and 1958. In 1957, for example, Cushenberry operated for nine months, whereas Gresik operated for only six months. This affected the first-year base for each plant.

The dollar costs of Cushenberry were converted to rupiahs only for 1959 and 1960, and for these periods the rupiah costs of Gresik substantially exceeded those of Cushenberry. If we divide the total rupiah cost per ton at Gresik by the total dollar costs per ton at Cushenberry for 1957 and 1958, we secure the *rate of exchange* which would have made the rupiah costs equal for the two plants. For 1957 the equalizing rate was 32.53 rupiahs to the U. S. dollar, and for 1958 the rate was 50.82 rupiahs to the U. S. dollar. Since the Indonesian auction or *de facto* rate moved from about 22 to 1 in July, 1957, to about 30.8 to 1 at the end of December, we may conclude that any monthly average of the *de facto* rate would provide a lower rupiah cost for Cushenberry than for Gresik in 1957. The auction rate in 1958 moved from the December, 1957, level of 30.8 to 1 to 37.85 to 1 in April, at which level it was fixed by government policy for the remainder of 1958 and through 1959 to the devaluation of August 24. Since the 1958 level was below that necessary to equalize costs, we may conclude that the money costs per ton of cement at Gresik in 1958 were higher than those at Cushenberry.

The fact that for Gresik the rupiah cost per metric ton increased in each period in relation to that of the preceding period is evidence of the inflation in Indonesia during the period. The inflationary forces are suggested by the following tabulation of the money supply by calendar quarters during the period 1957–1959. Figures are in billions of rupiahs, and are taken from Bulletin No. 19 of Bank Indonesia.

End of month	Money supply			Per cent of December, 1956
	Currency	Bank deposits	Total	
1956				
December	9.4	4.0	13.4	100
1957				
March	9.3	4.0	13.3	102
June	10.9	4.3	15.2	117
September	12.5	4.3	16.8	129
December	14.1	4.8	18.9	145
1958				
March	14.0	5.6	19.6	151
June	15.4	6.2	21.6	166
September	16.5	7.5	24.0	185
December	19.9	9.5	29.4	226
1959				
March	20.1	9.9	30.0	230
June	22.8	9.5	32.3	250
September	20.2	4.1	24.3	187
December	26.4	8.5	34.9	269

To understand the impact of domestic inflation on rupiah costs per metric ton for Gresik, we must remember that the procedure used in this study for computing depreciation and interest is such as to make these charges decline each year in the absence of any change in the domestic costs of construction or in the official rate of exchange. This is the result of the declining balance method of determining the base for depreciation and interest. This is seen in the dollar costs per metric ton for depreciation and interest at Cushenberry. In spite of an assumed increase in the replacement cost of a compound rate of 5 per cent per year, the unit costs of depreciation and interest declined at Cushenberry.

The current cash costs per metric ton provide a better measure of the effects of inflation than do those for total unit cost. Using 1957 costs as 100, the Gresik cash costs per ton increased to 238 per cent in the first six months of 1960, and to 168 per cent in 1959. Although the simple quantity theory of money is not advanced as an adequate explanation for price or cost changes in Indonesia, it is interesting to compare the relative changes in cash costs at Gresik and the relative changes in the money supply. Since the cash costs are the average costs for the period, we shall regard the average of the beginning and ending money supply for the period as the basis for computing the change in the supply. The costs and money supply compare as follows for Gresik:

Year	Average cash cost per metric ton		Average money supply	
	Rupiahs	1957 = 100	Billions of rupiahs	1957 = 100
1957	183	100	17.0	100
1958	228	125	24.2	142
1959	307	168	32.2	189

There are too many variables affecting both cash costs at Gresik and the money supply in Indonesia to permit the refinement of the data required for a satisfactory test of the precise effect of a change in money supply on the cash costs at Gresik, but the tabulation suggests that the relationship may be rather close. A comprehensive study by Ralph Anspach of the University of California Economics Project at the University of Indonesia suggests a quantity of money-retail price level relationship even closer than that of the tabulation above.[2]

In the preceding chapter it was pointed out that the use of the official rate of exchange should provide a relative advantage to Gresik over Cushenberry in an accounting period in which the rupiah fell relative to the dollar. Since the data of table 6–1 do not include conversion of Cushenberry dollar costs to rupiahs in 1957 or 1958, the only evidence to test the contention might appear to be for 1960 in relation to 1959. The costs per metric ton for depreciation cast doubt on this contention. The costs and their relative position were as follows:

| | Depreciation cost per metric ton | | Gresik unit cost as a percentage of Cushenberry |
Year	Gresik	Cushenberry	unit cost
1959	Rp. 334.11	Rp. 160.65	208
1960 (6 months) . . .	328.48	137.25	239

The reason for the deterioration of the Gresik costs relative to those of Cushenberry is that the official rate of exchange did not change between the two periods with respect to depreciation charges. In this study the assets are revalued at the *end of each year*. The rupiah was devalued August 24, 1959; hence the official rate of 45 to 1 was used for both 1959 and 1960 in valuing the portion of the Gresik plant represented by foreign exchange expenditures. Since the procedure employed for depreciation and interest is to convert Cushenberry dollar costs to rupiahs at the official rate at the *end of the period*, and we had to have such a rate to revalue the foreign exchange portion of the Gresik plant, we can actually convert dollars to rupiahs for depreciation and interest without making a decision as to the average rate for the year. The results are as follows:

---

[2] Ralph Anspach, "Monetary Aspects of Indonesia's Economic Reorganization in 1959," *Ekonomi dan Keuangan Indonesia* (Economics and Finance in Indonesia), Tahun Ke XIII, No. 1/2 Djanuari/Pebruari, 1960, pp. 2–47.

	1957	1958	1959
Year-end effective auction rate used to revalue foreign exchange portion of Gresik investment in fixed assets (see table 3–1)	270%	330%	—
Official rate, rupiahs to one U. S. dollar	11.475	11.475	45.00
Effective official rate, rupiahs to one U. S. dollar	30.98	37.87	45.00
Depreciation cost per ton at Cushenberry:			
Dollars	6.42	4.45	3.57
Rupiahs	199.00	169.00	161.00
Depreciation cost per ton at Gresik	360.00	377.00	334.00
Gresik as percentage of Cushenberry	181%	223%	207%

The improvement in depreciation cost per ton for Cushenberry relative to that for Gresik in 1958 compared to 1957 was primarily the result of the fact that the 15 per cent declining balance method *assigned a larger percentage of original cost to 1958* for Gresik than for Cushenberry. This was because Cushenberry operated nine months in 1957, whereas Gresik operated only six months. This relative effect would not continue into 1959 and subsequent years; hence its relative force is zero after 1958: the ratio of the cost per ton for Gresik to that for Cushenberry would, other things being equal (no change in relative inflation rates or in output rate), remain constant. This can be demonstrated as follows:

	Gresik	Cushenberry	Gresik as a percentage of Cushenberry
Original investment	Rp. 200,000	Rp. 100,000	200
15 percent depreciation, year 1957	30,000	15,000	200
Gresik, 6 months	15,000	} 133	
Cushenberry, 9 months		11,250	
Production: assumed figures at actual ratio, metric tons	40	67	60
Depreciation per ton	375	168	223

	Gresik	Cush-enberry	Gresik as a percentage of Cushenberry
Declining balance for 1958 depreciation	185,000	88,750	208
1958 depreciation at 15 percent	27,750	13,313	208
1958 production, 190 percent of 1957	76	127	60
1958 depreciation cost per ton	365	105	348
Declining balance for 1959 depreciation	157,250	75,437	208
1959 depreciation at 15 percent	23,588	11,316	208
1959 production, same as in 1958	76	127	60
1959 depreciation cost per ton	310	89	348

Returning to the improvement in the Gresik ratio (in percentage terms) of depreciation per metric ton relative to that for Cushenberry in 1959 (207 per cent) over 1958 (223 per cent), we conclude that this had to be almost entirely the result of a change in the official rate of exchange which exceeded the rate of cost increase for the local currency portion of the Gresik investment. The change in the rate of exchange was from 30.98 to 1 at the end of 1958 to 37.87 to 1 at the end of 1959, or approximately 23 per cent. The inflation rate used was 10 per cent; hence we may regard the result as consistent with our expectations. Since interest is always 50 per cent of depreciation, the same result would follow for relative interest costs per metric ton. A small part of the relative improvement was due to the relatively greater increase in output at Gresik.

BEHAVIOR OF SEPARATE ELEMENTS OF COST IN 1959

Table 6–2 compares the major elements of cost at Gresik and Cushenberry in 1959 on two bases: full costs and current expenditures or cash costs. The data for Gresik in table 6–2 were developed in table 6–6 and those for Cushenberry in table 6–8.

Readers familiar with costing problems of continuous process operations will recognize that the costs developed by elements of cost are approximations of those which would be obtainable by using a flow sheet for each single element of cost. For non-accountants this is equivalent to saying that the cost per metric ton is not quite that obtained by dividing the total money cost for the particular element by the number of metric tons actually completed in the accounting period. The method adjusts for changes in the level of the clinker inventory (changes in the level of quarried rock are ignored for each plant.) In deriving table 6–2 some of the separate cost items were combined to facilitate comparison, and some were split and combined with others. For example, the separate costs in table 6–6 for power, fuel, pier and oil storage, and water at Gresik were combined in a single cost called "utilities" in table 6–2. An example of splitting and combining is to use the cost of purchased silica sand and iron ore as "purchased material for raw grinding" at Gresik and to compare this with the costs reported by Cushenberry for clay and limestone spalls. The Gresik cost so designated does not include labor and power required to handle the raw materials at the plant, or depreciation and interest on the facilities required. The costs of purchased material for raw grinding are thus more nearly comparable for the two plants.

In table 6–2 all costs except operating labor are adverse to Gresik when the so-called full-cost basis is used. When the relevant depreciation and interest charges are removed from maintenance, utilities, and general and factory administration, however, all the remaining costs (the cash costs of the period) are lower for these items at Gresik than at Cushenberry. In 1959 only the costs of supplies and purchased raw materials are higher at Gresik than at Cushenberry. This is attributable chiefly to two factors: import duties and differences in the composition of limestone. Import duties affected operating and factory supplies, and to some extent gypsum. The limestone deposit at Gresik is relatively deficient in silica and iron compared to that at Cushenberry; therefore more of these had to be purchased at Gresik than at Cushenberry. Silica sand must be brought by small boats from another island at a great distance from Gresik, and sand containing iron from another part of Java. The quality of local gypsum is poor and erratic in Indonesia, and the cost per ton very high. Some imports were required to supplement local sources in 1959, and a larger percentage was required in 1960.

Although Gresik could obtain its utilities at a lower cash outlay than could Cushenberry in 1959, the very substantial investment in plant and equipment required to generate power and to transport and process water (see Chap. 2) made the capital cost for these utilities so high that total utility costs at Gresik were approximately 30 per cent higher than for Cushenberry. This we may associate primarily with differences in the stage of economic development of the two countries in which the plants function. The rates paid to the private utilities in California provide a rate of return rather close to the 7½ per cent used for the interest factor at Gresik.

The advantage of Gresik over Cushenberry in labor cost represented by wages and salaries and fringe costs such as food, but excluding the fringe costs of housing and transportation, is very great in percentage terms—: the Gresik costs are less than one-third of those at Cushenberry. This is an important problem in inter-economy comparisons, and will be discussed further after we consider the costs for the first six months of 1960.

In summary, the largest single factor contributing to the higher unit costs per ton at Gresik in 1959 was the high investment in fixed assets. The fact that the total investment at Gresik was more than twice that at Cushenberry was reinforced by the fact the plant capacity was less. In 1959 Gresik produced approximately 67 per cent of the tonnage produced by Cushenberry.

BEHAVIOR OF SEPARATE ELEMENTS OF COST IN 1960

Table 6–3 compares production and costs under the two methods of full-costing and cash-costing for the first six months of 1960. The Gresik output increased relative to that of Cushenberry over 1959; hence we might expect this to result in a relative improvement in the cost per ton for depreciation and interest. These factors compare as follows:

	Gresik	Cush-enberry	Gresik as a percentage of Cushenberry
Production in 1960, tons	137,496	197,406	69.65
Production in 1959, tons	282,804	422,631	66.92
Depreciation per metric ton, 1960	328.48	137.25	
Interest per metric ton, 1960 ..	164.24	68.85	
Total	492.72	206.10	239.00
Depreciation per metric ton, 1959	334.11	160.65	
Interest per metric ton, 1959 ..	167.01	80.55	
Total	501.12	241.20	208.00

The fact that combined depreciation and interest charges per metric ton at Gresik were 239 per cent of those at Cushenberry in 1960 (first 6 months) and only 208 per cent of those at Cushenberry in 1959, when the output showed a relative increase, indicates the differences in rate of change in the estimated costs of capital construction in the two economies. Since the official rate of exchange did not change between the end of 1959 and the end of 1960, the Cushenberry capital costs were converted at the same rate in each period. The fact that the official rate did not change also meant that, under the procedure used, there was no change in the estimated replacement cost of that portion of the Gresik plant represented by foreign exchange expenditures. At the original rate at the time of construction, the dollar equivalent of the *local cost* was $16,642,697, and the total dollar investment in Cushenberry was $14,539,715. Since we used an estimated construction cost inflation rate of 10 per cent for Gresik and 5 per cent for Cushenberry, the effect was to increase the slightly larger Gresik base by a factor twice that applied to the Cushenberry base. The relative rate of change in output for Gresik was about 4 per cent greater than that for Cushenberry. A rate of inflation in the cost base greater than the rate of improvement in output had the effect of increasing capital costs per metric ton for Gresik relative to those for Cushenberry.

Table 6–3 shows the same general relationships for total cost per metric ton in the first six months of 1960 that we found in table 6–2 for 1959. In cash costs, however, in 1960 Gresik no longer enjoyed an advantage in the costs of maintenance or utilities. Cash costs for maintenance at Cushenberry declined in the first six months of 1960 by a small amount, whereas the costs at Gresik went up sharply—by about 53 per cent. Based on tables 6–6 and 6–7 at the end of this chapter, comparisons of the cash components of repair and maintenance at Gresik are as follows:

	Rupiahs per metric ton		Increase in 1960	
	1959	1960	Amount	% of 1959
Repair labor	3.31	4.07	0.76	23
Repair supplies	19.80	25.09	5.29	27
Repair overhead	35.87	60.83	24.96	70
Total	58.98	89.99	31.01	53

Information made available to the writer indicated that wage and salary rates at Gresik in 1960 were at least 10 per cent higher than in 1959; therefore it would appear that the size of the maintenance force was increased at least 10 per cent. This agrees substantially with data from the labor force reports made available. The increase in repair supplies probably was in part a result of price increases and in part a result of using more supplies and parts. Since most repair parts are imported and a large stock is maintained, it was not possible, with the average rupiah cost system employed for the inventory, to determine the relative contribution of increased usage and increased prices. The increase in overhead was caused both by increased wages and salaries and size of staff, and by a sharp increase in power cost as a result of an increase in the price of refined petroleum products in January, 1960.

One of the considerations advanced by the writer for the use of the declining balance method of computing depreciation in the large state enterprises in Indonesia is the possibility that costs of repairs and maintenance will increase substantially each year and offset the lower depreciation charges. The charges per metric ton compare as follows for the years for which data were available:

	Rupiahs per metric ton		
	1958	1959	1960
Depreciation, full-cost basis	198	160	141
Maintenance	93	105	161
Total	291	265	302

The depreciation and maintenance costs at Cushenberry on a full-cost basis compare as follows:

	U.S. dollars per metric ton			
	1957	1958	1959	1960
Depreciation	$4.58	$3.25	$2.59	$2.26
Maintenance	1.89	1.72	1.88	1.64
Total	$6.47	$4.97	$4.47	$3.90

	Rupiahs per metric ton	
Depreciation	117	102
Maintenance	77	74
Total	194	176

At Gresik the increase in maintenance in 1959 did not offset the decline in depreciation, but it did in 1960. The change in maintenance cost at Gresik is not far out of line with what we would expect in terms of the rate of inflation. At Cushenberry, maintenanace costs per metric ton were relatively constant for the period 1957–1960.

The adverse costs of maintenance at Gresik seem to result largely from the cost distribution system employed. The system charged the maintenance department with its share of general and plant administration on the basis of the labor cost. Since the cost of general administration is quite high at Gresik, the result is to "inflate" the maintenance cost. The writer is strongly of the opinion, however, that it is necessary to include the costs of administration, and particularly of general administration, to obtain the most useful picture of the underlying economic structure. This, to repeat what has been emphasized before, is that the factor of social capital cost, or of the cost of factors internal to Gresik but external to Cushenberry, is of primary importance in the inter-economy comparison. As will be shown in detail later in this chapter, Gresik employs a larger number of maintenance workers and supervisors than does Cushenberry. This large number of employees requires the social services which comprise the bulk of the items in general administration, and so it seems necessary to assign to maintenance cost a share based on the money labor cost of maintenance.

The use of a large maintenance force reflects primarily the differences in the stages of economic development of Indonesia and the United States. In the first year the Indonesian plant had to train its workers to do maintenance work. The workers are not the product of an industrial and mechanical environment, but of a village agriculture or fishing economy which is labor-intensive in the extreme and where capital equipment is primitive and small in quantity. Gresik further must contend with high costs of imported repair parts and an irregular supply. This in turn requires that the maintenance force make many parts that would be purchased in a more industrialized economy.

It would seem that the maintenance costs should be compared by components, rather than in total, to avoid the influence of the high "distributed cost" of general administration. The three components are labor, parts and supplies, and overhead. Differences in organization and accounting create some problems of comparability. To limit the analysis to the cement-producing departments may not give as clear a picture of the inter-economy differences as will a total plant basis. The following data relate to the most recent period for which comparable data could be obtained, the first six months of 1960.

The larger repair labor force at Gresik involves a lower total repair labor cost than does a smaller one at Cushenberry. Even when the larger force is related to a total output of about two-thirds that at Cushenberry, the cost per ton for *all repair labor* at Gresik is only 14 per cent of that at Cushenberry. Data on the repair labor forces are not exact, but a figure of 230 maintenance workers and supervisors at Gresik at the end of 1959 and

	Repair salaries and wages	Direct repair materials
CUSHENBERRY		
Costs for entire plant, first 6 months of 1960	$ 245,902	$ 172,618
Less supervision and employee benefits	55,694	
	$ 190,208	$ 172,618
Convert to rupiahs at 45 to 1	8,559,360	7,767,810
Metric tons of finished cement	197,406	197,406
Cost per metric ton ....Rp.	43.36	Rp. 39.35
GRESIK		
Costs for entire plant, first 6 months of 1960	776,189	4,512,459
Metric tons of finished cement	137,496	137,496
Cost per metric ton ....Rp.	5.64	Rp. 32.82
Costs for cement production departments only, first 6 months of 1960	542,942	3,332,075
Metric tons of finished cement	137,496	137,496
Cost per metric ton ....Rp.	3.95	Rp. 24.23

of 60 at Cushenberry at the end of April, 1961, indicates the general relationship.

The fact that the cost per metric ton was less for repair parts at Gresik is contrary to what the writer expected. Part of the explanation probably is in the rate of exchange. All Cushenberry dollar costs were converted at 45 to 1, whereas it is likely that a substantial part of the items charged out of inventory at Gresik in the first half of 1960 were purchased in 1959 or earlier. This would mean that they were acquired at a rate of 39 to 1 or less. The money costs would be comparable if Gresik revalued its inventory of imported materials and parts whenever there is a change in the rate of exchange. At the time the writer was at Gresik this procedure was under discussion and was strongly supported by the executives. The chief barrier is the clerical work required. A second possibility is that there was *under-maintenance* at Gresik. If we take the view that the parts and supplies charged to cost in 1960 were actually acquired at a rate of exchange of about 39 to 1, the Cushenberry costs might be reduced about 13 per cent. For all repair parts in each plant, Cushenberry would then have a cost of approximately 35 rupiahs per ton, and Gresik 33 rupiahs per ton. Since Gresik must pay ocean freight and insurance plus about 20 per cent import duty, it apparently *did not use as many parts per ton of output* as did Cushenberry—and this in the face of maintaining a power plant and a larger fleet of cars and trucks. Admittedly, the maintenance of such social capital as housing and roads would have some effect on the cost per ton, but it can scarcely be argued that the cost should be lower when the total investment is more than twice that at Cushenberry and imported parts must carry transportation, insurance, and import duties. We may conclude that there was less "real" maintenance at Gresik in the first six months of 1960 than there was at Cushenberry. This conclusion was supported by the views of the top production executives at Gresik and by the Morrison-Knudsen International engineers in charge of the construction of the third kiln and related facilities. During the period covered by this study there was a severe shortage of foreign exchange in Indonesia, and Gresik was unable to secure allocations sufficient to meet the requests of the management for spare parts. Although data are not available concerning the difference between the level of expenditure considered desirable by the Gresik management and the level made possible by actual foreign exchange allocations, the writer received the impression that it was rather large.

In the expansion program for the third kiln the Morrison-Knudsen International engineers made extensive surveys of equipment condition and, to the extent feasible, the program included renovation of worn equipment. All parties concerned at Gresik believed that the maintenance program should be much more extensive than it was during the period of this study. The comparative data above support this view. A more liberal foreign exchange policy would not necessarily mean a larger maintenance force, for in a developing economy a large force is often required to *make parts* that in an industrialized economy are purchased from the manufacturer of the original equipment. Certainly inadequate maintenance leads to equipment failure and shortens the physical life of the plant. Inadequate *preventive* maintenance in the long run increases rather than reduces expenditure for both repair labor and repair parts and increases the cost per ton because of loss of production when equipment fails.

The sharp increase in the cash cost per metric ton for utilities at Gresik in the first six months of 1960 of Rp. 77, or 81 per cent was caused primarily by an increase in the prices of diesel fuel and bunker oil of approximately 100 per cent in January, 1960. This was the only price change in oil during the four years covered by the study, and was necessary because domestic prices of refined petroleum products had become so low in relation to other prices and the money incomes of consumers that an extensive black market developed and rationing of refined products had become a major operation. Both the refiners and the government were losing at the prevailing prices, the one because rupiah income was less than the current rupiah expenditures for refining and distributing, and the latter through loss of excise tax revenue and of foreign exchange earnings to the extent that the low domestic prices diverted petroleum to the domestic market. The price advance in 1960 eliminated the cash advantage in utilities enjoyed by Gresik in 1959. It is likely that a petroleum pricing policy more in line with the market situation in 1959 would also have eliminated or substantially reduced the advantage in cash expenditures for utilities of Gresik over Cushenberry.

In 1960, operating labor costs at Gresik continued to be lower than at Cushenberry. Labor costs increased at each plant in 1960, but by nearly the same percentage. The labor cost comparison is more complicated than simply comparing the figures for operating and repair labor, and we shall examine this in the following section for both 1959 and 1960.

In summary, inflationary forces in Indonesia in 1960 increased the cash costs per metric ton at Gresik in relation to those at Cushenberry, and also the costs per metric ton for the non-cash items of depreciation and interest. The favorable cash expenditure margin of Rp. 54 per metric ton at Gresik in 1959 gave way to an unfavorable cash margin of Rp. 54 per metric ton in the first six months of 1960.

COMPARING LABOR AND ADMINISTRATIVE COSTS

We turn now to the interesting and complex question of the "real cost" of labor in relation to the "money costs" in newly developing economies and advanced industrial economies. The data of table 6–2 and 6–3 give the advantage to Gresik for operating labor, but we must consider the nature of the charges included in labor cost at each plant before arriving at a conclusion regarding the absolute or relative significance of such costs in terms of the cost per ton of finished cement.

At Gresik in particular and in Indonesia in general the cash payment to both workers and supervisors is an incomplete measure of income for the worker, and therefore of labor cost for the enterprise. This is accentuated in a period of severe inflation, when virtually all employing units resort increasingly to payments in kind in order to assure the workers the minimum basic requirements for subsistence. Payments in kind take the form of free or subsidized rice, clothing, meals at work, organizing and financing workers' cooperatives to enable them to buy scarce items, and the like. For management and classified monthly workers (called *pegawai* in Indonesia), housing and transportation are often provided. Given the institutional environment in Indonesia, the first problem is to attempt to develop the "cash employment costs" of the enterprise. These will be defined as the total rupiah payments to the employee in the form of regular time and overtime, annual bonus, vacation pay, and the cost of payments in kind exclusive of housing and transportation. Since we are interested primarily in costs through the finish grinding department only, we can approximate the required result by adding to the operating labor, repair labor, and wages and salaries for factory administration and general administration, the costs of overtime, annual vacation, Lebaran (fasting month) bonus, and payments in kind. To make the comparison of the cost of cement production only, we must develop figures which exclude costs for departments after finish grinding. But to make an inter-economy comparison it appears best to use the total costs for all operations at each plant.

Our first task is to develop the cash costs of supervision and labor. This is done for 1959 in the following computations. The details of supervision and labor are taken from the *Annual Statistical Report* of P. N. Pabrik Semen "Gresik."

Cost items	Charged to factory costs	Charged to general administration
Direksi (resident directors)		Rp 228,205
Gadji/Upah (wages and salaries) ... Rp.	6,351,981	4,712,440
Total base pay	6,351,981	4,940,645
Other wage and salary payments:		
Upah lembur (overtime)	2,545,199	1,350,543
Bulan ke 13 (annual Lebaran bonus)	457,600	475,015
Hari libur (vacation pay)	12,688	64
C.D.C. 1958 (retroactive pay)	705,851	575,138
Other	4,961	68,282
Total	3,726,299	2,469,042
Total for 1959 .... Rp.	10,078,280	Rp. 7,409,687
Other wage and salary payments as a percentage of base pay	58.7%	50.0%
Cost of payments in kind:		
Food (lunches) .... Rp.	337,508	
Tea and coffee	200,723	
Work clothing	381,000	
Rice	840,840	
Total .... Rp.	1,760,071	
Payments in kind as a percentage of total cash employee compensation	17.5%	

With the foregoing data we may develop the costs of labor and supervision for Gresik and compare them with the costs for Cushenberry for the production of cement through finish grinding. The computations and comparisons for 1959 are presented in table 6–4. To make the comparison as useful as possible, the portion of the Cushenberry labor cost charged to steel rock was removed from the total costs, as was done in developing the unit costs of cement produced. The repair labor costs for 1959 for Cushenberry were estimated by applying to the 1959 maintenance costs for the cement-production departments the percentage of maintenance cost represented by repair labor in a period in 1960.

Based on the estimates and approximations of table 6–4, the cost per ton of finished cement for all cash payments for supervision and labor at Gresik was Rp. 53.27 per metric ton. This compares with Rp. 97.21 for Cushenberry and represents about 55 per cent of the Cushenberry cost per metric ton. This is significant in evaluating the economies of the two countries when we keep in mind that the total supervisory and labor force at Gresik at the end of 1959 was 996, and at Cushenberry 217. We have seen that the cash payment and the payment in kind for food and clothing do not represent the full cost of employment because the costs of housing and transportation are omitted. In the time available in Indonesia it was not possible for the writer to obtain detailed information concerning either the money outlays for housing and other benefits, or the distribution of such outlays between those in the managerial group, in the foreman group, and in the labor group. The costs for housing would be a function of the method of valuing the fixed assets and of taking depreciation and interest into the costs. As a rough approximation, however, virtually all the costs of *general administration* represent, in one way or another, supplementary or direct employment costs to Gresik. The lower half of table 6–4 shows the derivation of the general administration costs assigned to cement production alone. The total employment cost for cement-producing departments assigned from the combined costs of factory administration and general administration, but not including the cash employment costs in these departments, amounted to Rp. 33, 819, 317, or Rp. 119.59 per ton of finished cement. This cost when added to the direct payments in cash and kind raises the cost per ton for supervision and labor to Rp. 172.86. This in relation to a cost of Rp. 97.16 for Cushenberry suggests that the low cash payment system at Gresik may provide an inaccurate index of both labor income and labor cost.

The data of table 6–4 cover only the estimated costs for the production of cement through the finish grinding operation. For Gresik they do not include the costs of bag manufacture, packing, and loading, or locomotive and railroad costs; and for Cushenberry they do not include the cost of packing and loading or payments to the drivers who deliver a portion of the plant output in company trucks. The costs of getting the cement from the storage silos to the trucks, railroad cars, and boats at Gresik will be developed in the next chapter, when an attempt is made to evaluate the contribution of Gresik to the economy of Indonesia. Since cement is shipped and handled in the United States in a way quite different from that in Indonesia, no attempt will be made to develop and compare the separate elements of cost. To make the inter-economy comparison of employment costs as useful as possible, it is desirable to look at the total labor force at each plant. To do so we shall regard all the costs of general administration at Gresik, excluding payments to employees, as a supplementary employment cost. For Cushenberry, all social security payments by the employer and all so-called fringe benefit costs will be included as a part of total employment cost and of employee income. The data are compared below.

The costs per metric ton and per employee as computed here must be used and interpreted with caution. The assertion that all the original direct charges to general administration, excluding

CUSHENBERRY

Total salaries, wages, and employment benefits, 1959	$1,618,940
Convert to rupiahs at average rate of 41 to 1	Rp. 66,376,540
Metric tons of finished cement produced, 1959	422,631
Total number of employees at plant, end of 1959	217
Employment cost per metric ton of cement	Rp. 157
Employment cost per employee at plant	Rp. 305,882

Item   GRESIK
no.

1. Wages and salaries charged to factory cost
   (p. 135) .... Rp. 10,078,280
2. Wages and salaries charged to general
   administration (p. 135) 7,409,687
3. Costs represented by payments in kind: food and
   work clothing (p. 135) 1,760,071
4. Subtotal .... Rp. 19,248,038
   Total direct charges to general administration
      (Appendix A, table A–5) :
5.   Cash expenditures only ..... Rp. 28,405,593
6.   Less wages and salaries above   7,409,687
7.   Subtotal, cash basis 20,995,906
8. Subtotal .... Rp. 40,243,944
9. Depreciation of assets required by general
   administration only (table A–5) 26,645,099
10. Interest on assets required by general
    administration only (table A–5) 13,322,550
11. Total .... Rp. 80,211,593
12. Metric tons of finished cement produced, 1959 282,804
13. Total number of employees at plant, end of 1959 .. 996

	Cost per ton of finished cement	Cost per employee
Cash payments and payments in kind (item 4÷items 12 and 13)	Rp. 68	Rp. 19,325
Cash payments plus cash portion of general administration (item 8÷items 12 and 13)	Rp. 142	Rp. 40,405
Cash payments plus depreciation and interest on assets employed by general administration (item 11÷items 12 and 13)	Rp. 284	Rp. 80,523

the items involving payment to employees, are really *costs of the
kind of employment at Gresik* appears tenable to the writer,
based on what he observed during his stay at Gresik. For example,

expenditure for office supplies is in large measure determined by the state of development of the economy, that is, many employees and relatively little office machinery. It was necessary to maintain and operate a large fleet of cars and buses because of inadequate public transportation. A sizable community of homes had to be built and related facilities maintained, partly as a result of constructing the plant in a relatively isolated location. The same situation, however, is found for large enterprises even in the largest cities of Indonesia. In fact, the costs for general administration understate the real costs attributable to employment because they omit charges for utilities. What is most significant to the writer is that the cash employment costs plus the direct cash charges to general administration (item 8) provide a cost per ton of finished cement (Rp. 142) at Gresik which is not much below that at Cushenberry (Rp. 157). This contrasts with the cost per employee of Rp. 40,405 at Gresik and Rp. 305,882 at Cushenberry. Clearly, a low cash outlay *per worker* must not be equated with a low cash cost *per metric ton of cement produced.* When we include the high cost of depreciation and interest resulting from the 15 per cent declining balance method, Gresik employment costs per ton are substantially above those at Cushenberry—Rp. 284 in relation to Rp. 157, whereas costs per employee are still relatively small—Rp. 80,533 in relation to Rp. 305,882.

Another factor which must be mentioned in evaluating the employment costs is that the Permanente Cement Corporation maintains a large administrative and sales staff in Oakland, California, whereas only a small staff at the State Development Bank and the Department of Basic Industry and Mining is concerned with the administration of Gresik. The state trading company that distributes Gresik cement, however, maintains a rather large staff for cement distribution. Adding costs for central administration and sales undoubtedly would change the relative employment costs in favor of Gresik on a *per employee* and *per ton* basis. Data were not available from either enterprise for such a comparison.

The general conclusion emerges that relatively low cash employment cost per worker at Gresik does not result in an equally relatively low employment cost per ton of cement. This is because of the larger number of employees at Gresik. To this factor we now turn our attention.

SIZE AND COMPOSITION OF MANAGERIAL AND LABOR FORCES

Officials at each plant made available to the writer a complete manning table, or force report, in which the number of workers and their wage or salary classification were shown for each department. The Gresik report was for the end of 1959 and the Cushenberry report for April 30, 1961. Since the total force at Cushenberry was 204 in 1961 and 217 at the end of 1959, the use of the 1961 report will not provide a picture significantly different from that at the end of 1959. What is probably of more importance is that Cushenberry reduced its force between 1959 and early 1961, whereas Gresik expanded its force. The exact size of the Gresik force at the end of April, 1961, is not known to the writer, but part of the expansion was for training in anticipation of the requirements of the third kiln to come into operation late in 1961.

Gresik classifies its employees in the following eight major groups:

1. Central administration.
2. Commercial section.
3. Personnel and employee relations.
4. Community relations.
5. Financial section.
6. Public works and housing.
7. Service and utilities departments.
8. Factory operation.

Cushenberry divides its employees into fifteen groups. At Cushenberry a single group consists of those performing a particular function under a single supervisor. At Gresik each of the eight major groups consists of several subgroups—a total of forty. In general, it appears that the forty subgroups at Gresik can more nearly be equated with the fifteen major groups at Cushenberry. To provide a comparison of the work force, the writer decided to use the major groups at Gresik but to divide the production group into three parts: cement production, packing and loading, and bag manufacture. It was necessary to add another category, that of distribution, for Cushenberry, since it does deliver a part of its cement in its own gondola trucks. The grouping adopted brings out the number of employees in areas in which the differences in the technical structure or distribution method would seem to require differences in the number of workers even if the two plants were located in the same country. There was no particular difficulty in assigning the Cushenberry force to the Gresik categories, since the force report is very complete as to the type of work and location within the plant. The employees at each plant were divided into two groups: daily or hourly workers, and monthly employees. The force report for Cushenberry employs four categories: union, non-union, exempt, and non-exempt. In table 6–5, employees designated as union and non-union were treated as daily or hourly workers, and the exempt and non-exempt as monthly employees. The distinction between exempt and non-exempt is based on the wages and hours legislation which sets a minimum salary for the purpose of exempting supervisory personnel from the overtime payment provisions of the law. Exact counterparts of compensation obviously will not exist in two different economies, and the distinction between daily and hourly workers on the one hand and monthly employees on the other hand cannot be interpreted precisely.

Table 6–5 shows the total force (management and workers of all groups) at Gresik and Cushenberry. The preceding discussion brought out the fact that the total force at Gresik received wages, salaries, and related fringe benefits (excluding items such as housing and transportation in general administration) which aggregated about Rp. 68 per ton of cement produced in 1959, whereas the Cushenberry cost of wages and salaries and employee benefits aggregated about Rp. 157 per ton. Since productivity (tons of finished cement) of the 217 employees at Cushenberry was nearly 150 per cent of the productivity of the 996 at Gresik, we would expect the cost per ton at Cushenberry to be lower if the total employee cost in rupiahs were equal at the two plants. A general picture of the level of compensation in total, per metric ton, and per employee is provided by the following:

	Gresik	Cushenberry	Gresik as a percentage of Cushenberry
Total wages and salaries:			
Charged to factory costs (p. 135)	Rp. 10,078,280		
Charged to general administration (p. 135)	7,409,687		
Costs paid in kind (p. 135)	1,760,071		
Total	Rp. 19,248,038		
Total wages and salaries and employee benefits (p. 137)		$ 1,618,940	
Convert to rupiahs at 41 to 1		Rp. 66,376,540	
Total compensation	Rp. 19,248,038	Rp. 66,376,540	29
Number of employees ...	996	217	459
Annual compensation per employee	Rp. 19,325	Rp. 305,882	6
Annual compensation per employee	$ 471	$ 7,460	6

The foregoing estimate of average annual compensation does not reflect accurately the differences in employee income. First, it does not include the value to the employee of such services as housing and transportation; second, it does not reflect differences in purchasing power unless we can say that the official rate of exchange was a close approximation to the so-called purchasing power parity of the two currencies. The rate of exchange did not reflect relative purchasing power. A rough estimate by the writer is that the purchasing power in real terms was about half that indicated by the official rate of exchange, for the Indonesian employee. Since less than one-third of the Gresik force had company housing in 1959, we do not get a good *per employee* estimate when we attribute all the general administration, exclusive of wages and salaries, to employment costs. For those receiving housing and related community services, the effect was to provide a real income substantially in excess of the averages shown.

At Gresik the monthly employees have what amounts to civil service status, and daily workers have a degree of job security which is probably somewhat greater in the legal sense than union workers have at Cushenberry. In the writer's view, all classes of employees at each plant have unusually high job security because of the year-round near-capacity operation.

The monthly employees at Gresik are classified in three groups for compensation and status—groups corresponding closely to those of the regular government civil service. Classification is based almost entirely on education. Although there are in-grade gradations in salary according to experience, it is difficult for an employee to advance to a higher status if he does not have the appropriate education. At the end of 1959 the daily and monthly compensation rates and related family benefits were as follows at Gresik:

Type of compensation	Daily workers	Classified monthly employees		
		Lower group	Middle group	Upper group
		Compensation in rupiahs		
Base pay before overtime, annual bonus, food allowances, etc.:				
Rupiahs per day for 6-day week of 40 hours:				
Minimum	8.00			
Maximum	30.60			
Estimated average	15.00			
Rupiahs per month:				
Minimum		280	894	1,474
Maximum		1,675	2,755	2,650
Overtime limit in any one pay period as a percentage of base pay	150%	150%	150%	

		Classified monthly employees		
Type of compensation	Daily workers	Lower group	Middle group	Upper group
		Compensation in rupiahs		
Family allowances, per month:				
Wife		70	100	150
Each child, limit of 5:				
Pre-school		40	40	40
Elementary school		60	60	60
High school (age limit 21 years)		80	80	80
University (age limit 25 years)		120	120	120
Approximate education requirement		Elementary through junior high	High school	Technical high school through university

The compensation range at Cushenberry at the end of 1959 was as follows:

	Lowest	Highest
	Compensation in dollars	
Hourly employees, rate per hour for 40-hour work week	$ 2.04	$ 3.14
Monthly employees, salary per month	$343.00	$1,000.00
	Compensation in rupiahs at 41 to 1	
Hourly employees, rate per hour	Rp. 83.64	Rp. 128.78
Hourly employees, rate per day of 7 hours, roughly comparable to Gresik workday	Rp. 585.48	Rp. 901.18
Monthly employees, per month	Rp. 14,063.00	Rp. 41,000.00

The hourly worker in the Cushenberry plant is paid at a rate much higher in relation to the daily worker at Gresik than is the top supervisor. The margin for the upper ranges of management is reduced substantially when housing, transportation, and recreation facilities are added to the cash income of the Gresik employee. The tabulation indicates why the Cushenberry management has an incentive to minimize the size of the work force, and why a similar pressure does not apply to the Gresik management.

Factors Influencing the Size of the Work Force at Gresik

The comparison of the number of employees provided by table 6–5 raises many questions concerning employment in a developing economy. Does a developing economy require more people to man a particular mechanical production operation than does a plant in an industrialized economy? It might be argued that the Gresik plant, being of United States design and construction, should inherently be about as labor-saving in terms of technical operation as the Cushenberry plant. Assuming that the smaller capacity at Gresik probably would not significantly reduce the number of workers required for the actual production stations, we might ask: Does not the machinery itself determine the manpower in such a way that differences in the work force indicate deliberate overemployment? In Group 8 of table 6–5, cement production, the total number of employees at Gresik was 148, whereas Cushenberry had 74, a ratio of about 2 to 1. This suggests that *where technical conditions were most nearly comparable Gresik had the smallest work force relative to Cushenberry.* The ratio was much higher for maintenance and utilities, but here the technical conditions were not as similar as in the cement-production departments, mainly because utilities were produced at Gresik and purchased at Cushenberry. We would expect larger maintenance crews at Gresik for two reasons: lack of training and experience, and because more equipment must be maintained and many items made that can be purchased outside by Cushenberry. The fact that the original investment at Gresik was more than twice that at Cushenberry would suggest a ratio of 2 to 1. The fact that it is about 4 to 1 means that the work force for maintenance and utilities actually bears about the same 2 to 1 ratio that we find for the cement-producing departments. The larger force for packing and loading reflects the differing economic conditions of the two countries:–individual sacks and related handling in Indonesia, and bulk loading and hauling in the United States. The workers at Cushenberry in the "distribution" classification performed a function that in Indonesia is performed by the State Distributing Corporation, USINDO. No bags are manufactured at Cushenberry.

The areas in which the work force is largest at Gresik relative to Cushenberry are in clerical and personal services. The financial and accounting section has a ratio of 4 to 1. This reflects in part differences in mechanization, and in part more paper work at Gresik than at Cushenberry. Housing and public works at Gresik have no counterparts at Cushenberry, and reflect the differences in the structure of the two economies. The very large force in central administration, the commercial section, personnel, and community relations is both cause and effect of the larger force in the rest of the plant at Gresik. The Gresik plant is one of Indonesia's major enterprises, and two important pressures exist because of this: to provide employment and to provide a model of social welfare for the employees. Since labor cost is so low per person for practically all classes, the pressure to economize on labor that one finds in a plant in the United States is replaced by internal and external pressures to add workers. The internal pressures are many, of which personal prestige of the managerial staff is important. But the dominant pressure is unemployment and misery. Java is one of the most densely populated areas in the world, and the rate of increase is very high. If we consider that in 1959 the plant transfer price of a single sack of cement, Rp. 55, was about eight times the minimum cash daily wage, we realize the relative poverty of even the employed cement worker, and why many guards are necessary at the plant and on the vehicles transporting cement. In an underdeveloped economy with great unemployment, industrialization is virtually the only solution to unemployment. In seeking public support for the sacrifices necessary to industrialize, the government would provide visible evidence that an industrial plant does in fact mean substantial employment.

CAPITAL COSTS AS A DETERMINANT OF TOTAL COST
PER METRIC TON OF CEMENT PRODUCED

Having developed rather detailed comparisons of cost by elements of cost, we must now return to the data shown in table 6–1 for final consideration of the unit costs of depreciation and interest. As we have noted, Gresik had lower so-called cash costs per ton of finished cement produced in the departments through finish grinding than did Cushenberry in 1959, but this cash-cost advantage was more than offset by the disadvantage of higher costs for depreciation and interest. In the first six months of 1960, inflation erased even the cash-cost advantage for Gresik.

We must now consider the general effect of the arbitrary valuation of fixed assets to reflect inflation and the related depreciation and interest charges. A plant with higher initial investment per ton of capacity will show higher total unit costs than one with lower investment per ton of capacity in the first few years of operation if the time period for computing depreciation and interest is short enough. An obvious way of looking at this is to assume that both plants are fully written off in the first year. In this year the plant with the highest investment cost per ton of capacity will show extraordinarily high costs for depreciation and interest. But in subsequent years it will show lower total costs than the *less capital-intensive* plant if the initial higher investment accounted for the lower costs per ton of cash variable and cash fixed costs of regular operation.

In evaluating the costs of Gresik and Cushenberry, therefore, we must look at the probable physical life of the plants and not just at the book-life selected for computing depreciation and interest. In effect we must ask: What physical life will equalize the costs of the two plants, other things being equal? This reduces to the simple mathematical problem of determining the physical life necessary to equalize total unit cost. In terms of Gresik versus Cushenberry, we may pose the question somewhat as follows: Is it possible that the Gresik plant will last long enough to give a total unit cost per metric ton that is equal to or below that attainable with the Cushenberry plant?

Although it is impossible to provide a definitive answer to

the sort of question just posed, we can develop a useful approximation. The difficulty, of course, lies in projecting the future behavior of cash costs per ton. If we use 1960 as the base, Gresik will always have money costs above those for Cushenberry, and this independent of the rate of exchange used. The situation in 1959, and also in 1957 and in 1958, did provide the possibility that total costs at Gresik, over the actual physical life of the two plants, be equal to or below those at Cushenberry. For the purpose of demonstrating the issues, let us assume the following:

1. Price stability in each country after 1959, at the 1959 level.
2. No further changes in the official rate of exchange.
3. Cash costs per ton at the same level for each plant as in 1959.
4. Annual output at rated capacity of 250,000 tons for Gresik and 425,000 tons for Cushenberry.

To see the arithmetic involved in the problem, we may compare the cash cost per ton (table 6–1) for each plant in 1959, as follows:

	Rupiahs per metric ton
For the Gresik plant in Indonesia	307
For the Cushenberry plant in the United States	361
Advantage for Gresik	54

The next problem is the valuation to be used for computing depreciation and interest. In Appendix table A-2 the fixed assets at Gresik changed from Rp. 347,864,380 on the basis of original cost to Rp. 967,739,717 at the end of 1959. For Cushenberry the increase in replacement cost was estimated to be 5 per cent per year starting in 1957. The replacement cost at the end of 1959 was assumed to be 115.76 per cent of the original cost of $14,539,715, or $17,673,024. If we convert dollars at the end of 1959 to rupiahs at the rate of 45 to 1 we would obtain a value of Rp. 795,286,080. This is a rather questionable basis for our analysis, for the valuation method employed, as explained earlier, changed the original money ratio of investment from roughly 2 to 1 to 1.22 to 1. If we use the original approximate relationship of 2 to 1, the revalued rupiah investment at Cushenberry at the end of 1959 would be half that of Gresik, or Rp. 483,869,858. Using this value in relation to Rp. 967,739,717 for Gresik, we may develop annual depreciation charges for each plant on the straight-line basis for a series of years of possible life. We shall use 15, 20, 25, and 30 years. The results are as follows:

	Gresik	Cushenberry
Value of depreciable assets	Rp. 967,739,717	Rp. 483,869,858
Annual depreciation:		
15 years	64,515,981	32,257,990
20 years	48,386,986	24,193,493
25 years	38,709,569	19,354,784
30 years	32,257,990	16,128,995
Annual production in metric tons	250,000	425,000
Annual depreciation per ton:		
15 years	258.06	75.90
20 years	193.55	56.93
25 years	154.84	45.54
30 years	129.03	37.95
Difference in depreciation per metric ton:		
15 years	182.16	
20 years	136.62	
25 years	109.30	
30 years	91.08	

On the the basis of the 1959 cash cost difference of Rp. 54 per metric ton, even a physical life of 30 years will not give Gresik a combined cost for cash and depreciation that would be lower than that for Cushenberry. If this is so, no rate of interest above zero would change the situation, assuming that the same rate is applied to each plant investment. This conclusion would not be changed if we assumed a different rate of exchange, for any other rate would, in effect, apply the same multiplier to the cash margin of Rp. 54 that would be applied to the depreciation differential.

Although we have found the actual costs per ton of finished cement to be generally adverse to Gresik, this should be interpreted chiefly as reflecting the basic underlying differences in the economies of the two countries, and not as a criticism of either the decision to build Gresik or as a criticism of its operating management. Having compared the costs of the two plants, we now turn to the achievements and problems of Gresik in its own economic environment. What has been its cash contribution in relation to the cash requirements? What has been its contribution to the foreign exchange situation? What has it contributed, in a broad sense, to the economic and social development of Indonesia? These and related questions will be the concern of Chapter 7.

PART III

---

*Achievements and Problems
of the Gresik Plant*

VII

Contributions of the Gresik Cement Plant to the Economy of Indonesia

It is necessary to preface this analysis with a brief review of the internal political and economic conditions in Indonesia during the years covered by the study, from the middle of 1957 through the first half of 1960. This was a period of internal warfare in which economic warfare may be regarded as more important than the relatively short and sporadic military engagements. The extreme inflation of the period was not associated with a policy of industrial development, but was chiefly the product of a very high level of expenditures for internal security. During the early part of the period the Permesta rebel group in West Sumatra and in Northern Sulawesi made substantial inroads on the supply of foreign exchange by diverting exports of rubber and copra to their own account. The shortage of sea transport resulting in part from the difficulties with the Netherlands contributed to the shortage of foreign exchange and to the domestic inflation. Inflation was thus a political and military development more than a deliberate economic policy associated with an economic development program. Under such circumstances the problems of national unity and national survival quite properly were given precedence over those of adjusting domestic prices. Few countries engaged in a major struggle for survival have succeeded in avoiding inflation or in attempting to mitigate the burden on the population by attempts at price control.

In view of the conditions in Indonesia during the years 1957–1960, it would be improper to associate moral value judgments with the domestic inflation. In dealing with inflation, therefore, the writer was concerned with an economic fact of life that cannot be ignored in using the money price system of modern life. For the individual enterprise keeping its accounts in money units, inflation is much the same problem, regardless of the factors which lead to the money supply changes associated with inflation. The Gresik plant is not a war plant, and when it was planned and built the officials almost certainly did not expect that the country would be plunged into civil discord as soon as the plant began operations. In attempting to evaluate the contributions of the Gresik plant, therefore, we must keep in mind that it had to operate under rather special conditions. The plant is regarded as an instrument of peace and economic development, and our concern should be with these aims and not with those of domestic civil strife.

Of the many possible areas of analysis, we shall limit ourselves in this chapter to four: (1) contributions to the foreign exchange position of the Government of Indonesia; (2) the money earnings or losses of the plant; (3) the funds generated by the operations in relation to those required; and (4) the social and psychological contributions to the economy. It is possible to develop useful objective measures of the first three, but for the fourth item the writer must venture personal opinions.

CONTRIBUTIONS TO THE FOREIGN EXCHANGE POSITION OF THE GOVERNMENT

A soverign state may develop or preserve certain plants or enterprises which are unable to survive under the usual conditions of free competition and freely convertible foreign exchange. Examples of this are the infant industry and the national defense enterprises. A newly independent nation may want to develop certain manufacturing industries in order to gain experience with such operations. Such plants or enterprises may actually involve higher real costs to the country than if the equivalent product or service were imported. As the writer understands the situation, Gresik in particular and new industrial plants in general do not come under the infant industry program in Indonesia. Basic to industrialization in Indonesia is unemployment. Related to this is the possibility that many if not all purely domestic materials and supplies required for a plant such as Gresik would not be produced or utilized in the economy if the plant did not operate. This amounts to saying that the real costs represented by managerial and operating personnel and by domestic materials and supplies can be regarded as zero. Thus the significant real cost for Gresik is not its total cost but that portion represented by foreign exchange expenditures. The justification for Gresik, and for most manufacturing plants planned for Indonesia, is a *saving in foreign exchange.* Plants built to serve the domestic market in Indonesia are not intended to *earn* foreign exchange, but rather to *conserve* the available supply in such a way as to permit a higher level of domestic production and employment. In terms of this program, the amount of foreign exchange required to keep Gresik operating should be less than the landed cost in terms of foreign exchange of an equivalent tonnage of cement. This must be regarded as a minimum requirement, for it ignores both the real costs of purely domestic resources invested in the plant and the real costs of purely domestic resources employed in operating the plant after it is built. These, of course, are important costs, but they should be considered in evaluating the earnings of the plant, not in evaluating the foreign exchange effects.

If the Gresik plant keeps its accounts entirely in rupiahs and does not go through the accounting and financial formalities of buying foreign exchange for payments of principal and interest, the concern of its operating management will be with the foreign exchange required for current operations. An important aspect of this is that, once the cement plant is built, it may appear to the foreign exchange officials as a *drain on foreign exchange.* If foreign exchange is scarce (and it almost always is) the officials charged with rationing foreign exchange may provide either too little to keep the plant operating at capacity, or too little for adequate maintenance. If, for any reason, foreign exchange available to the plant management is inadequate, the contribution of the plant to the net foreign exchange position will diminish if imports of cement increase to offset the reduction in domestic production. The value in foreign currency of the *lost production* does not appear as *income* in the eyes of the group rationing foreign exchange, whereas the extra foreign exchange required for full capacity operation does appear as a current expenditure. In evaluating the contribution of Gresik, we should ideally attempt to estimate two things: (1) what it actually did "save" with its actual production, and (2) what it was prevented from "saving" as a result of lack of foreign exchange. The first item can be estimated with sufficient accuracy to permit useful conclusions, but the second could not be determined with the information available. It would be improper to argue that the difference between maximum possible output and actual output was entirely attributable to a lack of foreign exchange. It may be, and often was, attributable to a shortage of transport so that the plant must cut back when its storage silos are full.

Contributions attributable to actual production.—The Gresik accounting procedures in the period covered by this study did not provide supplementary records for the particular expenses requiring foreign exchange. As a result of this lack of data, it was impossible to obtain complete data on costs involving foreign exchange, and it has been difficult for the plant management to document its case with the foreign exchange control officials for adequate foreign exchange for capacity operations. It is possible, however, to obtain approximate figures sufficient to indicate the achievement of the plant and to show the nature of the problem. The estimating procedure adopted is to treat all the expenditures for certain elements of cost as involving foreign exchange. To the extent that some items represent local materials, the procedure will overstate the foreign exchange required.

To be on the conservative side with respect to the gross saving in foreign exchange, it was decided to deduct from the tonnage produced that amount used by the Gresik plant itself. The cost in foreign exchange to produce this quantity is included in foreign exchange requirements, whereas the tonnage is regarded as contributing nothing to the gross saving. To simplify the computations, we shall treat gross production in a given time period less tonnage for plant use as the equivalent of cement imported in the time period. By so doing we can apply against this *saving* the cost of imported items charged to production in the period concerned.

The first problem in developing data for gross saving is to arrive at the landed cost per ton of cement in terms of foreign exchange. Import statistics for Indonesia show gross weight in kilograms and landed cost in rupiahs at the official rate of exchange. By dividing the value by the weight we obtain an approximate figure that can be expressed in rupiahs per ton. We shall confine our data to the years 1956–1959 when the official rate of exchange used in the import value statistics was 11.475 rupiahs to the U. S. dollar. The data are as follows:

Year	Gross weight, metric tons	CIF value	Approximate value per ton	
1956	396,087	Rp. 129,264,000	Rp. 330	$29
1957	312,707	109,067,000	350	30
1958	112,417	37,351,000	332	29
1959	303,853	83,309,000	275	24

The decline in landed cost per ton in 1958 and 1959 possibly was the result of the volume contributed by the Gresik plant. For the purpose of this analysis we shall use the average landed cost for each year, although it might well be argued that the value of $30 per ton should be used for all years. To the extent that we compute losses attributable to a lack of foreign exchange, the prevailing price for the year should, of course, be used.

Having obtained a value per ton in foreign exchange, we may compute the net tonnage of Gresik available for sale, as follows:

Year	Total production	Tons for plant use	Net production	Value in U.S. Dollars	
				Per ton	Total
1957	109,445	388	109,057	$ 30	$ 3,271,710
1958	215,065	2,056	213,009	29	6,177,261
1959	282,804	2,666	280,138	24	6,723,312

In estimating the foreign exchange required for Gresik we shall use two amounts, actual expenditures and imputed costs. The imputed costs are those of gypsum and oil. Although most of the gypsum used in the years 1957–1959 was from domestic sources, the quality was variable and the rupiah cost went up each year. The plant management had to import gypsum in 1960, and it is likely that this will be true in the future. We shall assume that all gypsum used in the years 1957–1959 was from local sources, but in developing a net marginal contribution in foreign exchange for the future we shall assume that gypsum must be imported. Treating the cost of fuel at Gresik as an imputed cost in foreign exchange seems reasonable because it is a domestic product that will produce foreign exchange if exported. The dollar cost obtained by converting the rupiah cost at the official rate of exchange is probably an understatement of the value because of the low domestic price set by the government.

We may divide the foreign exchange requirements for Gresik into two categories: fixed and variable. We shall consider as fixed outlays those required for the payment of interest and principal on the Export-Import Bank loan, and those required for the maintenance of machinery and equipment. The payments of interest and principal are not fixed in the sense of being the same amount each year, but in the sense that they are not a function of the tonnage produced. Interest on the loan is at the rate of 5¾ per cent per year, and the loan is to be repaid over a period of 25 years. Assuming that 1/50th of a principal of $14,000,000 is paid each six months, and that interest is paid on the outstanding balance, the requirements for 1957–1959 are computed as follows:

	Required in U. S. dollars		
	1957	1958	1959
Interest payment at June 30		$ 394,450	$ 378,350
Principal payment at June 30		280,000	280,000
Interest payment at December 31	$402,500	386,400	370,300
Principal payment at December 31	280,000	280,000	280,000
Total	$682,500	$1,340,850	$1,308,650

The progressive devaluation of the rupiah from May, 1957, until April, 1958, under the exchange auction system makes it difficult to convert rupiah costs of these years to dollars. To simplify the problem of estimating, we use the rupiah costs of 1959, convert them to dollars at the average rate of 41 to 1, and allow for import duties and a special added tax called TPI (Tambahan Pembajaran Impor, an additional import payment usually assessed as a percentage of landed cost plus regular import duty—not all items being subject to the extra tax). The rate of 41 to 1 may understate the dollar requirements if a part of the imported items were acquired when the rate was lower, but this will be offset by treating all expenditures for materials as requiring foreign exchange. The estimate for 1959 was computed as follows:

	Costs in 1959 in rupiahs	Total import and TPI duty, %	Rupiahs net of import duty	Dollars at 41 to 1
Variable costs				
Operating supplies				
Bag material	35,922,488	50%	17,961,244	$ 438,080
Other	9,859,711	40	5,915,826	144,288
Factory supplies	9,315,788	40	5,589,473	136,328
Fuel	17,209,937	—	17,209,937	419,461
Subtotal	72,307,924		46,676,480	$1,138,157
Approximate net production available for sale, tons				$ 280,000
Estimated cost per metric ton, U. S. dollars				$ 4.35
Fixed costs represented				
by repairs (supplies)	8,319,318	40%	4,991,590	$ 121,746
Add estimated increase to level involved in				
1960 request by Gresik management				$ 128,254
Total				$ 250,000

The foregoing estimate may be on the low side for the variable cost items, but using the figure of $250,000 for repairs would seem to provide adequately for proper maintenance. The estimate used is supported by the Cushenberry expenditure in the first six months of 1960 of approximately $100,000 for the cement plant alone, excluding motorized equipment. The Cushenberry figure of $200,000 for a full year would be increased by at least 15 per cent for ocean freight and insurance; hence a figure of $250,000 does not appear unreasonable. Using the figure of $4.35 per ton for the variable costs of the separate years 1957, 1958, and 1959, we may estimate the contribution to foreign exchange as follows:

	1957	1958	1959	Total
Net tonnage available for domestic sale	109,057	213,009	280,138	602,204
Estimated landed cost per ton	$ 30.00	$ 29.00	$ 24.00	
Gross value of production	$3,271,710	$6,177,261	$6,723,312	$16,172,283
Required for interest and principal, Export-Import Bank loan	682,500	1,340,850	1,308,650	3,332,000
Margin for current operations	$2,589,210	$4,836,411	$5,414,662	$12,840,283
Required for spare parts	125,000	250,000	250,000	625,000
Margin for variable operating costs	$2,464,210	$4,586,411	$5,164,662	$12,215,283
Variable operating supplies and fuel	474,398	926,589	1,218,600	2,619,587
Estimated net saving in foreign exchange	$1,989,812	$3,659,822	$3,946,062	$ 9,595,696

Based on the estimates above, it is clear that the Gresik plant fulfilled the expectations of the Indonesian government and of the Export-Import Bank that it would contribute favorably to the foreign exchange position of the Indonesian government. This conclusion would apply even if we had increased the estimate for oil, and if the plant had used imported gypsum. At the 1959 rate of production, gypsum from the United States would have required an expenditure in foreign exchange of approximately $225,000. Even the use of an estimate for oil of three times that employed would add only about $800,000 to the 1959 total outlay. Thus oil and gypsum together would amount to about $1,025,000, and would reduce the 1959 contribution to $2,921,062, or $3,000,-000 in round numbers. This means that the loan from the Export-Import Bank might have involved more stringent terms—a shorter time for repayment or a higher rate of interest or both—before it would have made the Gresik investment undesirable to Indonesia in terms of its effect on the foreign exchange position.

It must be emphasized, in regard to the contribution of Gresik to foreign exchange saving, that the marginal increment per metric ton is far higher than the average per ton. This arises from the fact that the payments for principal and interest and for spare parts are not a function of output, whereas the variable current operating costs involving foreign exchange are substantially constant per ton. The marginal contribution in 1959 was about $19.65 per ton. This should be reduced for imported gypsum by about $0.83. Increasing the cost for oil by a factor of 200 per cent of the 1959 cost would add another $3.00 per ton; hence a conservative figure for the marginal net contribution is about $16.00 per metric ton. This points up the importance of allocating enough foreign exchange to Gresik to permit capacity operations.

The allocation of foreign exchange is not just that of enough funds in total for a fiscal or calendar year, but of developing the related procedures necessary to get the material and parts in the hands of the producing plant before a reduction in output is necessary. The Indonesian government's system of pre-audit of purchase orders is likely to constitute a bottleneck in the efficient scheduling of orders and shipments, with the possibility that critical items will arrive too late to prevent either complete shutdown or a reduction in output. Production capacity not utilized can never be regained. Another likely difficulty of a detailed and time-consuming pre-audit of purchase orders by exchange control officials is that it inevitably forces the management of a plant to seek the maximum stock so as to minimize the possibility of shutdown. This in turn ties up an enormous amount of foreign exchange in inventories. Domestic inflation adds to the pressure to accumulate maximum stocks.

At the time of the field study (1960) the technical management staff at Gresik was engaged in a program which would have a significant bearing on the savings in foreign exchange. This program was concerned with methods of increasing the output of the plant above the so-called rated capacity of 250,000 tons per year. The capacity figure was based on using the kilns for approximately 86 per cent of the available hours during a year. In several months this performance level was exceeded, and the technical staff had established a new target of 90 per cent. This would mean an achievement comparable to the best practice in industrial countries. The management hopes that a steady increase in the rate of utilization will actually reduce maintenance costs for the kilns, particularly for rebricking. When output is increased by about 10 per cent above the so-called designed capacity, the unit costs will be reduced nearly 10 per cent because almost all the cash costs and non-cash costs are fixed in the short period of kiln shutdowns, with the exception of operating supplies represented by imported items. Raising output by 10 per cent will contribute an additional $20 per ton (ignoring oil costs that would not be increased by the improvements in output), or about $500,000 per year. This will represent a substantial achievement by the plant.[1]

EARNINGS OF THE GRESIK CEMENT PLANT

In the preceding section we saw that Gresik has justified its existence in terms of savings in foreign exchange. We must now ask whether the savings in foreign exchange have been accompanied by revenues in rupiahs sufficient to cover the full economic costs in rupiahs as developed in this study. Related to this is the question: Did the plant generate enough rupiahs through the sale of cement to provide all the funds required? These two questions are closely related but not necessarily identical. To answer these questions the writer found it necessary to develop a set of cost and financial statements somewhat different from those prepared by P. N. Pabrik Semen "Gresik" for its regular annual reports. These statements appear in tables 7–1 through 7–11 in Appendix 1.

In 1957 the operating group from the United States used a rather simple cost accounting procedure at Gresik, and on the basis of the 1957 experience the system was changed in 1958. The 1958

---

[1] The rated capacity of 250,000 tons per year really applies to the production of clinker rather than to finished cement. In finish grind at least 3 per cent by weight is added in the form of gypsum. A part of the large production of finished cement in 1959 came from the use of over 11,000 tons of clinker carried over from 1958. Nevertheless, the plant exceeded the rated clinker capacity of 250,000 tons by 11,000 tons in 1959. This increase was in part the result of operating slightly above the level of 86 per cent of available kiln hours, and in part because the output per kiln hour slightly exceeded that used in arriving at the rated capacity of 250,000 tons.

system, with few changes, was employed in 1959 and in 1960. Table 7–1 states the costs of 1957 on the same general basis as those for the other years. The general procedure was to include the general administration charges omitted from the cost accounts of Gresik, and to use the 15 per cent declining balance method of depreciation and the 7½ per cent interest computation—the depreciation and interest being based on the revaluation to reflect the *de facto* devaluation of the rupiah resulting from the auction exchange system at the end of 1957. The development of the estimated cash costs, depreciation, and interest was necessary to obtain the 1957 figures for table 6–1 of the preceding chapter.

Tables 7–2, 7–3, and 7–4 were prepared to show in detail the costs incurred at Gresik after the cement is placed in the storage silos. The cost flow sheets of Appendix A show the details of cost and inventory movement to the clinker storage inventory and to the inventory of finished cement in the storage silos. Tables 7–2 through 7–4 utilize the cost data of the separate departments of Appendix A to develop the details of cost and inventory movement of cement transferred to the State Distributing Corporation, USINDO, or used by Gresik itself for construction or sale to the surrounding community. For the latter, some is given away and some is sold at reduced prices. Since the costs of depreciation used in this study were usually higher than those used by Gresik, and since interest was treated as a cost, the unit costs are higher than those obtained by Gresik's own cost procedure. Differences in cost are handled by adjusting the cost of construction in progress or by adjusting the profit and loss account (table 7–5). The procedures used in table 7–2, 7–3, and 7–4 might be employed to advantage by Gresik, for they require a complete accounting for all quantities of cement. The statements employed in this study always associate quantities and total cost to obtain unit costs, and are prepared in such a way as to account for all material as it moves through the production process to final sale or use by the plant.

Table 7–5 is one of the most important tables for our analysis. It uses the same data that the Gresik Plant used in preparing its annual statements of profit and loss, with the following exceptions:

1. The cost of sales is based on the computations of this study,

and so has higher depreciation and includes the imputed interest on fixed assets.

2. The price adjustments at the end of the year shown by the corporation as income are treated as revaluation of inventories. In effect the revaluation is treated in the same way as the net revaluation of fixed assets. In the time available at Gresik it was not possible for the writer to satisfy himself as to the nature of the price adjustments; hence the conclusion that they represented chiefly or entirely adjustments resulting from changes in the rate of exchange may be in error. The writer strongly recommends that all state enterprises in Indonesia maintain two valuations for inventories representing imports, one in foreign currency and one in rupiahs. At the end of each year the inventory of imported items should be revalued upward in rupiahs if there was a devaluation of the rupiah. Unless this is done, current rupiah costs will be understated in terms of the foreign exchange required to replace the items consumed during the period.

Table 7–5 indicates that the Gresik plant suffered substantial operating losses in 1957 and in 1958, earned a small profit in 1959, and was again heading for a substantial loss in 1960. It must be emphasized, however, that these conclusions involve the use of hindsight: the use of the official rate of exchange at the end of the year to revalue the dollar component of plant investment, and the use of estimated actual domestic increases in construction costs to revalue the local rupiah cost component of plant investment. If we contend that depreciation and interest should be taken into account by a socialist enterprise in pricing its product, it is reasonable to conclude that this can be done only from month-to-month on the basis of the current price and exchange rate situation. In a dynamic situation in which prices are moving upward, *the average price or rate for the year would be below those prevailing at the end of the year.* But if table 7–5 overstates cost because of the use of year-end values of fixed assets, it also omits an important cost, that of interest to the State Development Bank on net working capital. (Presumably any funds borrowed from other banks, such as Bank Indonesia, involved actual interest payments included in the regular costs.) Let us now attempt to estimate the magnitude of these factors.

A useful estimate of the overstatement of cost for depreciation and interest on fixed assets may be obtained by assuming that the increases in rupiah costs proceeded at the same rate throughout the year, and that any *de jure* devaluation occurred on June 30 and that the *de facto* devaluation of the auction exchange system occurred equally by months during the year. The *de jure* devaluation of 1959 in fact took place at the end of August, and the *de facto* devaluation of the auction exchange system was steadily upward (as a percentage of the parity rate: hence the *de facto* rate fell for the rupiah relative to the dollar) in 1957 and for the first four months of 1958, after which it was frozen at 332 per cent of parity. Although the assumption of a constant rate of inflation from changes in the rate of exchange is not exactly in accordance with the facts, it is sufficiently close to warrant its use. In using this assumption, we shall deduct from depreciation and interest on fixed assets in the years 1958 and 1959 22½ per cent of half of the annual net revaluation of fixed assets. For the first five months of 1960 we shall deduct 5/12 of 22½ per cent. No adjustment will be made for 1957 because the exchange auction system was inaugurated in May and the change from July through December was not large enough to warrant the correction, particularly in view of the offsetting factor of parts and supplies probably acquired during the construction period at the 11.475 to 1 rate.

The adjustment for depreciation and interest on fixed assets is computed as follows:

Year	Half of net revaluation	Depreciation and interest at 22½ percent
1958	Rp. 61,958,844	Rp. 13,940,739
1959	69,770,632	15,698,391
1960 (5 months; estimated)	31,991,536	3,000,000 (estimated)

The foregoing data are for cost decreases, whereas interest on average net working capital represents a cost increase. We may compute interest on average net working capital for 1958, 1959, and 1960 by using the data of table 7–10. Thus the average for 1958 is half of the sum of the net working capital at the end of 1957 and that at the end of 1958. The computations are as follows:

Year	Average net working capital	Interest at 5 per cent
1957 (year end)	Rp. 73,943,050	Rp. 1,848,576 (6 months)
1958	105,356,055	5,267,803
1959	175,226,830	8,761,342
1960 (estimated)	240,000,000	5,000,000 (5 months)

The profit or (loss) figures of table 7–5 may be adjusted as follows:

	1957	1958	1959	1960
Profit/(loss)	Rp. (37,363,742)	Rp. (87,729,580)	Rp. 7,259,879	Rp. (13,044,799)
Interest on working capital	1,848,576	5,267,803	8,761,342	5,000,000
Profit/(loss) before adjustment for depreciation and interest	(39,212,318)	(92,997,383)	(1,501,463)	(18,044,799)
Adjust for depreciation and interest	. .	13,940,739	15,698,391	3,000,000
Adjusted profit (loss)	Rp. (39,212,318)	Rp. (79,056,644)	Rp. 14,196,928	Rp. (15,044,799)
Number of sacks sold	1,938,288	4,352,973	5,602,864	1,841,063
Price increase/ (decrease) per sack to recover full ecomomic cost	Rp. 20.00	Rp. 18.00	Rp. (2.00)	Rp. 8.18
Actual average price	27.62	33.26	55.45	57.14
Economic price ...	Rp. 48.00	Rp. 52.00	Rp. 53.45	Rp. 65.32

The foregoing analysis illustrates the primary problem of P. N. Pabrik Semen "Gresik," that of obtaining from the government officials the proper economic price for its product. Certainly in 1957 and 1958 the government was caught in the web of a political and fiscal policy that produced enormous inflationary pressures, yet it is understandable that it wanted to keep down the prices of consumer goods. By keeping the official price of domestic cement below the price required for imported cement, the government produced a black market in cement in Indonesia. The result was not so much cheaper cement (except to the government agencies using Gresik cement) but profits for the black marketeers—profits that possibly were not reported in full for tax purposes. The low prices in 1957 and 1958 diverted funds from P. N. Pabrik Semen "Gresik," and hence from the State Development Bank, and channeled funds to other government agencies by allowing them to buy Gresik cement below full economic cost. The low prices also may be said to have diverted to the black marketeers funds required by the Gresik corporation and the State Development Bank.

We may conclude that the price situation was corrected in 1959, but that it appeared to be out of balance again in the first half of 1960. It seemed to the writer that the correction in 1959 was chiefly the result of permitting Gresik to use approximately the same price that effectively applied to imported cement. An additional price of Rp. 10 per sack was added in 1960 as a so-called economic development tax. This tax went directly to the Department of Finance and from there to the State Development Bank. The foregoing computations suggest that the tax revenue should have gone to Gresik and then to the State Development Bank in payment of interest.

At the time the writer completed the field research at Gresik (early December, 1960) the last monthly cost report available was for the month of July. July was the first month in 1960 in which cash manufacturing costs did not increase by a significant percentage. In general it seemed likely that Gresik would not maintain the average level of costs for the first six months throughout the last half of 1960, but might maintain the July level.

Although the preceding chapter emphasized the steady increase in unit costs of cement produced, additional data on the nature and extent of the increases may be in order. Table 7–11 summarizes the unit cash costs from the cost statements prepared by the cost accounting department at Gresik. Attention is directed to the importance of the increase of more than 100 per cent in the price of diesel fuel and bunker fuel in January, 1960. Table 7–11 was prepared to bring out two separate features of the unit cost problem at Gresik. The first is the persistent upward movement over the first three years, shown by the data in the upper half of the table. The second is the effect on unit costs of cutbacks in production, particularly during the Moslem fasting month, when transportation facilities in Indonesia were inadequate to handle the volume produced at Gresik, and when storage facilities were insufficient to permit continued operation at full capacity.

The fact that revenue from sales did not cover the full economic cost as developed in this study presents some problems in interpreting the balance sheets of table 7–8A and 7–8B. The rupiah amounts for the total assets of table 7–8A are substantially greater for each year than those shown in the balance sheet of the Gresik plant. Tables 7–6 and 7–7 show in detail the changes made by the writer as a result of the procedure of revaluing fixed assets to estimated replacement cost at the date of the balance sheet. Readers familiar with the controversies over the adjustment of financial statements to reflect changes in the price level will note that the writer adjusted only the inventory accounts and the fixed asset and depreciation allowance accounts. The writer does not believe any useful purpose is served by adjusting all accounts except cash on the basis of an index of consumer purchasing power. This method involves gains and losses that are really a function of the financial structure, that is, the proportion of total assets represented by debt. In a socialist system this is irrelevant, for it does not make much practical difference whether the State Development Bank contributes funds in the form of loans or in the form of capital stock. What is important is that the internal pricing structure should not ignore the effects of inflation and in so doing divert funds from the investment sector (represented by the State Development Bank) to the current account of the government. This is done if illusory money profits are taxed at a high rate, as they are in Indonesia.

The liabilities and capital section of the Gresik plant (table 7–8B) contains two important items added in this study. The first is the amount of the net revaluation of fixed assets, and the second is the liability for imputed interest on fixed assets. The first must be recovered in *earned* depreciation if the real capital in money units is to be recovered in the selling price of cement and returned to the State Development Bank to pay off the funds advanced. The second must be earned by Gresik and paid to the State Development Bank if the Gresik plant is to earn the real interest involved in the employment of funds. In fact, this liability might well be increased for interest on net working capital. As we have seen in Chapter 3, there is substantial merit not only in allowing the imputed interest in computing taxable income for Gresik, but also in exempting such interest from corporation income tax for the State Development Bank.

FLOW OF FUNDS AT THE GRESIK PLANT

Since depreciation accounting is arbitrary in that it must employ estimates of time and rate and, when assets are revalued, estimates of current reproduction cost, we need an analytical technique by which to test conclusions that rest in part on the arbitrary bases of depreciation and interest on fixed assets. The analytical device most satisfactory for this purpose is usually called the statement of sources and uses of funds. There are several ways of presenting such a statement. Table 7–9 shows one of the most common forms, and table 7–10 supplements table 7–9 by analyzing the change in net working capital, which is usually defined as the difference between current assets and current liabilities.

The general idea of the sources of funds is that the funds represent equivalent cash. Funds are derived mainly from two sources: current operations, and either long-term loans or new capital provided by the shareholders. Funds are used to acquire fixed assets, to acquire long-term investments such as bonds or stocks, to pay debts, to pay dividends, and to increase net working capital. Under depressed conditions, funds may be made available to the enterprise by a reduction in net working capital. On occasion, funds will be provided by the sale of assets.

In table 7–9 we treat 1957 as the first year of operation and compress all the construction activities from the formation of P. N. Pabrik Semen "Gresik" through December 31, 1957, into the single period of the year 1957. It is conventional to show funds provided by operations as the first item on the statement, even though in a particular year it may be a relatively small percentage of the total funds made available to the enterprise. Here the object is to use the cash concept of operations. This means that we remove all arbitrary charges for depletion and depreciation and, for Gresik, the interest on fixed assets and the amount involved in the revaluation of inventories. The latter is called a wash transaction in accounting, in that the same amount appears as both a source of funds and a use of funds. The foregoing is accomplished simply by adding the total of the non-cash expenses for the period to the reported profit or loss. Since we ignore corporation income taxes in this study because of the book losses, we simply start with the profit or loss figures of table 7–5 and adjust for depreciation, interest, and inventory revaluation. Thus, no matter how high or how low the depreciation and interest and inventory revaluation might have been, the funds provided by operations will be relatively unaffected by such charges. The only effect is on the inventory values of work in process and finished goods, and this tends to cancel out in the change in net working capital. We conclude that funds generated by operations were as follows:

1957 . . . . .Rp.	40,498,805
1958	83,007,099
1959	180,276,036
Total . . . . .Rp.	303,781,940

This is to say, approximately, that if all sales had been for cash and all expenses except depreciation and interest had been paid in cash, the sales exceeded the cash expenses by a total of Rp. 303,-781,940 for the three years.

Examination of the uses of funds of table 7–9 discloses that the State Development Bank (at that time, Bank Industri Negara) received a net of Rp. 18,181,466 in the three-year period (Rp. 34,088,357—Rp. 15,906,891). Here in the socialist economy of Indonesia we encounter a question which has often been asked by the stockholders of private corporations in the United States in the past 20 years: How is it possible for an enterprise to generate so many money units and still have so few available for distribution to the owners? The answer in both countries is that virtually all the funds generated by operations have to go back into the business, either in the form of fixed assets or in the form of an increase in net working capital. With reference to Gresik, Rp. 6,092,733 in 1958 and Rp. 23,082,486 in 1959 were required for additional fixed assets. The largest use, however, was for working capital.

The increase in net working capital is analyzed in table 7–10. Since the tonnage increase was small in relation to the increase in net working capital, why was so much working capital required? The answer is to be found in the *inflation of the currency* in Indonesia in the period under review. More rupiahs were required each year than in the previous year for wages, inventories, and purchased materials, and to carry accounts receivable. As table 7–10 indicates, the State Distributing Corporation for the State Development Bank enterprises, USINDO, accounted for about 50 per cent of the total net working capital requirements of Gresik. Since there was no opportunity to expand the scope of the study to include the distributing operations of USINDO, it is not possible to explain why a distributing agency should have so large a balance with the manufacturing company. The amount represented by cement cars, of course, is a policy problem for the three agencies concerned: the State Development Bank, Gresik, and USINDO. In general, however, good accounting and financial practice would suggest the desirability of having the State Development Bank transfer the cement car investment from the books of Gresik to those of USINDO. By keeping the investment on the Gresik books it is likely that depreciation was not taken by either agency, since Gresik would not consider it as a cost of producing cement. At the end of 1959 the current account balance of USINDO, nearly Rp. 87,000,000, represented the shipments of nearly three and a half months. The writer understands that USINDO sells on a combination of cash with order and cash on delivery; hence it seems strange that it takes so long to pay its account with Gresik. Further analysis by the State Development Bank or the Department of Basic Industry and Mining would appear desirable.

Although table 7–9 shows that the State Development Bank received a net cash payment of only Rp. 18,000,000 from the Gresik plant, the Bank received indirectly the amount of Rp. 76,-184,900 shown as used for government bonds as a result of the monetary devaluation of August 24, 1959. It is the understanding of the writer that the State Development Bank will receive as investment capital in rupiahs the amount of the bank deposits taken by the government in the devaluation of August 24, 1959 (90 per cent of the balance in each depositor's account in excess of

Rp. 25,000). Thus, in a monetary sense, P. N. Pabrik Semen "Gresik" returned funds to the State Development Bank in the net total of approximately Rp. 94,000,000. How does this compare with its implied obligation under the depreciation and interest methods employed in this study? The sum of interest and depreciation for the three years 1957–1959 in table 7–9 is about Rp. 408,-000,000, of which Rp. 272,000,000 represents depreciation and Rp. 136,000,000 represents imputed interest.

The conclusion seems inescapable that inflationary forces in Indonesia adversely affected the financial position of Gresik and its parent, the State Development Bank. This conclusion is reinforced when we ask about the relationship between the maximum rupiah funds applied to the State Development Bank (Rp. 94,-000,000) and the rupiah funds the Bank would have required to buy dollars in the amounts shown on page 158 for the interest and principal on the Export-Import Bank loan. We may estimate the rupiah requirements as follows, overstating the case somewhat by using the year-end rates of exchange:

Year	Total dollars	Official rate of exchange at end of year	Rupiahs required
1957	$ 682,500	31 to 1	Rp. 21,157,500
1958	1,340,850	38 to 1	50,952,300
1959	1,308,650	45 to 1	58,889,250
Total required			Rp. 130,999,050
Made available by Gresik			94,000,000
Shortage			Rp. 36,999,050

The financial picture of Gresik, particularly its implied obligations to the State Development Bank, illustrates well the difficulties of inflation. It is true that the recognition of inflation in the balance sheets in tables 7–8A and 7–8B resulted in a large increase in the book value of fixed assets. But this is offset by a similar increase in the implied obligation to the State Development Bank. Why was the offsetting credit for the revaluation of assets not added to the capital account of Gresik? This would be the usual treatment for a private enterprise firm, but it hardly seems logical for a state corporation, particularly when the greater part of the revaluation represents the change in the official rate of exchange. The debt to the Export-Import Bank must be paid in dollars purchased with rupiahs at the official rate of exchange; hence it appears better to treat the entire revaluation as an adjustment of the loan account with the State Development Bank. This is especially true when the Bank is the sole owner of a small number of capital shares. By crediting the net revaluation to the loan section of the balance sheet there is also the psychological attraction of not using the results of inflation to erase the deficits from operations. An additional advantage of the procedure is that it keeps before the government officials concerned with financial policy the monetary measures of the real effects of inflation on the flow of funds within the relevant government agencies and between the investment sector and the current expenditure sector of the state.

SOCIAL AND PSYCHOLOGICAL CONTRIBUTIONS OF GRESIK TO THE INDONESIAN ECONOMY

Although the financial position of Gresik vis-à-vis its implied obligations to the State Development Bank has suffered from a combination of inflationary forces and government price policy which kept rupiah income substantially below rupiah outgo requirements, there are other and perhaps more important measures of the contributions of Gresik to the Indonesian economy. In the first section of this chapter it was shown that the savings in foreign exchange were indeed significant. The financial difficulties themselves have advanced the understanding of monetary factors on the part of the officials concerned.

In regard to the intangible contributions, apart from the practical lessons in fiscal policy, the writer can venture only personal opinions. The Gresik experience establishes the ability of Indonesia to qualify its men and women for the complex tasks of operating a modern continuous process manufacturing plant. The fact that cement is produced 24 hours a day every day in the year means continuous and not intermittent responsibility. The small group of technical and administrative personnel sent to the United

States for a period of one year for training and observation was able to take over full charge of the entire operation of the Gresik plant within a year and a half from the time it started operation in July, 1957. The output of the plant had increased steadily until in mid-1960 it was above the so-called designed capacity of 250,000 tons per year. What is perhaps more important, the plant has continued to maintain a very high quality of product, in every respect above the minimum specifications for standard Portland type cement. The cement is tested not only in the laboratory at Gresik, but at the Engineering College in Bandung, West Java, and was tested at the French government laboratory in Paris for use in the dam being constructed by French contractors in West Java, the Djati Luhur Project.

Gresik stands today as an eloquent testimonial to the proposition that coöperation between a developing nation and an advanced industrial Western nation can, in a short time, overcome the psychological handicaps of the inferior status of a people under colonialism. The pride of management and workers in their work and in their plant at Gresik is very great, and justifiably so. They have done a tremendous thing. The technical and administrative performance at Gresik was given tangible recognition by the two governments of Indonesia and the United States in the 50 per cent expansion program.

Gresik has added greatly to the social capital of the community in setting an example in housing, educational, and recreational facilities. The housing facilities are modest, but represent a substantial advance over those generally available to workers and their families in Indonesia. The value of this investment in human dignity is incalculable. That it is regarded as a good investment by the workers is evidenced by their pride in their homes, for the houses are well maintained and the competition in gardening is intense.

Gresik is a microcosm of what the new Indonesia is attempting to build. That it has had difficulties was expected, most of all by the Indonesian authorities. But that it would survive the difficulties of the first few years and go on expanding its facilities and improving its operation was also expected by the people of Indonesia. It has justified the hopes and aspirations of those who struggled to bring it into existence and to take it through its first three years.

In the years ahead Gresik will continue to have many problems. Not the least of these is to obtain the proper price for its product, and enough foreign exchange to operate the plant at full technical capacity and maintain it properly. In the long run, maintenance may be the most critical problem, for improper maintenance does not always affect output immediately. With so large a capital investment in the plant, the authorities both in Djakarta and at Gresik should make every effort to improve the maintenance of the plant. Great strides have already been taken in developing maintenance mechanics out of personnel who had little or no prior training or experience in such work. What is more important, the maintenance personnel must be drawn from an environment in which mechanical appliances are rare and comparatively simple. Given adequate maintenance, good operating and cost control, and proper pricing, the future of P. N. Pabrik Semen "Gresik" will continue to be a source of pride to Indonesia.

VIII

Financial Policy and Organization Theory in Relation to Operating and Financial Responsibilities of State Enterprises

Although the Gresik experience in the period 1957–1960 was affected by the rather severe inflation arising from the internal security situation, principally the rebellion in West Sumatra and Northern Sulawesi, the experience nevertheless has a more general application. This arises from the fact that the rebellion has ended and the leaders have returned to civilian life in Indonesia under very generous terms. Prior to the surrender of the last of the leaders, Indonesia in 1960 completed a bold and ambitious Eight-Year Development Plan in the context of its guided democracy and guided economy. The nation now faces the problems of reconstruction in the former rebel areas and those of an ambitious plan of industrial and agricultural development. The instrument for development will be socialism. This means not only that there will not be a significant role for private foreign capital, but that the state and not domestic private enterprise will be responsible for the major industrial projects. The government has indicated that it will seek foreign loans and grants for the foreign exchange

---

The views expressed in this chapter go beyond the scope of the original investigation. The material grew out of discussions with the executives of Gresik, the State Development Bank, and the Department of Basic Industry and Mining. The first draft of the chapter was prepared in the form of a memorandum to the President-Director of Gresik and one of the directors of the State Development Bank for use in connection with a conference of Bank officials and those of the enterprises it had financed and for whose management it was responsible.

component of its industrial projects. The general pattern of financing used for Gresik will be employed for most future industrial projects requiring substantial foreign exchange and, in the initial stage, training abroad for the managerial and technical staff and a short operating contract during which foreign personnel will operate the plant and the Indonesian personnel will gain experience and eventually assume full responsibility for management and operation.

The Gresik experience suggests that the limiting factor in the rate of industrial development in Indonesia will be local currency and not foreign exchange. This may be contrary to what many expect. The supply of rupiahs for development projects such as Gresik comes chiefly or entirely from inflation; the money is created first in the form of advances (demand deposits) to the government by Bank Indonesia, and when the government draws cash, new paper money is issued. The fact that the money can be created does not mean that there is an unlimited supply. The inflation of 1957–1960 was severe, and the experience demonstrated that price control is not very effective. Early in January, 1960, the new price regulations adopted by the government were rather close to the prices which would have been established in a free market. For some commodities, notably textiles, the official prices were too high to move the volume of goods that importers and domestic producers wanted to sell. The price inflation, particularly in 1959 and 1960, created a psychological climate in which further price increases will cause increasing political unrest. Not the least of the resistance would come from government officials who have seen their standard of living, already very low in 1957, steadily eroded by prices which advanced faster than their salaries.

Although industrialization is regarded as the ultimate solution to unemployment in Indonesia, there is little unutilized arable land or land yielding less than the maximum amount per hectare. There is much land that is not cultivated intensively, but it is in the Outer Islands of Sumatra, Kalimantan (Borneo) and Sulawesi, and requires a substantial investment in both time and capital to make it productive. The Eight-Year Development Plan includes several large projects for new rice land, and a urea plant in South Sumatra to produce nitrogen fertilizer. These projects will eventually help the food supply situation, but for the next few years a substantial amount of food will have to be imported.

Since Indonesia does not have significant idle resources for the production of the basic necessities of food, clothing, and shelter, a large industrial development program will not have the multiplier effect on real income that a similar program usually has in industrialized countries such as the United States. The initial effect of the construction of a plant such as Gresik is inflationary, for the construction workers compete for a rather limited supply of basic consumer goods. There is more employment, but not more consumer goods. This is not to say that industrial development should not be undertaken, but to point out that the *real* saving in the economy is the *forced* saving that results from inflation. Consumer resistance does not take the form of refusing to save because the rate of interest is too low, but rather takes the form of political unrest. Public opinion cannot be ignored in a guided democracy. This is particularly true when a substantial percentage of the articulate group in the country consists of civil service and military personnel. A policy which leads to a large civil and military force, as in Indonesia, creates important barriers to economic policies which affect adversely the individual members of the government service.

An ambitious development program that almost certainly implies inflation of the currency to provide a substantial part of the local currency requirements for construction work will be subject to serious difficulties if the internal management of funds does not keep in the investment or capital formation sector the funds required by the nature of the commitments. It will also encounter difficulties if the system of organization and delegation of authority and responsibility is not effective and the various agencies work at cross purposes. The comments which follow are based not only on the study of Gresik and Cushenberry, but on extensive field investigation of the problems and achievements of medium and large government manufacturing plants throughout Java and parts of Sumatra. As a result of these investigations the writer agrees with the view that socialism is the best avenue to industrial development in Indonesia for at least a decade ahead, for the primary consideration is not so much economic as social and psychological.

Foreign enterprises with foreign personnel in all or most of the top managerial and technical positions are incompatible with the aspirations of the Indonesian people. In a very real sense the Indonesian revolution will not be complete until Indonesians manage their own major enterprises. This is the basic consideration, and beside it all real and imaginary claims for greater efficiency and more rapid development are of minor importance. The claims of greater efficiency for private foreign enterprises are often hard to substantiate. When we take into account the combination of a high Western standard of living which requires large imports and the repatriation of savings by foreign personnel, the real gain to Indonesia from foreign management often disappears and is replaced by a loss. The rate of growth argument has real merit, but the real objective of Indonesia is not the maximum rate of growth but the maximum rate of growth consistent with Indonesian ownership and management.

Given the objectives of Indonesia, particularly in the new Eight-Year Development Plan, we may consider the application of some of the Gresik experiences to the possible areas of difficulty in implementing the plan.

ORGANIZATION ASPECTS OF THE EIGHT-YEAR DEVELOPMENT PLAN

It seems that the financing of the Eight-Year Plan will be the joint responsibility of the Department of Finance and Bank Pembangunan (State Development Bank). The Department of Finance is to handle the foreign exchange secured from foreign loans and grants, and the rupiah counterpart will be made available to Bank Pembangunan for direct investment in the state enterprises. Bank Pembangunan will be an investment capital institution only, and regular banking transactions of the state enterprises as operating units are to be conducted through the commercial banks. It appears now that each enterprise will be a separate state corporation. The precise form of managerial organization and policy control had not been made public when the writer was in Indonesia, but it seems likely that the individual corporations will not be treated as subsidiaries of Bank Pembangunan. The state cor-

porations developed under the predecessor of Bank Pembangunan, Bank Industri Negara, were established for the most part
as subsidiaries of the bank. For P. N. Pabrik Semen "Gresik," the
actual share capital was held entirely by Bank Industri Negara.
The nominal share capital is small, however, being only Rp. 2,-
000,000 out of total liabilities and capital of Rp. 514,000,000 at
the end of 1959.

Bank Industri Negara does not appear to have had a uniform
policy for handling the funds representing foreign loans or grants.
On some occasions such loans were treated as capital participation
by the Department of Finance in the particular enterprise; on
other occasions the funds were treated as participation in Bank
Industri Negara. For Gresik, the accounting statements indicate
that the participation of the Department of Finance was by way
of Bank Industri Negara. This was the basis for the accounting
treatment developed in the last section of Chapter 2.

In the coming Eight-Year Development program Bank Pembangunan should be used in the way in which Bank Industri
Negara was used for Gresik; that is, the rupiah counterpart of the
foreign loans should be transferred to Bank Pembangunan by
the Department of Finance, and the rupiahs then transferred to the
account of the operating corporation in one of the commercial
banks. Choosing the best relationship between share or equity
capital and loan capital for the state corporations presents difficulties of two sorts: those involving policy control for the operating
units, and these involving actual financial arrangements. If the
operating control of the state corporations is to rest in the departments (ministries) and not in Bank Pembangunan, as appears to be
the case, the financial obligations of the operating companies with
respect to Bank Pembangunan should be defined. Control by the
department concerned should be with respect to general policies
and not to personnel or production practices; these should be the
responsibility of the operating management. To make as clear as
possible the nature of the recommendations advanced, terminology drawn from practice in the United States will be used. This
practice applies to public corporations, regulated enterprises, and
private profit enterprises. It should be regarded as deriving from
the functions and policies common to any large organization, and

not to firms conducted for private profit. Perhaps an advantage of the terminology is that it may be free from traditional or habitual meanings associated in Indonesia with Dutch business organization.

The terms employed are Board of Directors, Board committees, officers of a corporation, executives of a corporation, and executive committees. The terms and their possible use in Indonesia are discussed below.

The Board of Directors is that group of individuals acting on behalf of the relevant government agencies in formulating over-all policies for the operating corporation. There would be substantial advantages in grouping all like operating units together and having the same Board of Directors serve all the units. The Board should have at least one and possibly two representatives from Bank Pembangunan, two from the Department responsible for the operation of the unit (for Gresik, the Department of Basic Industry and Mining). Consideration should be given to including a representative of the Department of Labor and one from the Department of Defense. In an ideal sense, perhaps the Board of Directors of all units of production in a given area might include representatives of all the government agencies having important interests in that area. This would require a large board as opposed to a small or inside board. If the principle of the large board is is adopted, a smaller group or Board Committee might be used.

The basic responsibilities of the Board of Directors should be in establishing production and financial targets and in determining that the operating unit has at its disposal the resources necessary to reach the target. Indonesia's ship of state is passing through turbulent waters at present, and this condition may be expected to prevail for a few years longer. It should be the primary responsibility of the Board of Directors to match goals and resources. In a developing economy there is often a tendency to give more attention to what is desirable than to what is possible. The Board of Directors of the cement-producing units, for example, should not plan for full capacity output without doing everything possible to secure and enforce the delivery of the foreign exchange, transportation equipment, and domestic raw materials required for capacity operation.

In his field surveys of the problems of Indonesian factories the writer found two major barriers to effective production by existing enterprises: lack of foreign exchange for materials and spare parts, and long delays in transporting incoming material and the finished products of the factory. In large measure the reason for failure to employ existing resources effectively is that operating executives are expected to deal with matters that in the nature of the system they cannot handle. The primary responsibility for policy commitments which match goals set should be that of the Board of Directors. This conception of responsibility would result in a more forthright approach to the major bottleneck of Indonesia, the supply and allocation of foreign exchange and the processing of necessary documents. Two agencies are concerned with foreign exchange, Lembaga Alat-Alat Pembajaran Luar Negeri (referred to as LAAPLN hereafter), which rations foreign exchange to individual units, and Biro Devisen Perdagangan, the foreign trade bureau that issues the actual import licenses for specific purchases (referred to as BDP hereafter). It is the writer's impression that the existing foreign exchange system gives LAAPLN in general and BDP in particular rather too much control over the details of purchasing of imported items.

A clear distinction should be made between (1) budgeting and allocating foreign exchange among the various major industry groups, and (2) responsibility for the effective use of the amounts budgeted or allocated. The former is properly entrusted to a single top government agency (LAAPLN). The latter, in the long-run interests of Indonesia, should be performed by the state corporate units. To relate this to the cement industry in general and to Gresik in particular, the Board of Directors of the Indonesian cement factories should be in charge of developing the foreign exchange budgets of the separate units and presenting them as a consolidated budget or program to LAAPLN, the rationing agency. LAAPLN should make a firm commitment to the Cement Board for a definite period of time in advance, at least every six months. Once the commitment is received, the Cement Board should establish production targets for the separate producing units in accordance with the foreign exchange it has available. It should be the responsibility of the officers of the producing units to use the amount of foreign exchange allocation in accordance with its production target. With this approach to foreign exchange, an agency such as the State Accounting Office (Djawatan Akuntan Negara) should develop post-audit procedures to make sure that the foreign exchange was used for the purposes authorized. It is the writer's impression that the existing system places great reliance on pre-audit procedures by BDP. In the nature of things, a single agency is not competent to make decisions about the need for or the propriety of the specific purchases of all producing units. The pre-audit system is likely to create a serious bottleneck for placing orders for imported material, and to divert executive talent and time to the mechanics of procurement. In the long run it may develop irresponsibility rather than responsible, competent, and honest purchasing of imported materials. The purchasing function should be entrusted to the operating management and not, in effect, to the exchange control authorities.

If the principle of the large board is used, it is suggested that the Board as a whole meet at regular intervals for consideration of an agenda placed before it by one or two small Board committees.

Board committees.—In most organizations, large bodies function better as *reviewing* bodies than in *originating* plans and data. The latter is done more efficiently by small committees. Board committees would consist of relatively small, say three to five-member, groups selected from the Board of Directors. They should consist of men who are most familiar with the actual operating problems and procedures of the producing units. In terms of organization theory and practice, it is desirable to have a small liaison group which serves to connect the operating management of an enterprise and the policy-making Board of Directors. Such a liaison group is usually composed of the top officers of the enterprise who would have ex-officio positions as members of the Board of Directors. For the state enterprises in Indonesia, it is suggested that at least three of the officers should be ex-officio members of the Board: the President-Director, the Factory Production Manager, and the chief financial officer (Controller). The Board committees should include at least one of the ex-officio members. There should be at least two Board committees, a General Policy Committee and a Finance Committee. The General Policy Committee should be charged with developing policy issues and supporting data for periodic consideration by the entire Board—such as production targets, expansion plans, employee compensation, and the like. It should then supervise the operations of the producing enterprises. The Finance Committee should prepare and present the financial budget of the enterprise, and carry out the detailed programming of financing, including expansion. It would be desirable, of course, to have the major department heads of the operating enterprises participate in preparing the initial draft of their budget, and to give copies of the budget to them, as well as monthly reports comparing costs and production with the budget.

Officers of the state corporations.—The officers, appointed by the Board of Directors, should conduct the day-to-day affairs of the corporation in accordance with the plans and budgets adopted by the Board of Directors. For most state enterprises there should be a President-Director, an Executive Vice-President, a Controller or chief financial officer (performing the duties usually assigned to Kepala Administrasi), a Vice-President for Production, a Vice-President for Personnel and Social Affairs, and a Vice-President for Distribution. The latter should work as a liaison executive with the distributing agency for the products of the company. Certainly Gresik should have a senior officer who would also be on the Board of Directors of USINDO to assist in coördinating distribution with production.

If it is possible to decentralize foreign exchange controls, particularly the work of BDP, it would seem desirable to have a man of officer rank to supervise procurement in the large manufacturing enterprises. The purchasing function might be included in the duties of the chief financial officer, or there might be a Vice-President for Purchasing.

Executives of the operating corporations.—Not all members of the management group have the rank of officer in Indonesia or in the United States. Officers are appointed by the Board of Directors, but is is likely to promote efficiency and harmony if the responsibility for nominating (and hence for developing men of officer caliber) candidates for the other officers is that of the President-Director. In addition to the officers, most enterprises require a number of other executives for the supervision of the affairs of the enterprise. In conventional Indonesian organization structure these are the Kepala Bagian (department or section heads) and their subordinate supervisors. Executives below the rank of Officer of the Corporation should be elected by the President-Director.

The internal and external pressures in Indonesia for employment of a large staff create problems for the executives, chiefly because of the length of the chain of command. Orders and reports often must pass through several subordinate executives before reaching the foremen and workers. Gresik apparently has experienced some difficulty with distortion of orders, particularly those given verbally, and with determining whether orders have been carried out and at what level an order was not executed properly.

Executive committees.—These are composed of officers or other executives of the enterprise. The use of such committees is standard practice in Indonesia. Certainly it would appear necessary to have an Executive Committee in each enterprise whose major responsibility would be to develop the preliminary production and financial budgets for presentation by the President-Director to the Board of Directors, and for coördinating the work of the separate departments or sections in accordance with the general plan as finally adopted by the Board of Directors. The Executive Committee as used in this section seems to correspond closely with the local directors of a plant such as Gresik. It is the writer's understanding, however, that the present practice is for the Board of Directors (usually in Djakarta) to select the directors of a local plant. The selection by the President-Director might eliminate some sources of friction, particularly when membership on the local directors' Board is assigned to a man regarded as junior to one or more of the top management group not appointed as directors.

FINANCIAL RELATIONS BETWEEN THE OPERATING CORPORATIONS AND BANK PEMBANGUNAN

If Bank Pembangunan is to function only as an investment bank, there may be merit in making it the exclusive source of permanent capital in the state enterprises. If this is so, what is the most suitable legal form for the investment, share capital or loan capital? The writer is inclined to believe that the greatest advantage lies in the use of loan capital for the initial fixed investment in the enterprise, and the use of share capital in a nominal amount for voting control by the department in charge of the particular type of production in which the plant is to engage. This is substantially the arrangement for Gresik, except that the 2,000,000 rupiahs of share capital would be in the hands of the Department of Basic Industry and Mining, not the State Development Bank. In this conception, fixed investment would be the funds represented by the cost of the plant and equipment and the necessary stock of raw material, inventory in process, spare parts, and finished material. If Bank Pembangunan is to act as a revolving fund for investment, it would be well to restrict its investment to plant and equipment and have the regular commercial banks finance all inventories and accounts receivable.

The writer's experience with the enterprises formerly financed by Bank Industri Negara is that the management prefers share capital because it does not want to incur a liability on the books for interest when the enterprise does not have earnings sufficient to pay the interest. As earlier chapters of this study have indicated, the writer favors a rate of return on fixed assets of at least 7½ per cent. This should be a *minimum* target for any enterprise financed by Bank Pembangunan. If the Eight-Year Development Plan is to promote capital formation, the capital invested through Bank Pembangunan should be invested in enterprises which can yield a substantial surplus of rupiah income over full rupiah costs.

For reasons set forth at length in Chapter 3, it is suggested that all state enterprises financed through the State Development Bank employ the declining balance method of depreciation, using a rate of 15 per cent. This rate should, for convenience and simplicity, be applied to all depreciable fixed assets, regardless of probable useful physical life. The rate is intentionally made higher than would be justified by the normal physical life of the assets, particularly as this is conceived by private enterprise standards.

The use of a high rate is, in the writer's view, quite necessary for financial soundness. Such a high rate is justified by two considerations. The first consideration is the nature of the machinery most likely to be placed in the new plants. Some of the machinery, as at Gresik, will be acquired from industrially advanced countries, and hence is likely to be of the type developed primarily for high labor cost conditions. The new machinery, compared with the pre-revolution Dutch machinery, will have more instrument controls and more delicate equipment to be maintained. The maintenance problems on such machinery in the existing and immediate future in Indonesia will be serious, and maintenance costs will probably mount at an increasing rate. Preliminary studies at Gresik indicate that this is a definite possibility. In regard to machinery and equipment acquired from Eastern Bloc countries, the experience to date indicates that the financing arrangements often do not include adequate stocks of spare parts. To a lesser extent this has been true of Western Bloc financing also. There is reason to believe that Indonesia will not in the immediate future be able to maintain the stock of spare parts required for good preventive maintenance according to the standards of the more advanced industrial countries. A major part of the development program of Indonesia is to train mechanics to maintain complex machinery and equipment. In the necessary learning process, mistakes will be made and the consequences may be a shorter life for the new and more complicated machinery. It would be an error to assume that the new equipment being purchased will have anything like the physical life of the machinery in the Indonesian sugar factories. The 15 per cent declining balance method may involve a book-life a little shorter than the actual experience, but this disadvantage seems unimportant in relation to the second consideration, the life of the foreign loans.

The decision to press for economic development through state socialism appears to the writer to be sound in terms of both theory and practical considerations. Experience in the next ten years, however, may show that the rate of capital formation possible under state socialism will be substantially below that regarded as desirable by the government and people of Indonesia. This, of course, is not the immediate problem. What is important is the source of funds relied on for new plants and for the expansion of old ones. The Eight-Year Development Plan proposes to rely on foreign loans and grants, not on direct private foreign investment. Although political and economic developments in the major power blocs may result in favorable loan conditions for Indonesia, the present prospects and most past actual credits have involved a relatively short repayment period. The Export-Import Bank loans have been for unusually long terms, but the interest rate is relatively high. Credits from Western and Eastern Europe have, on the whole, been for short periods, often 10 to 15 years. Since the government of Indonesia must either pay off its foreign loans in 10 to 15 years or incur high interest charges in the first 10 to 15 years because the long-term loans carry a high interest rate on the unpaid balance, there is a rather pressing need to program investment in areas in which the financial pay-out period is not longer than the commitment for loan pay-off. This is the second reason for suggesting the 15 per cent declining balance method of recording depreciation. The 15 per cent declining balance in effect employs an approximate book-life of 13 to 14 years. This seems close enough to the recent loan terms, especially from Western Europe, to make the 15 per cent declining balance method desirable.

If the state corporations financed by Bank Pembangunan are expected to record depreciation using the 15 per cent declining balance calculation, and to include in cost a rate of interest on assets employed of 7½ per cent per year, the use of these rates should be regarded as a firm policy decision implying commitments with respect to the use of funds by the operating corporations and by Bank Pembangunan. This is simply to say that investments should not be undertaken by Bank Pembangunan which do not promise earnings sufficient to cover cash variable operating costs plus the depreciation and interest. It is somewhat questionable practice for Indonesia to devote its scarce capital resources to projects which do not pay in the particular conditions of its own economy. The writer believes that there are enough investment opportunities open to state enterprises in Indonesia to employ all the *rupiah capital* realistically available to Bank Pembangunan at the rate of return required by the 15 per cent declining balance—7½ per cent interest targets. Investment opportunities should be carefully selected on the basis of their prospective economic yield.

FINANCIAL ARRANGEMENTS BETWEEN THE OPERATING
CORPORATIONS AND BANK PEMBANGUNAN

The Eight-Year Development Plan requires that Bank Pembangunan act as creditor of the state enterprises financed by it until at a minimum the financial commitments of the program are discharged. It is the writer's definite understanding that the state enterprises are to be a source of funds for economic development and not a drain on the economy of Indonesia. Assuming this to be the intention of the government, any arrangements for the management control of the producing units should minimize the possibilities, first, of uneconomic investment and, second, of methods of operation which ignore the implicit financial obligations of the enterprise to Bank Pembangunan. The latter would include uneconomic pricing of products and too rapid expansion of social services. The state enterprises best serve the economic and social objectives of economic development in Indonesia by seeking to maximize cash profits before depreciation and interest. This is what the private capitalist enterprise is supposed to do, and it should also be the objective of socialist production in Indonesia in the years ahead. This is not to urge a policy of exploiting the consumer, but one of intelligent promoting of the public interest. The writer supports the general theory of socialist economic development in Indonesia primarily because he sees no better way of forming capital and also realizing the legitimate and necessary objective of minimizing foreign influence and control. It is very desirable for Indonesia to develop slowly at first on its own. Admittedly, this is a social-psychological-political view and not one of seeking the maximum real economic product in the short run. The realities of present Indonesian life favor state socialism. If this is so, the problem is to approach economic development rationally within this framework. The basic economic reality is that capital formation requires saving in the real sense. The level and distribution of income in Indonesia does not permit a significant amount of individual saving by the Indonesian people, but it does permit social saving by means of the prices charged for consumer goods. A price policy which maximizes the margin of rupiah receipts over direct cash variable costs is simply a policy of securing a large social saving via state enterprises. The objective of this is to provide as much capital formation as possible. It would be unfortunate (and eventually disastrous) to dissipate the social saving by allotting too much to social services and too little to new productive capital. P. N. Pabrik Semen Gresik may have apportioned too much of its resources to social services and too little to productive capital formation in payments to Bank Pembangunan.

If the Government of Indonesia wants to promote the formation of real productive capital, the enterprises first selected for investment should provide a high margin of income over cost. Then this additional capital or seed should be used for the formation of more capital and not for immediate consumption.

Thus we return to the need for a relatively high rate of depreciation and the use of interest on capital employed. A high rate of book depreciation and an arbitrary charge for interest will not guarantee either good investment decisions or good financial policies. Depreciation and interest charges are only devices to help in making policy decisions. Intelligently used, the depreciation and interest charges have value in directing the employment of resources. The charges neither bring resources into existence nor do they guarantee that they will be used wisely once they are brought into existence.

What are the practical advantages of the relatively high 15 per cent declining balance method of depreciation and the treatment of interest as a cost? As in private enterprise countries, the important possibility is that they may serve first as a useful guide in selecting investments which can earn the charges involved. In socialist Indonesia this means that the economy or the people need and want the products to be produced to such an extent that the market price that can be obtained is sufficient to provide the necessary return. This is not ruthless and heartless exploitation, but intelligent channeling of resources.

Let us assume that Bank Pembangunan, with the assistance of the planning agencies, invests in enterprises which can provide the margin required. It should be emphasized that this appears to have been true for P. N. Pabrik Semen "Gresik." Having produced and sold the products (i.e., cement) at a price which produces a large cash margin, the use of the depreciation rate and the interest rate become a mechanism for dividing the funds generated by the enterprise between the Department of Finance in the form of the corporation income tax, the State Development Bank, and the state industrial enterprise itself. To use a simple illustration, assume that a state industrial corporation earns its depreciation and interest in the amount of Rp. 22,500,000 (for the present purpose, Rp. 15,000,000 in depreciation and Rp. 7,500,000 in interest) and in addition provides Rp. 10,000,000 in net profit after depreciation and interest. The use of the arbitrary charge for depreciation and interest would mean that Bank Pembangunan would secure Rp. 22,500,000 to be used in part to buy foreign exchange for payment of principal and interest on foreign loans, and in part for additional investment in new enterprises or the expansion of existing enterprises. Only after this return to capital would the Department of Finance be entitled to a share of the funds provided by the operations of the enterprise. Assuming this to be 50 per cent of net profits, the Department of Finance would receive 50 per cent of Rp. 10,000,000, or Rp. 5,000,000. The balance would be available to the enterprise for expansion or distribution to the shareholders, that is, the Department of Basic Industry and Mining in the case of Gresik.

THE FORM OF INVESTMENT BY BANK PEMBANGUNAN

To achieve the results set forth in the preceding discussion, it is suggested that the capital contributed by Bank Pembangunan be divided into two parts: that representing the original investment in fixed assets, and that representing the original investment in working capital. The first part should be regarded as a *loan* that will be repaid in rupiahs through *earned depreciation,* and on which interest will be paid at the rate of 7½ per cent per year. The investment in working capital presumably will be for the economic life of the enterprise. This also should earn interest for the State Development Bank at the rate of 7½ per cent, or perhaps at a lower rate equal to that charged by the commercial banks on working capital loans. To distinguish between the investment to be paid off through the use of funds provided by earned depreciation and the investment in working capital, it is suggested that the former be represented by bonds and the latter by share capital. The producing enterprises might issue two classes of share capital, A and B. Class A would be voting shares and be issued in a purely nominal amount to the department concerned with the operating policy, that is, the Department of Basic Industry and Mining in the case of Gresik. Class B shares would be issued to Bank Pembangunan for the original contribution for working capital. The bonds presumably would have a par value equal to the original rupiah investment in fixed assets. The liability would be paid off by distributing the funds provided by earned depreciation. The annual revaluation to reflect the net changes in replacement cost of the fixed assets would be regarded as an increase in the loan (assuming inflation) of the State Development Bank. Interest paid to the State Development Bank should be based on the declining balance for the bonds, and on the original rupiah investment in working capital for the Class B shares.

It is suggested that the Department of Finance agree to treat the interest received by the State Development Bank as nontaxable income. In effect this would exempt the Development Bank from the corporation income tax. The objective would be to keep funds earned and received by the Bank in the capital sector of the economy. For the operating enterprises, the definition of taxable income as that remaining after depreciation of 15 per cent on the declining balance, 7½ per cent interest on the declining balance of the fixed assets and 7½ per cent (or less) on the investment in working capital, would provide an incentive to the Department of Finance to assist Bank Pembangunan in selecting productive enterprises for capital investment. It might also assist the Department of Finance to establish more effective auditing control of the state enterprises—a development regarded as urgent by all parties concerned.

The Eight-Year Development Plan has substantial possibilities for advancing the economy of Indonesia, but it may require more funds than can be provided without an inflation rivaling or exceeding that of the years 1957–1960. Keeping investment funds in productive channels will be one of the major tasks under the Plan. It is hoped that this study may contribute to an understanding of the complex problems of socialist investment management, and to their solution.

Postscript

The foregoing was written in the spring of 1962, but the manuscript did not go to the press until the spring of 1964. In the intervening period the conditions of inflation have continued, if anything, with increasing force. It was thought that the settlement of the West Irian dispute and the return of the 1958 rebellion leaders would permit the Government of Indonesia to reduce its expenditures for military and security purposes and to give top priority to economic stabilization and development. Another *de facto* devaluation in the summer of 1963 changed the rate to approximately 312 rupiahs to the U. S. dollar. For a time it seemed that the minimum conditions for effective international assistance were in prospect. The position of Indonesia with respect to the formation of Malaysia postponed the possibility of effective international assistance in stabilizing and reviving the economy. The progressive decline in the total output of the economy during the period of this study (1957–1960) continues, and for a number of manufactured products is accelerating because of the shortage of repair parts.

Indonesia for at least eight years has allocated to military purposes an increasing share of its diminishing national product. The rate of change in each category may not be large, but the evidence suggests that there is a high degree of interdependence between the use of resources for military purposes and the change in the total product of the economy. The inflation which continues, apparently at an increasing rate, is not an intentional by-product of an ambitious program of domestic capital formation, but of the pursuit of political objectives believed to outrank those of economic development. It is to be expected that eventually the measures necessary to arrest economic disintegration will be taken, and that economic development will become possible. The longer the disintegration continues, the worse the morale of the people, and particularly of that group which wants to provide sound industrial planning and effective industrial leadership. Inflation of the magnitude experienced by Indonesia has a corrosive effect on physical capital, on people, and on the institutions by which men and women coöperate to live together in peace and harmony.

The deterioration of the economy of Indonesia does not seem to the writer to invalidate the recommendations contained in this study. If anything, the acceleration in the rate of inflation multiplies the problems of evaluation and decision with which the study is concerned. The administrative difficulties appear to have increased, and the proposals for change may have more merit now than when they were first presented to a small group in Indonesia in 1960. Continued decline in total output accompanied by continued increase in population will make it necessary to use external funds for rehabilitation as well as for new plant and equipment. International agencies and the governments of the Western industrial countries are increasingly concerned that economic assistance should be made available to the countries both able and willing to maintain certain minimum conditions of fiscal responsibility and internal administrative structure and organization. The minimum conditions vary from country to country and from time to time, but the objective is to advance economic development and not support regimes and programs clearly inconsistent with economic development. The achievements of Gresik demonstrate what can be accomplished under adversity. It is to be hoped that such people and such programs will eventually have a more favorable environment for their continued development.

APPENDIX 1

*Supplementary Tables for
Chapters 2, 3, 6, and 7*

TABLE 2-1

INVESTMENT IN THE GRESIK CEMENT PLANT IN INDONESIA
AND IN THE CUSHENBERRY PLANT IN THE UNITED STATES
(In U. S. dollars)

Category of plant facility	Total cost in dollars		Cost of facilities required in Indonesia but not in U.S.
	Gresik plant in Indonesia	Cushenberry plant in U.S.	
General administration, mainly housing and community development	$10,100,280	. . . . .	$10,100,280
Factory administration, comparable for both plants	1,564,872	$ 1,153,093	. . . . .
Machine shop and warehouse	552,198	237,526	. . . . .
Subtotal	12,217,350	1,390,619	10,100,280
Utilities and related facilities			
Ocean dock and oil storage facilities	1,590,261	. . . . .	1,590,261
Diesel power plant and electric lines	2,204,087	356,914	1,847,173
Water line and water treatment plant	1,265,003	501,129	. . . . .
Electrical equipment and installation	942,334	1,203,559	. . . . .
Subtotal	6,001,685	2,061,602	3,437,434
Cement production and storage facilities			
Clay department	765,745 ⎫		
Limestone quarry and crushing equipment	3,123,601 ⎬	2,636,393	
Silica sand facilities	98,753 ⎭		
Raw grinding department	1,105,621	1,561,899	
Kilns, cooling, and clinker storage	3,142,889	3,602,518	
Gypsum storage	12,644	. . . . .	
Finish grinding department	1,371,548	1,563,946	
Storage silos, packhouse, and loading facilities	2,046,992	1,436,264	
Subtotal	11,667,793	10,801,020	
Bag factory	520,714	. . . . .	520,714
Locomotive and railroad spur tracks	1,155,386	286,474	868,912
Subtotal	1,676,100	286,474	1,389,629
Total investment, all facilities	$31,562,928	$14,539,715	$14,927,340
Approximate annual capacity for producing cement, metric tons	275,000	425,000	
Investment required per ton of capacity	$114.00	$ 34.20	

TABLE 2-2

INVESTMENT BY TYPE OF CURRENCY IN THE GRESIK CEMENT PLANT IN INDONESIA
AND IN THE CUSHENBERRY PLANT IN THE UNITED STATES

Category of plant facility	Investment in Gresik cement plant in Indonesia				Investment in Cushenberry plant in U.S.	Amount by which investment in Gresik plant exceeded (or was below) investment in Cushenberry plant			
						Facilities required at both plants		Facilities required at Gresik only	
	Expenditure in dollars of foreign exchange	Local expenditure in rupiahs	Rupiahs converted to dollars at 11.475 to 1	Total		Foreign exchange only	Total investment	Foreign exchange only	Total investment
	(1)	(2)	(3) [2 ÷ 11.475]	(4) [1 + 3]	(5)	(6) [1 - 5]	(7) [4 - 5]	(8) [1 - 5]	(9) [4 - 5]
General administration, mainly housing and community development	$ 1,413,606	Rp. 99,679,582	$ 8,686,674	$10,100,280	....	....	....	$1,413,606	$10,100,280
Factory administration, comparable for both plants	436,211	12,951,381	1,128,661	1,564,872	$ 1,153,093	$ (716,882)	$ 411,779	....	....
Machine shop and warehouse	342,978	2,400,798	209,220	552,198	237,526	105,452	314,672	....	....
Subtotal	2,192,795	115,031,761	10,024,555	12,217,350	1,390,619	(611,430)	726,451	1,413,606	10,100,280
Utilities and related facilities									
Ocean dock and oil storage facilities	697,793	10,241,066	892,468	1,590,261	....	....	....	697,793	1,590,261
Diesel power plant and electric lines	1,902,518	3,460,509	301,569	2,204,087	356,914	(427,929)	....	545,604	1,847,173
Water line and water treatment plant	503,716	8,735,765	761,287	1,265,003	501,129	2,587	763,874	....	....
Electrical equipment and installation	619,317	3,706,624	323,017	942,334	1,203,559	(584,242)	(261,225)	....	....
Subtotal	3,723,344	26,143,964	2,278,341	6,001,685	2,061,602	(581,655)	502,649	2,243,397	3,437,434
Cement production and storage facilities									
Clay department	606,124	1,831,655	159,621	765,745	....	606,124	765,745	....	....
Limestone quarry and crushing equipment	2,208,464	10,501,191	915,137	3,123,601	2,636,393	(427,929)	487,208	....	....
Silica sand facilities	91,439	83,931	7,314	98,753	....	91,439	98,753	....	....
Raw grinding department	696,690	4,692,482	408,931	1,105,621	1,561,899	(865,209)	(456,278)	....	....
Kilns, cooling, and clinker storage	2,504,416	7,326,483	638,473	3,142,889	3,602,518	(1,098,102)	(459,629)	....	....
Gypsum storage	12,644	....	....	12,644	12,644	12,644	12,644	....	....
Finish grinding department	1,153,971	2,496,699	217,577	1,371,548	1,563,948	(408,975)	(192,398)	....	....
Storage silos, packhouse, and loading facilities	1,241,767	9,239,951	805,225	2,046,992	1,436,264	(194,497)	610,728	....	....
Subtotal	8,515,515	36,172,392	3,152,278	11,667,793	10,801,020	(2,285,505)	866,773	....	....
Bag factory	389,414	1,506,663	131,300	520,714	....	....	....	389,414	520,714
Switching locomotive and railroad spur tracks	178,932	11,204,811	976,454	1,155,386	286,474	....	....	(107,542)	868,912
Subtotal	568,346	12,711,474	1,107,754	1,676,100	286,474	....	....	281,872	1,389,626
Total investment, all facilities	$15,000,000	Rp.190,059,591	$16,562,928	$31,562,928	$14,539,715	$(3,478,590)	$2,095,873	$3,938,875	$14,927,340
Less investment in Cushenberry plant	14,539,715			14,539,715					
Excess of investment in Gresik plant	$ 460,285			$17,023,213					
Approximate annual capacity for producing finished cement, metric tons	275,000		275,000		425,000				
Investment required per ton of capacity	$ 54.00	Rp. 691	$ 60.00	$114.00	$ 34.20				

TABLE 3-1

P. N. PABRIK SEMEN "GRESIK":
COMPUTATION AND APPLICATION OF REVALUATION INDEXES,
MACHINE SHOP AND WAREHOUSE DEPARTMENT

Average % of value at beginning of year	Explanation	Computation of indexes			
		Portion of original cost in dollars	Convert dollars to rupiahs	Portion of original cost in rupiahs	Total cost in rupiahs
(1)		(2)	(3)	(4)	(5)
	Original costs incurred by Morrison-Knudsen International	342,978	3,935,675	2,400,798	6,336,473
	Year 1957				
	Convert $ portion at auction rate of 270% of rupiah equivalent		10,626,323		
	Convert local costs at 110% of original cost			2,640,818	
209.38%	Total rupiah cost as revised				13,267,201
	Year 1958				
	Convert $ portion at auction rate of 330% of rupiah equivalent		12,987,728		
	Convert local costs at 110% of 1957 revaluation			2,904,966	
119.79%	Total rupiah cost as revised				15,892,694
	Year 1959				
	Convert $ portion at new official rate of 400% of rupiah equivalent original cost		15,742,700		
	Convert local costs at 110% of 1958 revaluation			3,195,463	
119.16%	Total rupiah cost as revised				18,938,163
	Year 1960				
	No change in rupiah equivalent of $ portion		15,742,700		
	Convert local costs at 110% of 1959 revaluation			3,515,009	
101.69%	Total rupiah cost as revised				19,257,709

TABLE 3-2

P. N. PABRIK SEMEN "GRESIK":
COMPUTATION OF DECLINING BALANCE, DEPRECIATION, AND INTEREST,
MACHINE SHOP AND WAREHOUSE DEPARTMENT

Explanation	Declining asset value	Allowance for depreciation	Interest expense
	(1)	(2)	(3)
Year 1957			
Original rupiah cost	6,336,473		
Revaluation at end of year, 109.38%	6,930,728		
Revised value	13,267,201		
Depreciation, at 15% for ½ year	995,040	995,040 ·	
Interest, at 7½% for ½ year			497,520
Balance, at end of 1957	12,272,161	995,040	
Year 1958			
Revaluation at end of year, 19.79%	2,428,661	196,918	
Revised value	14,700,822	1,191,958	
Depreciation, 15%	2,205,123	2,205,123	
Interest, 7½%			1,102,562
Balance, at end of 1958	12,495,699	3,397,081	
Year 1959			
Revaluation at end of year, 19.16%	2,394,172	650,881	
Revised value	14,889,871	4,047,962	
Depreciation, 15%	2,233,481	2,233,481	
Interest, 7½%			1,116,740
Balance, at end of 1959	12,656,390	6,281,443	
Year 1960			
Revaluation at end of year, 1.69%	213,897	106,156	
Revised value	12,870,287	6,387,599	
Depreciation, 15%	1,930,543	1,930,543	
Interest, 7½%			965,272
Balance, at end of 1960 (estimated)	10,939,744	8,318,142	

TABLE 3-3

P. N. PABRIK SEMEN "GRESIK":
APPLICATION OF REVALUATION INDEXES,
MACHINE SHOP AND WAREHOUSE DEPARTMENT

Line		1957	1958	1959	1960
1	Revaluation index used	209.38%	119.79%	119.16%	101.69%
	Asset account				
2	Beginning balance	6,336,473	13,267,201	15,892,780	19,937,833
3	Revaluation at end of year	6,930,728	2,625,579	3,045,053	320,053
4	Revised beginning balance	13,267,201	15,892,780	18,937,833	19,257,886
5	Additions during year	. . . .	. . . .	. . . .	. . . .
6	Balance at end of year	13,267,201	15,892,780	18,937,833	19,257,886
	Allowance for depreciation				
7	Beginning balance	. . . .	995,040	3,397,081	6,281,443
8	Revaluation at end of year	. . . .	196,918	650,881	106,156
9	Subtotal	. . . .	1,191,958	4,047,962	6,387,599
10	Depreciation for period	995,040	2,205,123	2,233,481	1,930,543
11	Balance at end of year	995,040	3,397,081	6,281,443	8,318,142
	Net book value, end of year				
12	Line 6 minus line 11	12,272,161	12,495,699	12,656,390	10,939,744
	Net revaluation, end of year				
13	Line 3 minus line 8	6,930,728	2,428,661	2,394,172	213,897

TABLE 6-1

GRESIK AND CUSHENBERRY:
COMPARISON OF PRODUCTION COSTS PER METRIC TON,
1957, 1958, 1959, AND FIRST SIX MONTHS OF 1960

	(1) 1957	(2) 1958	(3) 1959	(4) First six months, 1960
Production in metric tons:				
Gresik	109,445	215,065	282,804	137,496
Cushenberry	192,250	375,670	422,631	197,406
Gresik as % of Cushenberry	56.93	57.25	66.92	69.65
Total cost per metric ton:				
Gresik: Rupiahs	723.00	794.00	Rp.808.00	Rp.925.82
Cushenberry: Dollars	19.15	15.62	$ 14.17	$ 13.01
Rupiahs			Rp.602.41	Rp.585.45
Gresik as % of Cushenberry			134.00	158.00
Gresik, 1957 = 100	100.00	110.00	112.00	128.00
Cushenberry, 1957 = 100	100.00	82.00	74.00	68.00
Cash cost per metric ton exclusive of depreciation and interest:				
Gresik: Rupiahs	183.00	228.00	306.88	433.10
Cushenberry: Dollars	9.52	8.94	$ 8.81	$ 8.43
Rupiahs			Rp.361.21	Rp.379.35
Gresik as % of Cushenberry			85.00	114.00
Gresik, 1957 = 100	100.00	125.00	168.00	237.00
Cushenberry, 1957 = 100	100.00	94.00	93.00	89.00
Depreciation cost per metric ton:				
Gresik: Rupiahs	360.	377.00	334.11	328.48
Cushenberry: Dollars	6.42	4.45	3.57	3.05
Rupiahs			160.65	137.25
Gresik as % of Cushenberry			208.00	239.00
Gresik, 1957 = 100	100.00	105.00	93.00	91.00
Cushenberry, 1957 = 100	100.00	69.00	56.00	48.00
Interest cost per metric ton:				
Gresik: Rupiahs	180.	189.	Rp.167.01	Rp.164.24
Cushenberry: Dollars	3.21	2.23	$ 1.79	$ 1.53
Rupiahs			Rp. 80.55	Rp. 68.85
Gresik as % of Cushenberry			208.00	239.00
Gresik, 1957 = 100	100.00	105.00	93.00	91.00
Cushenberry, 1957 = 100	100.00	69.00	56.00	48.00

Sources: For Gresik, tables 6-6 and 6-7 at end of Chap. 6 for 1959 and first six months of 1960. (Computations for 1957 and 1958 not shown.) For Cushenberry, tables 6-8 to 6-11 at end of Chap. 6.

TABLE 6-2

GRESIK AND CUSHENBERRY:
COMPARISON OF UNIT COSTS PER METRIC TON BY MAJOR ELEMENTS OF COST, 1959
(All costs in rupiahs)

| | Full-cost basis | | | | Cash-cost basis | | | |
| | (1) | (2) | (3) | (4) | (5) | (6) | (7) | (8) |
	Gresik	Cushen-berry	Favorable to Gresik	Adverse to Gresik	Gresik	Cushen-berry	Favorable to Gresik	Adverse to Gresik
Operating labor	8.08	26.65	18.57		8.08	26.65	18.57	
Repairs and maintenance	105.28	77.08		28.20	58.98	72.98	14.00	
Operating and factory supplies and various purchased services	45.65	29.11		16.53	45.66	29.11		16.55
Utilities	238.93	184.50		54.44	95.43	145.96	50.53	
Purchased material for processing:								
For raw grinding	20.52	18.86		1.66	20.52	18.86		1.66
For finish grinding	29.25	17.22		12.03	29.25	17.22		12.03
General and factory administration	120.88	68.06		52.82	48.96	50.43	1.47	
Subtotal	568.59	421.48		147.11	306.88	361.21	54.33	
Depreciation	159.58	116.55		43.03	334.11	160.65		173.46
Interest	79.83	58.50		21.33	167.01	80.55		86.46
Subtotal	239.41	175.05		64.36	501.12	241.20		259.92
Total costs	808.00	596.53		211.47	808.00	602.41		205.59

Sources: For Gresik, table 6-6. For Cushenberry, table 6-8. Some items were consolidated to provide comparable data.

TABLE 6-3

GRESIK AND CUSHENBERRY:
COMPARISON OF UNIT COSTS PER METRIC TON BY MAJOR ELEMENTS OF COST, FIRST SIX MONTHS OF 1960
(All costs in rupiahs)

	(1)	(2)	(3)	(4)	(5)	(6)	(7)	(8)
	Full-cost basis				Cash-cost basis			
	Gresik	Cushenberry	Favorable to Gresik	Adverse to Gresik	Gresik	Cushenberry	Favorable to Gresik	Adverse to Gresik
Operating labor	10.65	27.90	17.25		10.65	27.90	17.25	
Repairs and maintenance	160.81	73.80		87.01	89.99	69.75		20.24
Operating and factory supplies and various purchased services	39.53	20.70		18.83	39.52	20.70		18.82
Utilities	290.06	201.15		88.91	162.48	162.90	.42	
Purchased material for processing:								
For raw grinding	23.15	18.00		5.15	23.15	18.00		5.15
For finish grinding	51.85	22.50		29.35	51.85	22.50		29.35
General and factory administration	138.50	68.85		69.65	55.46	57.60	2.14	
Subtotal	714.55	432.90		281.65	433.10	379.35		53.75
Depreciation	140.91	101.70		39.21	328.48	137.25		191.23
Interest	70.36	50.85		19.51	164.24	68.85		95.39
Subtotal	211.27	152.55		58.72	492.72	206.10		286.62
Total costs	925.82	585.45		340.37	925.82	585.45		340.37

Sources: For Gresik, table 6–7, for Cushenberry, table 6–9. Some items were consolidated to provide comparable data.

TABLE 6-4

GRESIK AND CUSHENBERRY: COMPARISON OF COST OF SUPERVISION AND LABOR, 1959
(All Gresik costs in rupiahs)

	(1)	(2)	(3)	(4)	(5)	(6)	(7)	(8)	(9)	(10)
	Gresik						Cushenberry			
	Base wages and salaries	Less cost of depts. after finish grinding	Cost for cement production	Add over-time and other costs	Add net cost of pay in kind	Total	Total dollars	Less 9 per cent for steel rock	Balance to cement	Rupiahs at 41:1
Number employed, all depts.						996	217			
Direct operating labor	2,546,216	942,410	1,603,806	941,434	256,609	2,801,849	308,140	27,733	280,407	11,496,687
Repair labor	2,115,141	75,798	2,039,343	1,197,094	326,295	3,562,732	505,769	45,520	460,249	18,870,209
Wages and salaries:										
Factory administration	1,151,158	253,255	897,903	527,069	143,664	1,568,636	286,633	25,797	260,836	10,694,276
General administration:										
Wages	539,466	118,683	420,783	247,000	67,325	735,108				
Salaries	4,940,645	1,086,942	3,853,703	1,926,852	616,592	6,397,147				
Subtotal	5,480,111	1,205,625	4,274,486	2,173,852	683,917	7,132,255				
Total labor cost						15,065,472			1,001,492	41,064,172
Tons of finished cement						282,804				422,631
Cost per metric ton						53.27				97.16
Total general administration at Gresik						52,502,016				
Less 22 per cent for depts. after finish grinding						11,550,444				
Balance for cement production to silos						40,951,572				
Less wages and salaries, as above						7,132,255				
Balance, considered as cost of services for labor required for cement production only						33,819,317				
Cost per ton of finished cement						119.59				
Total cost per ton for wages, salaries, payments in kind, and general administration						172.86				97.16

Source: Data supplied by each enterprise.

TABLE 6-5

GRESIK AND CUSHENBERRY: HOURLY AND MONTHLY EMPLOYEES,
AT DECEMBER 31, 1959, FOR GRESIK; AT APRIL 30, 1961, FOR CUSHENBERRY

Item no.		(1)	(2)	(3)	(4)	(5)	(6)
		Gresik			Cushenberry		
		Number of hourly or daily employees	Number of monthly employees	Total employees	Number of hourly or daily employees	Number of monthly employees	Total employees
1	Central administration	11	17	28		2	2
2	Commercial section	38	25	63		7	7
3	Personnel and employee relations	48	102	150		7	7
4	Community relations	81	6	87	...	...	...
5	Financial and accounting	5	35	40	...	9	9
6	Public works and housing	78	10	88	...	...	...
7	Maintenance, utilities, and service	205	42	247	66	6	72
8	Cement production	148	20	168	57	17	74
9	Packing and loading	84	2	86	15	1	16
10	Bag manufacture	37	2	39	...	...	...
11	Distribution	...	...	...	12	5	17
	Total	735	261	996	150	54	204

TABLE 6-6

P. N. PABRIK SEMEN "GRESIK":
COMPUTATION OF COST PER TON BY ITEMS OF COST,
FULL-COST BASIS AND CASH-COST BASIS, 1959
(All costs in rupiahs)

	(1)	(2)	(3)	(4)	(5)	(6)
	Full-cost basis			Cash-cost basis		
	Total from cost flow sheet, App. table A–6	Per cent of total	Cost per metric ton	Cash costs from flow sheet, App. table A–8	Per cent of total	Cost per metric ton
Operating labor	2,217,891	1.00%	8.08	2,217,891	1.00%	8.08
Repairs: Labor	904,517	.41	3.31	904,517	.41	3.31
Supplies	5,406,418	2.45	19.80	5,406,418	2.45	19.80
Overhead	22,451,433	10.17	82.17	9,800,879	4.44	35.87
Subtotal	28,762,368	13.03	105.28	16,111,814	7.30	58.98
Operating supplies	22,884,734	10.37	83.79	22,884,734	10.37	83.79
Factory supplies	3,188,217	1.44	11.63	3,188,217	1.44	11.64
Fuel	13,658,039	6.19	50.02	13,658,039	6.19	50.02
Pier charges for fuel	8,059,364	3.65	29.49	964,927	.44	3.56
Power	32,482,109	14.72	118.94	8,070,269	3.66	29.57
Water	11,053,150	5.01	40.48	3,357,068	1.52	12.28
Subtotal	122,305,872	55.41	447.71	70,452,959	31.92	257.92
General administration	28,559,899	12.94	104.56	11,614,361	5.26	42.50
Factory administration	4,457,066	2.02	16.32	1,771,508	.80	6.46
Subtotal	155,322,837	70.37	568.59	83,838,828	37.98	306.88
Non-cash costs:						
Depreciation	43,603,223	19.75	159.58	91,259,230	41.35	334.11
Interest	21,801,613	9.88	79.83	45,629,615	20.67	167.01
Subtotal	65,404,836	29.63	239.41	136,888,845	62.02	501.12
Total costs	220,727,673	100.00%	808.00	220,727,673	100.00%	808.00
Cost of purchased material included in operating supplies: Material for raw grinding:						
Iron ore	2,605,625	1.18%	9.53	2,605,625	1.18%	9.53
Silica sand	2,996,442	1.36	10.99	2,996,442	1.36	10.99
Subtotal	5,602,067	2.54	20.52	5,602,067	2.54	20.52
Material for finish grinding: Gypsum	7,995,680	3.62	29.25	7,995,680	3.62	29.25
Total purchased material	13,597,747	6.16%	49.77	13,597,747	6.16%	49.77

Note: Depreciation and interest on the full-cost basis consists only of the charges for these items for the cement production departments. The cash costs exclude all depreciation and interest, therefore these charges together must be the difference between the total cost and the cash costs, or Rp. 220,727,673 − Rp. 83,838,828 = Rp. 136,888,845. Interest is 1/3 of the total and depreciation 2/3.

TABLE 6-7

P. N. PABRIK SEMEN "GRESIK":
COMPUTATION OF COST PER TON BY ITEMS OF COST,
FULL-COST BASIS AND CASH-COST BASIS,
FIRST SIX MONTHS OF 1960
(All costs in rupiahs)

	(1)	(2)	(3)	(4)	(5)	(6)
	Full-cost basis			Cash-cost basis		
	Total from cost flow sheet, App. table A-12	Per cent of total	Cost per metric ton	Cash costs from flow sheet, App. table A-14	Per cent of total	Cost per metric ton
Operating labor	1,420,213	1.15%	10.65	1,420,213	1.15%	10.65
Repairs: Labor	542,942	.44	4.07	542,942	.44	4.07
Supplies	3,332,075	2.71	25.09	3,332,075	2.71	25.09
Overhead	17,488,892	14.22	131.65	8,081,227	6.57	60.83
Subtotal	21,363,909	17.37	160.81	11,956,244	9.72	89.99
Operating supplies	12,998,286	10.57	97.86	12,998,286	10.57	97.86
Factory supplies	2,213,644	1.80	16.67	2,213,644	1.80	16.66
Fuel	14,371,062	11.69	108.23	14,371,062	11.69	108.23
Pier charges for fuel	3,052,254	2.48	22.96	192,897	.16	1.48
Power	16,409,186	13.35	123.60	5,531,863	4.50	41.66
Water	4,683,639	3.81	35.27	1,480,196	1.20	11.11
Subtotal	76,512,193	62.22	576.05	50,164,405	40.79	377.64
General administration	16,584,398	13.49	124.89	6,705,630	5.45	50.46
Factory administration	1,802,607	1.47	13.61	659,290	.54	5.00
Subtotal	94,899,198	77.18	714.55	57,529,325	46.78	433.10
Non-cash costs:						
Depreciation	18,710,950	15.22	140.91	43,624,199	35.48	328.48
Interest	9,355,476	7.60	70.36	21,812,100	17.74	164.24
Subtotal	28,066,426	22.82	211.27	65,436,299	53.22	492.72
Total costs	122,965,624	100.00%	925.82	122,965,624	100.00%	925.82
Cost of purchased material included in operating supplies: Material for raw grinding:						
Iron ore	1,369,555	1.11%	10.28	1,369,555	1.11%	10.28
Silica sand	1,703,240	1.39	12.87	1,703,240	1.39	12.87
Subtotal	3,072,795	2.50	23.15	3,072,795	2.50	23.15
Material for finish grinding:						
Gypsum	6,887,280	5.60	51.85	6,887,280	5.60	51.85
Total purchased material	9,960,075	8.10%	75.00	9,960,075	8.10%	75.00

Note: Depreciation and interest on the full-cost basis consists only of the charges for these items for the cement production departments. The cash costs exclude all depreciation and interest; therefore these charges together must be the difference between the total cost and the cash costs, or Rp. 122,965,624 − Rp. 57,529,325 = Rp. 65,436,299. Interest is 1/3 of the total and depreciation is 2/3.

TABLE 6-8

THE PERMANENTE CEMENT CORPORATION

CUSHENBERRY PLANT: COMPUTATION OF COSTS PER METRIC TON,
FULL-COST BASIS AND CASH-COST BASIS, 1959

(Costs in U.S. dollars)

	(1)	(2)	(3)	(4)	(5)	(6)	(7)	(8)	(9)
	Total, from cost flow sheet, App. table B-8	Full-cost basis Per cent of total	Full-cost basis Cost per metric ton, U.S. dollars	Convert to rupiahs	Adjust depreciation and interest[a]	Cash cost, column 1 minus column 5	Cash-cost basis Per cent of total	Cash-cost basis Cost per metric ton, U.S. dollars	Convert to rupiahs
				At 41:1					At 41:1
Labor	$ 280,983	4.62%	.65	26.65		280,983	4.62%	.65	26.65
Maintenance	807,881	13.29	1.88	77.08	(44,832)	763,049	12.55	1.78	72.98
Operating supplies	149,600	2.46	.35	14.35		149,600	2.46	.35	14.35
Utilities	1,929,880	31.73	4.50	184.50	(402,079)	1,527,801	25.13	3.56	145.96
Purchased services	23,873	.39	.06	2.46		23,873	.39	.06	2.46
Equipment operation	86,567	1.42	.20	8.20		86,567	1.42	.20	8.20
Material handling	43,805	.72	.10	4.10		43,805	.72	.10	4.10
Subtotal	3,322,589	54.63	7.74	317.34	(446,911)	2,875,678	47.29	6.70	274.70
Purchased materials:									
For raw grinding	199,713	3.28	.46	18.86		199,713	3.28	.46	18.86
For finish grinding	179,988	2.96	.42	17.22		179,988	2.96	.42	17.22
Subtotal	379,701	6.24	.88	36.08		379,701	6.24	.88	36.08
General administration	709,894	11.68	1.66	68.06	(184,006)	525,888	8.65	1.23	50.43
Total cash costs[a]	4,412,184	72.55	10.28	421.48	(630,917)	3,781,267	62.18	8.81	361.21
				At 45:1					At 45:1
Non-cash costs:									
Depreciation	1,112,951	18.30	2.59	116.55	420,611	1,533,562	25.22	3.57	160.65
Interest	556,475	9.15	1.30	58.50	210,306	766,781	12.60	1.79	80.55
Total non-cash costs	1,669,426	27.45	3.89	175.05	630,917	2,300,343	37.82	5.36	241.20
Total costs	6,081,610	100.00%	14.17	596.53	. . .	6,081,610	100.00%	14.17	602.41[b]

[a] These are the depreciation and interest included in the full-cost charges for maintenance, utilities, and general administration. The treatment here is consistent with that of tables 6-6 and 6-7, preceding.

[b] The unit cost under this method is higher in 1959 than the full-cost method of col. 4 because all depreciation and interest costs are converted at 45:1, whereas in col. 4 a portion of depreciation and interest is included in the cash costs of maintenance, utilities, and general administration and converted at 41:1.

TABLE 6-9

THE PERMANENTE CEMENT CORPORATION

CUSHENBERRY PLANT: COMPUTATION OF COSTS PER METRIC TON,
FULL-COST BASIS AND CASH-COST BASIS, FIRST SIX MONTHS OF 1960

(Costs in U. S. dollars)

	(1)	(2)	(3)	(4)	(5)	(6)	(7)	(8)	(9)
		Full-cost basis				Cash-cost basis			
	Total, from cost flow sheet, App. table B-10	Per cent of total	Cost per metric ton, U.S. dollars	Convert to rupiahs	Adjust depreciation and interest[a]	Cash cost, column 1 minus column 5	Per cent of total	Cost per metric ton, U.S. dollars	Convert to rupiahs
				At 45:1					At 45:1
Labor	$ 130,861	4.80%	.62	27.90		130,861	4.80%	.62	27.90
Maintenance	344,059	12.61	1.64	73.80	(19,642)	324,417	11.89	1.55	69.75
Operating supplies	31,329	1.15	.15	6.75		31,329	1.15	.15	6.75
Utilities	936,751	34.33	4.47	201.15	(178,823)	757,928	27.77	3.62	162.90
Purchased services	13,433	.49	.06	2.70		13,433	.49	.06	2.70
Equipment operation	37,512	1.37	.18	8.10		37,512	1.37	.18	8.10
Material handling	14,802	.54	.07	3.15		14,802	.54	.07	3.15
Subtotal	1,508,747	55.29	7.19	323.55	(198,465)	1,310,282	48.01	6.25	281.25
Purchased materials:									
For raw grinding	83,670	3.07	.40	18.00		83,670	3.07	.40	18.00
For finish grinding	105,234	3.85	.50	22.50		105,234	3.85	.50	22.50
Subtotal	188,904	6.92	.90	40.50		188,904	6.92	.90	40.50
General administration	319,984	11.72	1.53	68.85	(50,900)	269,084	9.87	1.28	57.60
Total cash costs[a]	2,017,635	73.93	9.62	432.90	(249,365)	1,768,270	64.80	8.43	379.35
Non-cash costs:									
Depreciation	474,230	17.38	2.26	101.70	166,243	640,473	23.47	3.05	137.25
Interest	237,115	8.69	1.13	50.85	83,122	320,237	11.73	1.53	68.85
Total non-cash costs	711,345	26.07	3.39	152.55	249,365	960,710	35.20	4.58	206.10
Total costs	2,728,980	100.00%	13.01	585.45	. . .	2,728,980	100.00%	13.01	585.45

[a]These are the depreciation and interest included in the full-cost charges for maintenance, utilities, and general administration.
The treatment here is consistent with that of tables 6-6 and 6-7.

TABLE 6-10

THE PERMANENTE CEMENT CORPORATION

CUSHENBERRY PLANT: COMPUTATION OF COST PER TON BY ELEMENTS OF COST, 1958

(All costs in U. S. dollars)

	(1)	(2)	(3)	(4)	(5)	(6)	(7)
	Full-cost basis				Cash-cost basis		
	Total, from cost flow sheet, App. table B-6	Per cent of total	Cost per metric ton	Eliminate depreciation and interest[a]	Cash costs, column 1 minus column 4	Per cent of total	Cost per metric ton
Labor	$ 233,547	4.07%	$ .64	$	$ 233,547	4.07%	$ .64
Maintenance	630,009	10.98	1.71	(46,114)	583,895	10.17	1.59
Operating supplies	60,215	1.05	.16		60,215	1.05	.16
Utilities	1,780,582	31.02	4.84	(447,913)	1,332,669	23.22	3.62
Purchased services	12,917	.23	.04		12,917	.23	.04
Equipment operation	109,355	1.91	.30		109,355	1.91	.30
Material handling	62,039	1.08	.17		62,039	1.08	.17
Subtotal	2,888,664	50.34	7.86	(494,027)	2,394,637	41.73	6.52
Purchased materials:							
For raw grinding	248,872	4.34	.68		248,872	4.34	.68
For finished grinding	153,484	2.67	.42		153,484	2.67	.41
Subtotal	402,356	7.01	1.10	. . .	402,356	7.01	1.09
General administration	657,971	11.46	1.79	(170,148)	487,823	8.50	1.33
Total, excluding depreciation and interest	3,948,991	68.81	10.75	(664,175)	3,284,816	57.24	8.94
Non-cash costs:							
Depreciation	1,193,147	20.79	3.25	442,783	1,635,930	28.51	4.45
Interest	596,573	10.40	1.62	221,392	817,965	14.25	2.23
Total non-cash costs	1,789,720	31.19	4.87	664,175	2,453,895	42.76	6.68
Total costs	$5,738,711	100.00%	$15.62	. . .	$5,738,711	100.00%	$15.62

[a]These are the depreciation and interest included in the full-cost charges for maintenance, utilities, and general administration. The treatment here is consistent with that of tables 6-6 and 6-7.

TABLE 6-11

THE PERMANENTE CEMENT CORPORATION

CUSHENBERRY PLANT: COMPUTATION OF COST PER TON BY ELEMENTS OF COST, 1957
(All costs in U. S. dollars)

	(1)	(2)	(3)	(4)	(5)	(6)	(7)
	Total, from cost flow sheet, App. table B-4	Full-cost basis		Eliminate depreciation and interest[a]	Cash-cost basis		
		Per cent of total	Cost per metric ton		Cash costs, column 1 minus column 4	Per cent of total	Cost per metric ton
Labor	$ 160,779	4.21%	$ .81		$ 160,779	4.21%	$ .81
Maintenance	376,504	9.86	1.89	(37,922)	338,582	8.86	1.69
Operating supplies	47,998	1.25	.24		47,998	1.26	.24
Utilities	1,120,374	29.33	5.61	(350,443)	769,931	20.16	3.86
Purchased services	22,375	.58	.11		22,375	.58	.11
Equipment operation	80,991	2.12	.41		80,991	2.12	.41
Material handling	15,584	.41	.08		15,584	.41	.08
Subtotal	1,824,605	47.76	9.15	(388,365)	1,436,240	37.60	7.20
Purchased materials							
For raw grinding	127,634	3.34	.64		127,634	3.34	.64
For finished grinding	75,806	1.99	.38		75,806	1.99	.38
Subtotal	203,440	5.33	1.02	. . .	203,440	5.33	1.02
General administration	421,767	11.04	2.11	(163,463)	258,304	6.76	1.30
Total, excluding depreciation and interest	2,449,812	64.13	12.28	(551,828)	1,897,984	49.69	9.52
Non-cash costs:							
Depreciation	913,449	23.91	4.58	367,885	1,281,334	33.54	6.42
Interest	456,724	11.96	2.29	183,943	640,667	16.77	3.21
Total non-cash costs	1,370,173	35.87	6.87	551,828	1,922,001	50.31	9.63
Total costs	$3,819,985	100.00%	$19.15	. . .	$3,819,985	100.00%	$19.15

[a] These are the depreciation and interest included in the full-cost charges for maintenance, utilities, and general administration. The treatment here is consistent with that of tables 6-6 and 6-7 preceding.

TABLE 7-1

P. N. PABRIK SEMEN "GRESIK"
DISPOSITION OF TOTAL PRODUCTION COSTS INCURRED, 1957
(All costs in rupiahs)

	(1)	(2)	(3)	(4)
Total costs, from statement of profit and loss (Lampir Rekening Untung Rugi)				Rp 27,348,540
Add: Back inventories at December 31, 1957:				
Clinker			Rp 377,355	
Cement in silos			1,875,184	
Bags			510,976	2,763,515
				30,112,055
Deduct: General administration costs			4,706,781	
Factory administration costs			1,566,618	6,273,399
Costs incurred for labor, supplies, and materials				Rp 23,838,656

	Cement production	Bag manufacture	Packing and loading	Total
Distribution of costs of labor, supplies, and materials, from cost statement	15,561,235	7,286,556	990,865	23,838,656
Distribute general and factory administration on basis of experience in 1958	4,974,806	345,037	953,556	6,273,399
Total cash costs incurred	20,536,041	7,631,593	1,944,421	30,112,055
Add: Depreciation (from App. table A-2):				
General administration on basis of 1959 dist.	7,248,983	502,767	1,389,464	9,141,214
Factory administration on basis of 1959 dist.	1,652,955	114,644	316,833	2,084,432
Factory departments, actual	30,927,636	1,029,176	4,987,953	36,944,765
Subtotal	39,829,574	1,646,587	6,694,250	48,170,411
Add: Interest, half of depreciation:				
General administration	3,624,491	251,383	694,733	4,570,607
Factory administration	826,477	57,322	158,417	1,042,216
Factory departments	15,468,818	519,588	2,493,977	18,482,383
Subtotal	19,919,786	828,293	3,347,127	24,095,206
Total	80,285,401	10,106,473	11,985,798	102,377,672
Less: Clinker inventory, adjusted to include depreciation and interest	1,207,536			
Cost of finished cement	79,077,865			
Tons of finished cement produced	109,445			
Cost per ton	722.54			

	Total costs incurred, as above	Per cent of total	Cost per metric ton	
Cash costs	20,536,041	25.58	183	
Depreciation	39,829,574	49.62	360	
Interest	19,919,786	24.80	180	
Subtotal	59,749,360	74.42	540	
Total	80,285,401	100.00%	723.00	

TABLE 7-2

P. N. PABRIK SEMEN "GRESIK":

COST OF BAG MANUFACTURING,
1957, 1958, 1959, 1960 (5 MONTHS)
(All costs in rupiahs)

	1957 (1) Number of bags	1957 (2) Rp. amount	1957 (3) Rp. per bag	1958 (4) Number of bags	1958 (5) Rp. amount	1958 (6) Rp. per bag	1959 (7) Number of bags	1959 (8) Rp. amount	1959 (9) Rp. per bag	1960 (5 months) (10) Number of bags	1960 (5 months) (11) Rp. amount	1960 (5 months) (12) Rp. per bag
Direct and indirect charges:												
Operating labor					283,746			425,897			244,275	
Repairs: Labor					6,046			10,553			6,043	
Parts		Not available			123,848			31,506			12,329	
Overhead					751,488			149,627			84,043	
Subtotal					881,382			191,686			102,415	
Operating supplies, paper, etc.					22,980,806			35,922,488			11,585,576	
Factory supplies					74,381			104,297			66,446	
Power		7,286,556			928,833			1,047,810			450,080	
Subtotal					25,149,148			37,692,178			12,448,792	
General administration		1,271,153			3,041,908			3,992,101			2,063,290	
Factory administration					545,859			623,009			420,065	
Depreciation		1,029,176			2,208,977			2,344,536			838,732	
Interest		519,588			1,149,489			1,172,268			419,366	
Total cost of dept.	2,221,895	10,106,473	4.55	4,540,282	32,185,381	7.09	6,121,670	45,824,092	7.49	1,987,828	16,190,245	8.14
Beginning inventory of finished bags	. . .	. . .	. . .	188,242	856,234	4.55	204,180	1,426,753	6.99	568,241	4,244,470	7.47
Finished bags available	2,221,895	10,106,473	4.55	4,728,524	33,041,615	6.99	6,325,850	47,250,845	7.47	2,556,069	20,434,715	7.99
Ending inventory of finished bags	188,242	856,234	4.55	204,180	1,426,753	6.99	566,241	4,244,470	7.47	599,892	4,795,890	7.99
Bags used	2,033,653	9,250,239	4.55	4,524,344	31,614,862	6.99	5,757,609	43,006,375	7.47	1,956,177	15,638,825	7.99
Disposition of bags used:												
For shipments or own use	1,943,239	8,838,978	4.55	4,369,264	30,531,093	6.99	5,627,670	42,035,825	7.47	1,909,671	15,267,037	7.99
Extra bags shipped to customer	40,315	183,376	4.55	117,689	822,378	6.99	103,621	773,996	7.47	40,251	321,790	7.99
Subtotal	1,983,554	9,022,354	4.55	4,486,953	31,353,471	6.99	5,731,291	42,809,821	7.47	1,949,922	15,588,827	7.99
Broken at factory	50,099	227,885	4.55	37,391	261,391	6.99	26,318	196,554	7.47	6,255	49,998	7.99
Total, as above	2,033,653	9,250,239	4.55	4,524,344	31,614,862	6.99	5,757,609	43,006,375	7.47	1,956,177	15,638,825	7.99

Notes: Original computations of cost per bag were carried to five decimal places and rounded to two decimals for this table; hence details may not add to totals. Original five-place figures used to obtain amounts shown. Costs of extra bags supplied to customers and of bags broken at factory are treated as part of cost of cement sold in table 7-4.

TABLE 7-3

P. N. PABRIK SEMEN "GRESIK":
PACKING AND SHIPPING AND LOCOMOTIVE AND RAILROAD COSTS,
1957, 1958, 1959, 1960 (5 MONTHS)
(All costs in rupiahs)

	(1)	(2)	(3)	(4)	(5)	(6)	(7)
	1957	1958		1959		1960 (5 months)	
	Packing and shipping, locomotive and R.R.	Packing and shipping	Locomotive and R.R.	Packing and shipping	Locomotive and R.R.	Packing and shipping	Locomotive and R.R.
Direct and indirect charges:							
Operating labor		694,864	23,032	1,092,726	19,400	681,286	16,849
Repairs: Labor		78,627	2,594	123,360	4,937	67,763	1,992
Supplies		356,719	16,504	1,021,223	27,156	391,439	15,935
Overhead		2,518,645	110,489	4,071,905	114,173	2,100,638	82,008
Subtotal		2,953,991	129,587	5,216,488	146,266	2,559,840	99,935
Factory supplies		256,771	16,590	400,814	18,416	216,898	22,677
Power		1,238,444	. . . .	1,397,080	. . . .	600,107	. . . .
Subtotal	990,865	5,144,070	169,209	8,107,108	184,082	4,058,131	139,461
General administration	3,513,003	8,119,232	268,993	11,123,240	222,603	6,174,358	153,419
Factory administration		1,456,985	48,270	1,735,896	34,740	1,256,997	31,618
Depreciation	4,987,953	8,075,660	2,821,277	8,172,539	2,727,491	2,945,810	1,028,280
Interest	2,493,977	4,037,830	1,410,639	4,086,270	1,363,746	1,472,905	514,140
Total cost of department	11,985,798	26,833,777	4,718,388	33,225,053	4,532,662	15,908,201	1,866,918

Note: For years after 1957 costs of packing and shipping are treated as a part of cost of cement bagged in table 7-4. Costs of locomotive and railroad are treated as a part of cost of cement sold in table 7-4. In 1957 the combined costs are treated as a part of the cost of cement bagged in table 7-4.

TABLE 7-4

P. N. PABRIK SEMEN "GRESIK":
COST OF CEMENT SOLD AND USED BY CORPORATION.
1957, 1958, 1959, 1960 (5 months)
(All costs in rupiahs)

	1957			1958			1959			1960 (5 months)		
	(1) Number of tons or bags	(2) Rupiahs amount	(3) Cost per ton or bag	(4) Number of tons or bags	(5) Rupiahs amount	(6) Cost per ton or bag	(7) Number of tons or bags	(8) Rupiahs amount	(9) Cost per ton or bag	(10) Number of tons or bags	(11) Rupiahs amount	(12) Cost per ton or bag
Data in terms of metric tons												
Cost of cement in silos beginning of year	...	...	...	12,283	8,874,434	722.54	8,885	7,017,222	789.78	10,305	8,315,671	806.96
Cost of cement produced	109,445	79,077,865	722.54	215,065	170,681,099	793.63	282,804	228,362,722	807.50	112,307	106,177,715	945.43
Cement available	109,445	79,077,865	722.54	227,348	179,555,533	789.78	291,689	235,379,944	806.96	122,612	114,493,386	933.79
Value of ending inventory	12,283	8,874,434	722.54	8,885	7,017,222	789.78	10,305	8,315,671	806.96	27,128	25,331,747	933.79
Cost of cement sacked, tons	97,162	70,203,431	722.54	218,463	172,538,311	789.78	281,384	227,064,273	806.96	95,484	89,161,639	933.79
Data in terms of sacks												
Cost of cement sacked, sacks	1,943,239	70,203,431	36.13	4,369,264	172,538,311	39.49	5,627,670	227,064,273	40.35	1,909,671	89,161,639	46.69
Add: Packing and shipping (table 7–3)	...	11,985,798	6.17	...	26,833,777	6.14	...	33,225,053	5.90	...	15,908,201	8.33
Add cost of bags (table 7–2)	...	8,836,978	4.55	...	30,531,093	6.99	...	42,035,825	7.47	...	15,267,037	7.99
Total cost of cement bagged	1,943,239	91,026,207	46.84	4,369,264	229,903,181	52.62	5,627,670	302,335,151	53.72	1,909,671	120,336,877	63.01
Less cement to corporation warehouse (see below)	7,763	363,650	46.84	41,121	2,163,705	52.62	53,325	2,864,726	53.72	265,156	16,708,540	63.01
Cost of cement bagged	1,935,476	90,664,557	46.84	4,328,143	227,739,476	52.62	5,574,345	299,460,425	53.72	1,644,515	103,628,337	63.01
Cost of cement transferred to USINDO					4,716,388	1.09		4,532,662	.81		1,866,918	1.14
Add: Cost of locomotive and R. R., table 7–3	(40,315)	183,376	4.55	(117,689)	822,378	.19	(103,621)	773,996	.14	(40,251)	321,790	.20
Cost of empty bags, table 7–2a	50,099	227,885	4.55	(37,391)	261,391	.06	(26,318)	196,554	.04	(6,255)	49,998	.03
Cost of broken bags, table 7–2a												
Total cost of cement sold, see income statement, table 7–5	1,935,476	91,075,818	47.05	4,328,143	233,541,633	53.96	5,574,345	304,963,637	54.71	1,644,515	105,867,043	64.37
Cost of cement to warehouse for own use												
As above	7,763	363,650	46.84	41,121	2,163,705	52.62	53,325	2,864,726	53.72	265,156	16,708,540	63.01
Beginning inventory	...	...	...	1,951	91,393	46.84	72	3,747	52.36	176	9,455	52.36
Total available	7,763	363,650	46.84	43,072	2,255,098	52.36	53,397	2,868,473	53.72	265,332	16,717,995	63.01
Ending inventory	1,951	91,393	46.84	72	3,747	52.36	176	9,455	52.36	851	53,576	63.01
Cement used by corporation, or given to community	5,812	272,257	46.84	43,000	2,251,351	52.36	53,221	2,859,018	53.72	264,481	16,664,419	63.01
Used in construction	3,000	140,532	46.84	18,170	951,327	52.36	24,702	1,326,989	53.72	67,833	4,280,323	63.01
Given to community	2,812	131,725	46.84	24,830	1,300,024	52.36	28,519	1,532,029	53.72	196,548	12,384,096	63.01
Total, as above	5,812	272,257	46.84	43,000	2,251,351	52.36	53,221	2,859,018	53.72	264,481	16,664,419	63.01

*Figures for number of bags are not included in total, but are provided to show computation of cost in "rupiahs amount" columns.

Note: Details of unit cost columns may not add to totals because of rounding.

TABLE 7-5

P. N. PABRIK SEMEN "GRESIK"

STATEMENT OF PROFIT AND LOSS 1957, 1958, 1959, AND 1960 (5 MONTHS)

(All costs in rupiahs)

	1957		1958		1959		1960	
	(1)	(2)	(3)	(4)	(5)	(6)	(7)	(8)
	Total in rupiahs	Rp. per sack	Total in rupiahs	Rp. per sack	Total in rupiahs	Rp. per sack	Total in rupiahs	Rp. per sack
Number of sacks:								
Transferred to USINDO	1,835,476		4,328,143		5,574,345		1,644,515	
Sold or given to community	2,812		24,830		28,519		196,548	
Total	1,838,288		4,352,973		5,602,864		1,841,063	
Revenue net of sales tax from:								
USINDO	53,536,931		144,599,336	33.41	309,337,608	55.49	93,967,587	37.14
Community	. . . . .		182,781	7.36	410,664	14.40	11,238,753	57.14
Sweepings					921,951			
Total	53,536,931	27.62	144,782,117	33.26	310,670,223	55.45	105,206,340	57.14
Cost of sales (table 7–4):								
USINDO	91,075,818	47.05	233,541,633	53.96	304,963,637	54.71	105,867,043	64.37
Community	131,725	46.84	1,300,024	52.38	1,532,029	53.72	12,384,096	63.01
Total	91,207,543	47.05	234,841,657	53.95	306,495,666	54.70	118,251,139	64.23
Margin (loss) from:								
Sweepings					921,951	.79		
USINDO			(88,942,297)	(20.55)	4,373,971		(11,899,456)	
Community			(1,117,243)	(44.99)	(1,121,365)	(40.30)	(1,145,343)	
Total	(37,670,612)	(19.43)	(90,059,540)	(20.69)	4,174,557	.75	(13,044,799)	(7.09)
Other income:								
House rent	1,950		60,990		93,514			
Equipment rental	12,300		73,490		64,906			
Sale of waste	87,300		733,306		509,575			
From use of autos	48,193		36,659		501,457			
Miscellaneous			1,550		232,137			
Refund of sales tax	137,127		1,383,393		377,444			
Interest earned					2,325,828			
Profit sales of cars	20,000		40,572		440,000			
Total other income	306,870		2,329,960		4,544,861			
Subtotal	(37,363,742)		(87,729,580)		8,719,418			
Other expenses:								
Adjustment of 1958 cement price with USINDO					1,081,089			
Loss from monetary devaluation of rupiah					378,450			
Total other expenses	. . . . .	: :	. . . . .	: :	1,459,539			
Net profit (loss) before corporation tax	(37,363,742)		(87,729,580)		7,259,879			

TABLE 7-6

P. N. PABRIK SEMEN "GRESIK":
COMPARISON OF DEBIT ACCOUNTS ON BALANCE SHEET
ACCORDING TO BOOKS AND ACCORDING TO REVISIONS MADE IN THIS STUDY,
DECEMBER 31, 1957, 1958, AND 1959
(All costs in rupiahs)

Debits	Balances, 1959			Balances, 1958			Balances, 1957		
	(1) Per books	(2) Used in this study	(3) Difference	(4) Per books	(5) Used in this study	(6) Difference	(7) Per books	(8) Used in this study	(9) Difference
Current assets									
Cash on hand and in banks	310,841	310,841		275,320	275,320		41,192	41,192	
State Development Bank:									
Revolving fund, Djakarta	14,006,369	14,006,369		762,409	762,409		4,777,184	4,777,184	
Dividend account, Djakarta	12,000,000	12,000,000							
Current account, Surabaja branch				16,212	16,212				
Time deposits				850,000	850,000		500,000	500,000	
Total cash	26,317,210	26,317,210		1,903,941	1,903,941		5,318,376	5,318,376	
Receivables									
P. T. USINDO: Cement	86,801,680	86,801,680		36,586,767	36,586,767		11,067,253	11,067,253	
Imports	2,157,058	2,157,058							
Cement cars	36,350,312	36,350,312		26,305,593	26,305,593		25,630,056	25,630,056	
Trade accounts	1,980,009	1,980,009		775,329	775,329		681,945	681,945	
Deposits with suppliers	4,593,367	4,593,367		33,370,335	33,370,335		10,849,247	10,849,247	
Miscellaneous	19,103	19,103							
Payments made in advance for goods in transit									
Total receivables	131,901,529	131,901,529		107,678,162	107,678,162		63,045,298	63,045,298	
Inventories									
Raw materials:									
Production supplies	25,609,034	25,609,034		54,669,703	54,669,703		25,486,145	25,486,145	
Operating supplies	48,798,667	48,798,667		4,824,628	4,824,628		3,816,102	3,816,102	
Other supplies	10,826	10,826					6,159	6,159	
Finished material and work in process:									
Cement in sacks	9,863	9,455	(408)	2,563	3,747	1,184		91,393	91,393
Cement in silos	7,326,916	8,315,671	988,755	7,323,550	7,017,222	(306,328)	5,636,262	8,874,434	3,238,172
Clinker	6,338,046	6,393,768	55,722	15,345,125	14,028,817	(1,316,308)	1,134,219	1,207,536	73,317
Finished sacks	4,114,065	4,244,470	130,405	1,918,468	1,426,753	(491,713)	1,535,372	856,234	(679,138)
Error on original statement				1,000		(1,000)			
Total inventories	92,209,417	93,381,891	1,172,474	84,085,035	81,970,870	(2,114,165)	37,614,259	40,338,003	2,723,744
Total current assets	250,428,156	251,600,630	1,172,474	193,667,138	191,552,973	(2,114,165)	105,977,933	108,701,677	2,723,744
Government bonds, from devaluation	76,184,900	76,184,900							
Fixed assets subject to depreciation:									
Original rupiah cost	365,963,905	362,196,048	(3,767,857)	356,927,030	358,638,232	1,711,202	348,683,585	347,864,380	(819,205)
Revaluation to estimated replacement cost		605,543,669	605,543,669		428,372,385	428,372,385		284,407,327	284,407,327
Total	365,963,905	967,739,717	601,775,812	356,927,030	787,010,627	430,083,597	348,683,585	642,271,707	293,588,122
Construction in progress	19,404,457	19,404,457		1,536,055	1,536,055		3,840,532	3,840,532	
Increase (decrease) in cost of cement used		(5,640)	(5,640)		333,720	333,720			
Total fixed assets	385,368,362	987,138,534	601,770,172	358,463,085	788,880,402	430,417,317	352,524,117	646,112,239	293,588,122
Error on original statement							(200)		(200)
Total debits	711,981,418	1,314,924,064	602,942,646	552,130,223	980,433,375	428,303,152	458,501,850	754,813,916	296,312,066

TABLE 7-7

P. N. PABRIK SEMEN "GRESIK":

COMPARISON OF CREDIT ACCOUNTS ON BALANCE SHEET ACCORDING TO BOOKS AND ACCORDING TO REVISIONS MADE IN THIS STUDY, DECEMBER 31, 1957, 1958, AND 1959

(All costs in rupiahs)

Credit accounts	(1) Per books	(2) Balances, 1959 — Used in this study	(3) Difference	(4) Per books	(5) Balances, 1958 — Used in this study	(6) Difference	(7) Per books	(8) Balances, 1957 — Used in this study	(9) Difference
Current liabilities									
State Development Bank, Surabaja branch									
Revolving fund	1,907,795	1,907,795							
State cash account	3,543,750	3,543,750							
Fee and interest, 1959	17,000,000		(17,000,000)	20,000,000		(20,000,000)			
Dividend, 1959	12,000,000		(12,000,000)						
Overdraft	307,732	307,732					9,700	9,700	
Accounts payable	3,198,146	3,198,146							
Corporation income tax, 1958	12,320,527	12,320,527		5,217,993	5,217,993		34,748,927	34,748,927	
Bankers and Guarantee Trust Co., U. S. A.	2,059,836	2,059,836							
Indonesian Embassy, U. S. A.	190,486	190,486							
Dollar accounts not billed				38,948,746	38,948,746				
Employee witholding taxes payable				151,496	151,496				
Sales taxes payable				618,371	618,371				
Paper received but not paid for	2,712,666	2,712,666							
Spare parts received but not paid for	11,675,092	11,675,092		9,847,308	9,847,308				
Total current liabilities	66,916,030	37,916,030	(29,000,000)	74,783,914	54,783,914	(20,000,000)	34,758,627	34,758,627	
Long-term liabilities									
State Development Bank, head office, Djakarta:									
For construction loans	385,455,568	385,455,568		369,548,677	369,548,677		383,637,034	383,637,034	
For interest (as computed in this study)		115,937,637	115,937,637		78,744,657	78,744,657		24,085,206	24,085,206
Total long-term liabilities	385,455,568	501,393,205	115,937,637	369,548,677	448,293,334	78,744,657	383,637,034	407,722,240	24,085,206
Revaluation of assets, regarded as part of loan capital account of P. N. Pabrik Semen Gresik with State Development Bank:									
Revaluation of fixed assets		605,543,689	605,543,689		428,372,395	428,372,395		294,407,327	294,407,327
Adjustment of allowance for depreciation		(47,677,382)	(47,677,382)		(10,047,381)	(10,047,381)			
Net revaluation of fixed assets		557,866,287	557,866,287		418,325,014	418,325,014		294,407,327	294,407,327
Revaluation of current assets		13,802,473	13,802,473		12,365,244	12,365,244		5,606,930	5,606,930
Total revaluation		571,668,760	571,668,760		430,690,258	430,690,258		300,014,257	300,014,257
Capital									
Common stock (held by State Development Bank)	2,000,000	2,000,000		2,000,000	2,000,000		2,000,000	2,000,000	
Accumulated earnings (loss):									
Balance, beginning of year	(27,778,250)	(122,870,832)	(95,092,582)	(20,699,856)	(37,851,619)	(17,151,763)	(20,699,856)	(37,363,742)	(16,663,886)
Profit (loss) current year (table 7-5)	87,580,419	7,259,879	(80,320,540)	(7,078,394)	(87,729,580)	(80,651,186)		(487,877)	(487,877)
Unallocated difference		(1,955,632)	(1,955,632)		2,710,367	2,710,367			
Balance, end of year	59,802,169	(117,566,585)	(177,368,754)	(27,778,250)	(122,870,832)	(95,092,582)	(20,699,856)	(37,851,619)	(17,151,763)
Total capital	61,802,169	(115,566,585)	(177,368,754)	(25,778,250)	(120,870,832)	(95,092,582)	(18,699,856)	(35,851,619)	(17,151,763)
Allowance for depreciation									
Charged to cost on basis of estimated reproduction cost at end of each year	197,807,651	271,835,272	74,027,621	133,575,882	157,469,320	23,913,438	58,803,345	48,170,411	(10,632,934)
Addition to reflect fact that depreciation base in prior years was below estimated reproduction cost at end of current year		47,677,382	47,677,382		10,047,381	10,047,381			
Total	197,807,651	319,512,654	131,705,003	133,575,882	167,536,701	33,960,819	58,803,345	48,170,411	(10,632,934)
Error in statement based on original book accounts							2,700		2,700
Total credits	711,981,418	1,314,924,064	602,942,646	552,130,223	980,433,375	428,303,152	458,501,850	754,813,916	296,312,066

TABLE 7-8A

P. N. PABRIK SEMEN "GRESIK"

COMPARATIVE CONDENSED BALANCE SHEETS
(BASED ON REVISIONS OF BOOK ACCOUNTS MADE IN THIS STUDY)
DECEMBER 31, 1957, 1958, AND 1959
(In rupiahs)

Item no.	Assets	Composition in terms of prior items	(1) 1959	(2) 1958	(3) 1957
	Current assets				
1	Cash on hand and in banks		26,317,210	1,903,941	5,318,376
2	Receivables		131,901,529	107,678,162	63,045,298
3	Inventories		93,381,891	81,970,870	40,338,003
4	Total current assets		251,600,630	191,552,973	108,701,677
5	Government bonds, from currency devaluation of August 24, 1959		76,184,900		
	Fixed assets				
	Plant, machinery, and equipment:				
6	Original cost		362,196,048	358,638,232	347,864,380
7	Revaluation to estimated replacement cost at date of balance sheet		605,543,669	428,372,395	294,407,327
8	Total	6 + 7	967,739,717	787,010,627	642,271,707
	Allowance for depreciation:				
9	Accumulated charges to cost		271,835,272	157,489,320	48,170,411
10	Applicable to revaluation at date of balance sheet but not charged to cost in prior years		47,677,382	10,047,381	. . .
11	Total	9 + 10	319,512,654	167,536,701	48,170,411
12	Net book value	8 - 11	648,227,063	619,473,926	594,101,296
	Construction in progress:				
13	Per books		19,404,457	1,536,055	3,840,532
14	Increase (decrease) for change in cost of cement used		(5,640)	333,720	. . .
15	Total	13 + 14	19,398,817	1,869,775	3,840,532
16	Total fixed assets	12 + 15	667,625,880	621,343,701	597,941,828
17	Total assets	4 + 5 + 15	995,411,410	812,896,674	706,643,505

Source: Tables 7-6 and 7-7.

TABLE 7-8B

P. N. PABRIK SEMEN "GRESIK"

COMPARATIVE CONDENSED BALANCE SHEETS
(BASED ON REVISIONS OF BOOK ACCOUNTS MADE IN THIS STUDY)
DECEMBER 31, 1957, 1958, AND 1959
(In rupiahs)

Item no.	Liabilities and capital	Composition in terms of prior items	(1) 1959	(2) 1958	(3) 1957
	Current liabilities				
18	(See table 7-7 for details)		37,916,030	54,783,914	34,758,627
	Long-term liabilities				
	State Development Bank:				
19	For construction loan		385,455,568	369,548,677	383,637,034
20	For interest on investment in net fixed assets		115,937,637	78,744,657	24,085,206
21	Total		501,393,205	448,293,334	407,722,240
	Revaluation of assets, regarded as adjustment of advances by State Development Bank:				
	For fixed assets subject to depreciation:				
22	Revaluation to estimated replacement cost at date of balance sheet		605,543,669	428,372,395	294,407,327
23	Deduct depreciation applicable to revaluation at date of balance sheet but not charged to cost in prior years		47,677,382	10,047,381	. . .
24	Net revaluation of fixed asset	22 - 23	557,866,287	418,325,014	294,407,327
25	For current assets-inventories, chiefly to reflect changes in rate of exchange between acquisition and date of balance sheet		13,802,473	12,365,244	5,606,930
26	Total revaluation	24 + 25	571,668,760	430,690,258	300,014,257
	Capital				
27	Statutory shares		2,000,000	2,000,000	2,000,000
	Accumulated earnings (deficit):				
28	Balance, beginning of year		(125,093,322)	(37,363,742)	. . .
29	Profit (or loss) for year, before corporation tax (see table 7-5)		7,259,879	(87,729,580)	(37,363,742)
30	Balance, end of year		(117,833,443)	(125,093,322)	(37,363,742)
31	Net capital (deficit)		(115,833,443)	(123,093,322)	(35,363,742)
32	Liabilities and capital, before adjustment	18+21+26+31	995,144,552	810,674,184	707,131,382
33	Unaccounted for gain or loss, presumably attributable to revaluation of assets		266,858	2,222,490	(487,877)
34	Total liabilities and capital	32 + 33	995,411,410	812,896,674	706,643,505

Source: Tables 7-6 and 7-7.

TABLE 7-9

P. N. PABRIK SEMEN "GRESIK":
STATEMENT OF SOURCES AND USES OF FUNDS,
1957, 1958, AND 1959
(In rupiahs)

Item no.		(1) 1959	(2) 1958	(3) 1957
	Sources of funds			
	Funds provided by operations:			
1	Net profit (loss)	7,259,879	(87,729,580)	(37,363,742)
	Add: Back non-cash charges:			
2	Depreciation	114,385,952	109,318,910	48,170,411
3	Interest	57,192,976	54,659,455	24,085,206
4	Revaluation of inventories	1,437,229	6,758,314	5,606,930
5	Total non-cash charges	173,016,157	170,736,679	77,862,547
6	Funds provided by operations (1 + 5)	180,276,036	83,007,099	40,498,805
7	Funds provided by State Development Bank as a loan	15,906,891	. . . . .	383,637,034
8	Funds provided by State Development Bank as share capital	. . . . .	. . . . .	2,000,000
9	Total funds available	196,182,927	83,007,099	426,135,839
	Uses of funds			
10	To construct original plant	. . . . .	. . . . .	347,864,380
11	To add to plant	3,557,816	10,773,852	. . . . .
12	To add to or (decrease) construction in progress	17,529,040	(1,970,755)	3,840,532
13	Adjustment of assets	1,995,630	(2,710,364)	487,877
14	Total expenditures for fixed assets	23,082,486	6,092,733	352,192,789
15	To reduce loan from State Development Bank	. . . . .	14,088,357	. . . . .
16	To pay interest to State Development Bank	20,000,000	. . . . .	. . . . .
17	Total paid to State Development Bank	20,000,000	14,088,357	. . . . .
18	Cash converted to bonds by devaluation of August 24, 1959	76,184,900	. . . . .	. . . . .
19	Subtotal (14 + 17 + 18)	119,267,386	20,181,090	352,192,789
	Balance of funds used			
20	For current working capital	75,478,312	56,067,695	68,336,120
21	To revalue inventories	1,437,229	6,758,314	5,606,930
22	Net increase in working capital (9 - 19) = (20 + 21)	76,915,541	62,826,009	73,943,050

TABLE 7-10

P. N. PABRIK SEMEN "GRESIK"
ANALYSIS OF CHANGES IN WORKING CAPITAL,
1957, 1958, 1959
(All costs in rupiahs)

	(1) Balance, end of 1957	(2) Balance, end of 1958	(3) Increase or (decrease) in working capital	(4) Balance, end of 1958	(5) Balance, end of 1959	(6) Increase or (decrease) in working capital
Cash	5,318,376	1,903,941	3,414,435	1,903,941	26,317,210	24,413,269
Receivables	63,045,298	107,678,162	44,632,864	107,678,162	131,901,529	24,223,367
Inventories	40,338,003	81,970,870	41,632,867	81,970,870	93,381,891	11,411,021
Total current assets	108,701,677	191,552,973	82,851,296	191,552,973	251,600,630	60,047,657
Current liabilities	34,758,627	54,783,914	20,025,287	54,783,914	37,916,030	16,867,884
Net working capital	73,943,050	136,769,059	62,826,009	136,769,059	213,684,600	76,915,541
Increase in net working capital represented by USINDO accounts:						
For cement sales	11,067,253	36,586,767	25,519,514	36,586,767	86,801,680	50,214,913
For imports	. . . . .	. . . . .	. . . . .	. . . . .	2,157,058	2,157,058
For cement cars	25,630,056	26,305,593	675,537	26,305,593	36,350,312	10,044,719
Total	36,697,309	62,892,360	26,195,051	62,892,360	125,309,050	62,416,690
Per cent of total	50%	46%	42%	46%	59%	81%

TABLE 7-11

P. N. PABRIK SEMEN "GRESIK"

CASH UNIT COST COMPARISON, EXCLUDING GENERAL ADMINISTRATION, 1957-1960
(Summarized from cost statements of corporation)

	(1)	(2)	Total cash cost, rupiahs per metric ton						(9)	Cash cost through finish grinding, rupiahs per metric ton						
	Equivalent prod., tons[a]	Total	Labor		Supplies		(7) Factory	(8) Fuel	Total cash cost through finish grinding	Labor		Supplies		(14) Factory	(15) Power	(16) Fuel
			(3) Operating	(4) Repair	(5) Operating	(6) Repair				(10) Operating	(11) Repair	(12) Operating	(13) Repair			
Data showing increases in unit cost for entire period:																
January, 1958	17,615	265.72	24.69	3.18	118.04	14.71	32.34	72.75	153.17	6.87	2.11	46.01	7.49	10.94	21.22	58.53
December, 1958	20,692	320.78	47.15	5.31	172.02	7.31	25.98	63.01	150.13	12.74	3.56	45.04	5.88	15.16	17.95	49.80
Average, 1958	18,205	281.92	26.66	4.02	143.85	14.06	23.45	59.88	150.15	7.70	2.82	44.15	10.22	11.08	17.66	56.52
Increase (decrease), January-December	3,077	55.07	22.46	2.13	53.98	(7.40)	(6.36)	(9.74)	(3.04)	5.87	1.45	(.97)	(1.61)	4.22	(3.27)	(8.73)
January, 1959	15,506	325.10	38.99	6.35	173.93	8.77	20.96	76.10	163.70	9.29	4.59	51.91	5.67	11.32	20.34	80.58
December, 1959	24,982	440.43	34.20	4.46	183.97	98.74	55.21	62.85	256.12	7.77	3.28	67.20	69.84	28.78	28.96	50.29
Average, 1959	22,023	383.70	33.13	4.78	215.22	90.66	34.99	64.92	209.90	8.91	3.43	86.59	20.54	16.71	22.04	51.68
Increase (decrease), January-December	9,476	120.34	.21	(1.89)	10.04	90.97	34.25	(13.25)	92.42	(1.52)	(1.31)	15.29	64.17	17.46	8.52	(10.29)
January, 1960	21,032	449.85	33.16	6.32	209.77	22.96	41.63	136.01	289.60	7.67	4.80	89.79	16.23	22.47	38.82	109.82
July, 1960	19,582	535.05	35.86	7.65	242.10	55.06	54.35	140.03	316.88	8.33	5.12	80.56	30.27	29.33	38.45	115.82
Average 7 months, 1960	20,830	495.72	45.69	6.20	225.41	38.05	41.25	139.12	314.72	10.88	4.40	99.46	28.05	22.67	35.59	113.57
Increase (decrease), January-July	(1,450)	85.20	2.70	1.33	32.33	32.10	12.72	4.02	27.28	.66	.32	(9.23)	23.04	6.86	(.37)	6.00
Increase, 1958 to 1959	3,818	37.17	6.47	.76	71.37	16.60	11.54	(4.96)	59.75	1.21	.81	42.44	10.32	5.63	4.38	(4.84)
Increase, 1959 to 7 months, 1960	(1,093)	231.44	12.56	1.42	10.19	7.39	7.00	74.20	104.82	2.07	.97	12.87	7.51	5.96	13.55	81.89
Increase, December, 1959-July, 1960	(5,400)	94.82	1.66	3.19	58.13	(61.89)	(.86)	77.18	60.76	.56	1.84	13.36	(30.57)	.55	9.49	65.53
Data showing combined effect on unit costs of increasing factor prices and fluctuating production volume:																
December, 1959	24,982	440.43	34.20	4.46	183.97	99.74	55.21	62.85	256.12	7.77	3.28	67.20	69.84	28.78	28.96	50.29
January, 1960	21,032	449.85	33.16	6.32	209.77	22.96	41.63	136.01	289.60	7.67	4.80	89.79	16.23	22.47	38.82	109.82
February, 1960	14,127	547.07	135.24	9.90	159.93	39.71	44.33	157.96	337.64	30.84	6.91	72.23	27.06	32.89	48.75	118.96
March, 1960	23,400	458.04	33.24	5.70	199.11	39.95	38.26	141.78	328.76	9.24	4.00	113.86	29.79	20.08	34.62	117.17
April, 1960	24,000	469.35	33.56	5.05	207.64	51.99	34.01	137.08	306.59	8.71	3.80	89.96	39.52	19.85	29.97	114.68
May, 1960	22,826	488.97	42.42	4.00	227.15	38.94	45.62	130.84	295.60	10.02	2.85	93.21	28.23	21.88	31.72	107.69
June, 1960	21,540	548.56	39.65	6.52	314.98	17.69	33.61	137.11	337.05	9.00	4.47	145.52	15.21	16.78	33.32	112.75
July, 1960	19,582	535.05	35.86	7.65	242.10	55.06	54.35	140.03	316.88	8.33	5.12	80.56	39.27	29.33	38.45	115.82

[a] The cost system employed by P. N. Pabrik Semen "Gresik" uses the concept of "equivalent tons" to apply to certain overhead costs. The "equivalent production" quantity contains an adjustment of actual tons of finished cement to reflect changes in the inventories.

INDEX

INDEX

Accelerated depreciation methods, 69–71
Accounting procedures, 9–10, 11–14, 33–35, 41, 50–56 *passim*, 61–68, 69–82 *passim*, 83–102, 103–115 *passim*, 116–145, 146, 155, 156, 161, 162–166, 168–172 *passim*, 183, 191. *See also* Depletion; Depreciation
Actual cost system, 85–86
Administration and management, 1, 33, 41–42, 85, 86, 88–95 *passim*, 96, 97, 129–130, 134–139 *passim*, 140–146 *passim*, 163, 174, 179–188 *passim*
American Society of Certified Public Accountants, 78
Anderson, A. J., 7
Anspach, Ralph, 121
Assets. *See* Capitalization; Revaluation of assets

Balance sheets, 102, 104, 117, 168
Bank Indonesia, 8, 34, 48, 50–55 *passim*, 120, 164, 177
Bank Industri Negara, 3, 8, 36–37, 47, 53, 72, 180. *See also* State Development Bank
Bank Pembangunan. *See* State Development Bank
Biro Devisen Perdagangan. *See* Foreign Trade Bureau
Black market, 81, 113–114, 133, 166–167
Board committees, 183–184
Board of Directors, 181–183
Brantas River, 44
By-products, 44

Capital consumption. *See* Depletion; Depreciation
Capital formation, 31–32, 47, 49–50, 55, 70, 71, 73, 82, 168, 170, 178, 187, 189–190, 195
Capitalism. *See* Private enterprise
Capitalization, 1–4, *passim*, 7–10 *passim*, 13, 14, 19–20, 21, 25–28, 30–39 *passim*, 40–41, 46, 59–82, 105, 116, 126, 147–150, 170, 180, 186, 191. *See also* Depletion; Depreciation; Expansion program; Financing; Interest; Revaluation of assets; Social overhead capital
Carman, C. MacArthur, 7
Cash costs, 83–102 *passim*, 103–115 *passim*, 117–150 *passim*, 155, 167
Cement making, 20–21, 44, 83–84, 99–101. *See also* Raw materials; Storage; Technology; Transportation
Chinese businesses, 4
Citizenship, 4
Cold war, 1–2
Colonial heritage, 37, 96, 174
Construction economics, 31–33, 42, 111, 114–115, 127, 178
Consumption demand, 31–32, 177–178
Cost accounting. *See* Accounting procedures
Costs. *See* Capitalization; Interest; Labor costs; Operating costs; Production costs
Counterpart funds, 50–53, 180. *See also* Export–Import Bank
Credit. *See* Financing; Interest
Cultural factors. *See* Labor force characteristics; Political and social factors; Socialist economy
Currency convertibility, 103–115. *See also* Currency valuation; Foreign exchange; Foreign investment
Currency valuation, 33–36, 68, 73, 74–75, 80, 105, 111–114 *passim*, 119–120, 122, 124, 127, 131–132, 142, 148, 159, 163–165, 171, 173, 195. *See also* Inflation
Current cash costs, 116–150 *passim*

Deficit financing, 70
Department of Basic Industry and Mining, 139, 171, 179, 186, 191
Department of Defense, 181
Department of Finance, 8, 14, 48–56 *passim*, 67, 167, 179–188 *passim*, 191

www.ingramcontent.com/pod-product-compliance
Lightning Source LLC
Chambersburg PA
CBHW021527210326
41599CB00012B/1405